AF553237

WOMEN AND CRIME

WOMEN AND CRIME

Dr M U Qureshi

2007

SBS Publishers & Distributors Pvt. Ltd.
New Delhi

All rights reserved. No part of this publication may be reproduced, stored in a retrieval system, or transmitted in any form or by any means, electronic, mechanical, photocopying, recording or otherwise, without the prior written permission of the publisher and the copyright holder.

ISBN : 81-903098-1-1

Indian Price - Rs 795

First Published in India in 2006
Reprinted in 2007

© Author

Published by:
SBS PUBLISHERS & DISTRIBUTORS PVT. LTD.
2/9, Ground Floor, Ansari Road, Darya Ganj,
New Delhi - 110002, INDIA
Tel: 23289119, 41563911
Email: mail@sbspublishers.com

Printed at Chaman Enterprises, New Delhi - 110002.

Contents

Preface

The society, where women being not revered is evidently despicable. A woman embodies the qualities like love, sacrifice, patience, etc. It is paradoxical that the so-called torch-bearers of women's cause, see to it that women's emancipation does not really take place at all costs in our country. Many a politician and the political party had initially taken up the cause of women's rightful representation in parliament, legislative assemblies and local bodies. However, unfortunately for about a decade, we have been witnessing the women's bill being tossed around.

The moment, the foetus in a womb is formed, the hunt for this unfortunate section in our country begins. Female babies are not allowed to take birth by the conservative, illiterate and even some literate sections of our society. Only in upper and highly educated class of society, women are given due recognition. A large chunk of women in our country remains to be stoic as for the atrocities being unleashed against them. They are merely considered as child-bearing and rearing machines.

Women's plight in our society should be highlighted in its deserving manner. Present work is the result of all painstaking efforts to cover all relevant aspects of crime against women in our society. The book has been prepared with a dint of hard work, research and using all the available sources. Hence, undoubtedly this will be greatly useful for all the sections of readership.

Please be forthcoming in sending suggestions and views freely, so that the undersigned can reciprocate to these, with due concern promptly.

— Author

1

Concept and Perception

In this book, we will start with a definition and meaning of violence and then will proceeds to discussing fluctuations in violence and certain factors, in order to give new dimensions to violence, by making it more crude and vulgar especially for women.

The Meaning of Violence

The Chamber's Twentieth Century dictionary describes violence as excessive unrestrained or unjustifiable use of force. Violence also means outrage, profanation, injury or rape. Infliction of injury on other people is the essence of violence. It may be either physical or mental. On the legal level it is illegal employment of methods of physical coercion for personal or group ends. The infliction of injury by police is exercise of state's force as long as it is legal. But as soon as it crosses the boundary of legality and inflicts injury for lust or for personal gain, it becomes violence and is more dangerous than the violence by ill armed and ill organized collectivity people.

The socio-cultural forces are important as determinants of

violence. The social structural approach emphasises the structural determinant of violence.

Value Consensus Basis of Social Order : The functionalist and conflict theorists explain violence in society in different ways. The functionalists make value-consensus the basis of social order. For them inequality in society is natural. Violence exists and persists for performing system maintenance function. Durkheim upheld normality of crimes. Universal conformity to normative expectations in unlikely. In a social order where women is held in contempt, she will be subjected to violence.

Power Demonstration Mechanism : The conflict theorists hold that violence is the primary mechanism that holds societies together. They do not put emphasis upon consensus. For them social relations are unequal and exploitative. Equality for them is un-natural and inequality has to be maintained by the use of force and violence. Power is the central concern of the conflict perspective. Criminal statutes are created and enforced according to the wishes of those having power. Violence against women like beating and rape is an assertion of male domination and control.

Ancestral : An offshoot of the social structural approach is the socio-biological view of human behaviour. It traces violence, war and rape to the violent background of the primitive ancestors. On this theme of ancestry, sociologists have based their analysis and attributed violence to the male and victimization to the female on human nature.

Exploitation : According to Gandhian analysis violence in its crudest form has always existed in society, every where in the world. The great mass of the people have suffered constantly from it and have been living in a state of violence perpetually. The life, dignity and the property of the poor, weak and women have always been unsafe. They have been living in perpetual state of peacelessness.

According to the same Gandhian analysis, the quantum of violence might not have increased. It is the logistics of its operations and the targets that have changed. Violence has touched the upper elite, disturbing peace of the ruling class, the politicians, the business executives and the intellectuals. Violence which was under the surface is now being seen and heard by those who had never encountered with it uptill now. Violence has acquired new dimensions recently with incidents like gang rapes upon women by men in police uniform.

Violence is thus a means to an end. It is used for system maintenance, assertion of power exploitation and victimization. On the other hand it is also used, for securing redressal of grievances of the oppressed.

Conflicting Views

There are subtle differences between violence with purpose, senseless violence, force, crime and terrorism.

According to Paul Wilkinson, Violence is the use of unauthorised and illegal use of coercive power, whether by the state, by factions or individuals. Violence is the illegitimate use or threatened use of coercion resulting or intended to result in the death, injury, restraint or intimidation of persons or the destruction or seizure of property.

Terrorism is organised and planned violence for achieving same goal. By its very nature it is indiscriminate arbitrary and unpredictable. It is rooted in a tradition of Nihilist political thought, that glorifies in the destruction of the structure of governmental power through violence for its own sake. They exhibit an indifference to all existing moral codes. Their main aim is to break the morale of their target.

Incidental large scale and often sanguinary epiphenomenal terror, (spasm), like mass violence, wars and riots are different from systematic regimes of terror.

Terrorism is used by politically motivated groups as well as by criminals who use it for ransom, for black-mail or for private gains.

Ordinary crimes are considered morally wrong if there is no ideology at the back of them. If they are backed by an ideology no moral guilt is presumed in those actions. For instance, if decoity murders and smuggling etc. are committed for over-throwing repressive regimes, they are considered terrorism with a moral purpose.

The essence of violence is thus infliction of injury. Its chief features are:

(i) Excessive, unrestrained and unjustifiable use of force,

(ii) Outrage, profanation, or rape,

(iii) Causing physical, injury,

(iv) Causing mental, injury

(v) Illegal employment of methods of physical coercion for personal or group ends,

(vi) Exploitation,

(vii) Violation of human rights of life, liberty, equality and dignity.

Thus in overall pattern of violence along with other weaker sections of the society, women becomes an object of violence.

The Categorization

Violence can be placed under different categories. According to Gandhian analysis these are (i) Societal violence (ii) Violence of protest and (iii) Counter violence.

Societal Violence : The establishment by upholding the system decides the infrastructure of violence. This infrastructure is made up of centralized bureaucracy, large institutions, monoliths of industry and big business monopolies of either power or position or wealth or merit. According to Gandhi's definition of violence in the above context, it is exploitation and exploitation hurts physically as well as mentally. Exploitation militates against life itself. It denies the majority of the weaker and exploited sections, their primary needs of survival, dignity of person and opportunity for growth.

The violence of the establishment is often unrecognised and unaccountable. It is not only the state or the economic institutions which perpetrate violence by exploitation but violence is enshrined in all big establishments including universities, law courts, parliaments and developmental plans.

Navjiwan Mandal of Orissa compiled a series of materials which go to prove that the machinery of law and order which is supposed to protect the citizens provides by itself an important device for violence and exploitation.

For an illustration, in the above quoted compiled series by Navjiwan Mandal, the main brunt of violence is borne by the tribal population of Orissa. These tribals account for 40% of its people's sufferings. It is violence of the establishment i.e. of the Police and of Forest Laws and state policies.

Thus one of the source of violence in society is the establishment itself. The total structure of violence and its content are determined by the establishment. "Violence is initiated by those who oppress, who exploit, who fail to recognize others as persons - not by those who are oppressed, exploited and unrecognized".

Rape of a woman by an individual is a violence upon her physique and psyche of highest intensity. She never surmounts the shock, the guilt and trauma she has to undergo during such an event. She carries the guilt on her conscience till the last of her breath. But when it is gang rape and that also by the custodians of law the immensity of trauma guilt and humiliation is unfathomable.

Taking example of India, never before have the Policemen been held in such dread as they are today. The incidents of humiliation, sex torture and gang-rapes inflicted upon Maya Tyagi of Baghpat, Brij Bala of Lucknow, Sheela Devi of Dabwali, Mathura of Maharashtra or Rameezabee of Hyderabad have shown the brutality and lawlessness of the cops which could be matched only with the criminals whom they are supposed to prosecute.

The Police terrorism is very much a part of India's system. The Police uniform gives the cops a false sense of security. They think themselves above law. The Policeman who is impoverished under the system, attempts to discover methods for extortion of extra money. He is sex starved because he is separated from his family for months and finds in what ever woman can be caught, an easy prey for his sex satisfaction. He can kill the husband if he puts forth any resistance because the system insulates the policeman from any kind of harm. No one is prepared to testify against a Policeman. The judicial system is slow to respond the stretched out enquiries and give him time to wipe out all evidences against him. Moreover politicisation of Police force has aggravated their sense of lawlessness. The crisis of character in the Police force has deepened. For instance, one of the investigative report in a journal, mentions about a former Inspector general of Police in Madhya Pradesh, who sent a confidential note some time back, advising his men not to rape any woman because the Assembly was in session.

Violence of Protest : The pathological deviants among the exploited people break laws and protest against the establishment surreptiously, in order to nibble profits from the system. These are not able to touch the lines of the upper elite and therefore often resort to open violence. The machinery of law protects the influential in the society. It is put in ever readiness to clamp down heavy boots upon the deviants with all the weight of counter violence at their command. The deviants attempt to direct their violence upon their own poorer and weaker kith and kin. Thus the poorer and the weaker are oppressed on the one hand by the establishment and on the other by those who protest and utilise them for their own purposes.

Counter Violence : Recently a transformation in the structure of violence has been taking place. In order to liquidate the violence of establishment, the violence of Protest has become grossly politicised and ruthless. For the sake of peace maintenance has come counter violence in reaction.

The quantum of violence of Protest and Counter violence has increased. These two kinds of violence are new phenomena. These have acquired new features. A non-political person was earlier more safe in the city as compared to a political activists and women in general were safer than men. The two new type of violence were directed against the decision makers. The men of establishment included both government as well as opposition. But now ordinary non-political common men and women have become target of violence. Men are murdered and maimed, but women are sexually tortured and raped.

Unsettling Impacts

In all the newly independent societies some unsettling influences have worked in fluctuations of violence. The following are some such factors.

1. Independence movements and introduction of universal franchise in developing nations have acted as catalysts for intense political participation of the public mass. Processes of politicisation have legitimised all forms of violence. Riots and revolts have often been employed to bring changes into governmental policies and programmes. In most of these developing nations violence has now become an inextricable part of the political process attending the elections in village, city, state and parliamentary bodies.
2. Corruption rampant even in high places is a problem to be reckoned with in almost all the newly independent developing countries. Younger generation has come to believe that the government and bureaucracy any where respond only to the language of violence and organized pressure.

   The Police force and army in some countries have entered into direct participation in politics. In most of the developing nations even minimum standards of administrative efficiency is absent. The government becomes incapacitated and is unable to cope with the problem of corruption stalking in every walk of life. The disorderly behaviour of the elders is aped by the younger generation and when masses are led to agitational movements, violence easily erupts. The media flashes in head lines, all these forms of social behaviour thus giving them prominence.

3. Decline in productivity, fall in per capita income, deterioration in health conditions and darkness because of illiteracy, throw the citizenry into the abyss of cynicism and fatalism. These provide fertile soil for violent collective behaviour in every walk of life.

4. Communal or ethnic violence have been rocking almost all the newly sovereign states. In most of the organized violence the man power is provided by the youth belonging to educational institutions. In consequence the establishment comes down with heavy hand on the young people. In cases of atrocities on peasants and workers the establishment often exceeds the limit of legitimate violence.

   If violence becomes a part of the temper of the society, the weaker section including women become easiest prey of violence.

5. The readily available arms, production of illegal weapons, private armies of the rich people, paralytic police force all have combined to accentuate the criminal tendencies amongst the exploiters.

6. If the economic, social and educational systems have not been able to come out of the feudalistic webs there is inequality on every level. Every one is engaged in finding out shortest route to money making. On social occasions like birth, marriage and death there is a throat cut competition to show off prosperity by vulgar display of wealth. The educational institution are divided into roofless and teacherless schools and the most sophisticated private

schools. In such an environment thinking itself becomes feudalistic. Women in such societies are added to the list of show pieces. If a woman happens to be a bread earner or contributor to family income, she becomes a bonded labour because she does not possess the decision making power. In such feudalistic societies women are held in contempt and are considered as property. They are sold and bought. Even in care homes and mental asylums they are not cared for or given proper treatment but are used as objects of sex satisfaction.

7. Another factor responsible for ascendency and fluctuations in violence against women is growing religious ritualism and fundamentalism. Women, children and the weaker people have to bear the brunt of sufferings inflicted upon them by the hypocrites of the society.

8. When violence is rampant, every one feels insecure about the future. Fatalism strikes root in such a society. Failure of the law and order machinery and inefficiency of bureaucracy all create an environment where women's activities are curbed. Their place is confined to the four walls of their homes.

The Objectives

1. Since violence is a means to an end it can be used to serve some purpose for the society. For instance in India the scheduled castes and scheduled tribes have been able to secure some benefits due to the Reservation policy of the Government. But women's lot has not been able to attract much attention. It is only when they have used pressure-tactics that they have been able to achieve some laws in their favour, and have been able to make the law and order machinery start moving.

2. Persistence of certain patterns of violence is an indicator that there is some thing basically wrong with the social system. It must be rectified before there is total anarchy.

3. Epiphenomenal violence throws light on many other related issues, which had been taken note of earlier. For instance violence in India has thrown light on the poor economic conditions of the lowest rung of the Policemen. It has shown how Policemen are often put in tight corners by their political masters and also how poor are their technical tools, with which they are expected to function in fast developing modernizing turbulent and violent societies.

The general temper of violence has intensified the atrocities upon women. They are objects of beating, torture, injury and rape because all these have been routinized in the society. Violent incidents are so numerous that no eye-brows are raised when a new incident is added to the old and infinitely long list.

Legal Status

There has been a growing trend towards violence against women, more so with development and liberalization and the hunger and greed for material things. The global campaign for elimination of violence against women in the recent years indicates the enormity as well as the seriousness of the atrocities committed against women that are being witnessed the world over. Development along with its progressive changes in personal lifestyle, living standards, varied economic growth caused by urbanisation and changes in social ethos contribute to a violent attitude and tendencies towards women which resulted in an increase in crimes against women.

The containment of such incidents is a necessity in our country so that the Indian women may attain their rightful share and live in dignity, freedom, peace and free from crimes and aspersions.

The battle against crime against women has to be waged by the various sections of society through campaigns and various programmes with social support alongwith legal protection, safeguards and reforms in the Criminal Justice System.

The State has enacted various legislative measures to uphold the Constitutional mandate. This intended to ensure equal rights, to counter social discrimination and various forms of violence and atrocities and to provide support services especially to the working women.

In spite of all these safeguards, the women in our country continue to suffer due to unawareness of their rights, illiteracy and oppressive practices and customs. The resultant consequences are many viz. a constant fall in the sex ratio, high infant mortality rate, low literacy rate, high dropout rate of girls from education, low wage rates, etc.

Types of Offences

Women may be victims of various crimes such as murder, robbery, cheating, etc. which are not specifically directed against them, there are crimes identified which are designated as Crime Against Women which are directed specifically against them.

Offences of Punishable Nature

(i) Rape (Sec. 376 IPC)

(ii) Kidnapping and abduction for different purposes (Sec. 363-373 IPC)

(iii) Homicide for Dowry, Dowry deaths or their attempts (Sec. 302/304-B IPC)

(iv) Torture, both mental and physical (Sec. 498-A IPC)

(v) Molestation (Sec. 354 IPC)

(vi) Sexual Harassment (Eve-Teasing) (Sec. 509 IPC).

(vii) Importation of girls (upto 21 years of age) (Sec. 366-B IPC).

Specific Laws for Investigation

Although all laws are not gender specific, the provisions of law affecting women significantly have been reviewed periodically and amendments carried out to keep pace with the emerging requirements. Some acts which have special provisions to safeguard women and their interests are:

(i) The Employees State Insurance Act, 1948

(ii) The Plantation Labour Act, 1951

(iii) The Family Courts Act, 1954

(iv) The Special Marriage Act, 1954

(v) The Hindu Marriage Act, 1955

(vi) The Hindu Succession Act, 1956

(vii) Immoral Traffic (Prevention) Act, 1956

(viii) The Maternity Benefit Act, 1961 (Amended in 1995)

(ix) Dowry Prohibition Act, 1961

(x) The Medical Termination of Pregnancy Act, 1971

(xi) The Contract Labour (Regulation and Abolition) Act, 1976

(xii) The Equal Remuneration Act, 1976

(xiii) The Child Marriage Restraint (Amendment) Act, 1979

(xiv) The Criminal Law (Amendment) Act, 1983

(xv) The Factories (Amendment) Act, 1986

(xvi) Indecent Representation of Women (Prohibition) Act, 1986

(xvii) Commission of Sati (Prevention) Act, 1987.

Conventional Crimes

The head-wise incidence of reported crimes during the period 1996 to 1998 along with percentage variation is presented in Table. It is observed that Crimes Against Women in 1998 reported an increase of 8.3 per cent and 4.8 per cent over previous years, 1997 and 1996 respectively. In absolute numbers, an increase of 10,073 cases were reported at all-India level in 1998 over 1997.

Incidence of Reported Crimes and Percentage Variations (1996-1998)

Sl. No.	Crime Head	Year 1996	1997	1998	Percentage variation in 1998 over 1997
1.	Rape	14846	15330	15031	–2.0
2.	Kidnapping and Abduction	14877	15617	16381	4.9
3.	Dowry Death	5513	6006	6917	15.2
4.	Torture	35246	36592	41318	12.9
5.	Molestation	28939	30764	31046	0.9
6.	Sexual Harassment	5671	5796	8123	40.1
7.	Importation of Girls	182	78	146	87.2
8.	Sati Prevention Act	0	1	0	–100.0
9.	Immoral Traffic (P) Act	7706	8323	8695	4.5
10.	Indecent Rep. of Women (P) Act	96	73	192	163.0
11.	Dowry Prohibition Act	2647	2685	3489	29.9
	Total	1,15,723	1,21,265	1,31,338	8.3

The proportion of IPC crimes committed against women towards total IPC crimes remained around 6.0 per cent during 1996-1998 as shown in Table.

Proportion of Crime against Women (IPC) toward total IPC Crimes

Sl. No.	Year	Total IPC Crime	Crime Against women (IPC cases)	Percentage to total IPC crime
1.	1996	1709576	115723	6.8
2.	1997	1719820	110183	6.4
3.	1998	1779111	118962	6.7

The available data indicates an increasing trend during the three years (i.e. 1996, 1997, 1998) in all the IPC crime against women except 'Rape', 'Sati (Prevention) Act' and 'Importation of Girls' which reported a declining trend during this period. All crimes against women reported under Special and Local Laws also resulted increasing trends during three years except 'Indecent Representation of Women (P) Act' which reported a declining trend.

All India Crime rate i.e. no. of crimes per lakh population for crimes against women reported to the police worked out to be 13.5 during 1998. However, when estimated with reference to female population this rate almost doubles to 28.1 per lakh female population. This rate of crime which does not appear alarming at first sight may be viewed with caution, as a sizable number of crimes against women go unreported due to social stigma attached to them.

Uttar Pradesh State reported highest incidence (13.3%) of crimes followed by Madhya Pradesh (12.1%) and Maharashtra (10.9%). In contrast, Delhi, which accounted for only 1.9 per cent of total crimes and shared only 1.3% of the population in the country reported third highest rate of such crimes at 19.6 after Madhya Pradesh (20.5).

Rape Cases : Incidence of rape cases (15,031) reported a decline of 2 per cent during 1998 over 1997 (15,330). Madhya Pradesh alone reported 22.3 per cent of total rape cases in the country. Delhi, which represented only 2.9 per cent cases reported fourth highest rate at 3.4 after Mizoram (9.3), Madhya Pradesh (4.3) and D & N Haveli (3.9).

Rape Victims : According to Table at national level there were 15,033 rape victims compared to 15,330 in the previous year representing a decrease of nearly 2 per cent. Of these 8,414 (56%) were in the age group of 16-30 years, 3,433 (22.8%) in the age group of 10-16 years and 626 (4.2%) of age 10 years and below. Similar to decrease (2%) in the number of rape victims over previous year, the child victims (below 10 years) of age also reported decrease of 18.7 per cent and the victims above 30 years of age reported an increase of 10.8 per cent, signifying decrease of incidents relating to rape of Children.

Victims of Rape by Age-groups during 1996-1998 and Percentage Changes during 1998 over 1997

Sl. No.	*Year*	*Below years*	*10-16 years*	*16-30 years*	*30 years & above*	*Total of all age-groups*
1.	1996	608	3475	8281	2485	14849
2.	1997	770	3644	8612	2310	15336
3.	1998	626	3433	8414	2560	15033
4.	Percentage change in 1998 over 1997	–18.7	05.8	–2.3	10.8	–2.0

Custodial Rapes : During the year 1998 only four cases of custodial rape (one each from Andhra Pradesh, Gujarat, Maharashtra, and Uttar Pradesh) were reported in the country.

Kidnapping and Abduction : Incidence of kidnapping and abduction reported an increase of 4.9 per cent in 1998 over 1997. The States of Uttar Pradesh and Rajasthan each reported more than 15 per cent of these cases at national level while Delhi with share of 6.0% cases reported highest rate at 7.5.

Dowry Deaths : Incidence of dowry deaths during 1998 reported have a rise of 15.2 per cent over the previous year. 32.2 per cent of these cases at national level were reported by Uttar Pradesh alone followed by Bihar 15.0 per cent.

Torture (Cruelty by Husband and Relatives) : Incidence of torture cases in the country increased by 12.9 per cent in 1998 over the previous year. 18.7 per cent of these were reported by Maharashtra while the highest rate in the country at 9.5 reported from Rajasthan compared to 4.3 national average rate.

Molestation : Incidence of molestation in the country in 1998 reported an increase of 0.9 per cent over the previous year. Nearly 23.5 per cent of total such cases were reported from Madhya Pradesh which was also significantly higher rate (9.4) than national average rate (3.2).

Sexual Harassment (Eve-Teasing) : The number of sexual harassment cases reported in 1998 in the country significantly rose by 40.1 per cent over the previous year. More than half (59.7%) of these cases were reported from Andhra Pradesh, Uttar Pradesh and Tamil Nadu. Jammu & Kashmir reported the highest rate at 3.8 compared to 0.8, the national average rate.

Importation of Girls : A total of 146 such cases were registered in 1998 compared to 78 cases in the previous year, a sharp increase of 87.2 per cent over 1997. Gujarat, Madhya Pradesh and Haryana reported 57, 26 and 25 cases respectively.

Transformed Methods

Sati Prevention Act : Though the practice of Sati is something unheard of in modern times, there have been few cases now and then. No such case from any of State/UT was reported in the country during 1998.

Immoral Traffic (Prevention) Act : Cases under this Act registered an increase of 4.5 per cent during 1998 as compared to 1997. More than half (68.3%) cases were reported from the State of Tamil Nadu only. This should be construed as an indicator of improved policing efforts by Tamil Nadu police in this area.

Indecent Representation of Women (Prohibition) Act (Torture) : A remarkable increase of 163.0 per cent was noticed for cases under this Act in 1998 as compared to cases reported in the previous year (1997). Nearly 45 per cent cases were collectively reported from Andhra Pradesh and Bihar put together.

Dowry Prohibition Act cases : These cases reported an

increase of 29.9 per cent in 1998 as compared to 1997. Of these, a sizable proportion (42.6 %) were reported from Bihar.

Disposal of Crimes Against Women Cases : The collection of detailed information on disposal of all the identified crimes committed against women has commenced from the year 1995. The comparative national level status of disposal of these cases by police and courts is presented in the succeeding paragraphs. However State/UT-wise details are presented in the main chapter on Disposal of crime cases.

Disposal by Police : During 1998, at national level, the disposal of IPC cases by police accounted for 76.5 per cent (including 0.4 per cent cases where investigation was refused). The crime-head-wise analysis of crimes against women cases revealed a fairly high disposal percentage for 'Sexual Harassment' cases (92.2%), 'Molestation' (85.1%), and 'Cruelty by Husband and Relatives' cases (79.3%). On the other hand, while at national level 87.5 per cent cases reported under SLL were disposed of by police (including 0.6 per cent where investigation was refused), the quantum of cases disposed under 'Dowry Prohibition Act' was comparatively low at 75.4 per cent.

The position of cases charge-sheeted to total cases for investigation was quite satisfactory for all the crimes committed against women when compared to national average of 55.2% for total IPC crimes. Only in case of 'Kidnapping and Abduction of Women and Girls' the percentage was lower (35.9%) than the national average.

The percentage of charge-sheeted cases under SLL at national level stood at 84.4. Comparatively, the charge-sheet percentage in cases of Dowry Prohibition Act and Indecent Representation of Women (Prohibition) Act was lower than the national average being 62.4 per cent and 62.1 per cent respectively.

Disposal by Courts : The crimes headwise, comparative details of cases of disposal of crimes tried, convicted or pending trial against women (IPC and SLL) by courts during the last two year (1997 and 1998) are presented.

As compared to 76.5 per cent disposal* by police in case of IPC crimes at national level and 87.5 per cent in case of SLL crimes, the disposal** of these cases by courts was reported to be very low at 19.0 per cent and 52.1 per cent respectively.

The disposal by courts of heinous crime cases such as 'Rape' and 'Kidnapping and Abduction of Women and Girls' was reported to be nearly17 per cent and 15.3 per cent respectively during 1998. At the end of the year 48,685 'Rape' cases, 39,103 'Kidnapping and Abduction' cases, 18,523 'Dowry Death' cases and 1,07,192 'Torture' cases were pending for trial in different courts of the country. Amongst SLL cases 42.9 per cent cases under 'Immoral Traffic (P) Act' remained pending for trial while pendency percentage was as high as 80.5 per cent and 86.1 per cent for cases registered under 'Dowry Prohibition Act' and 'Indecent Representation of Women (P) Act' respectively. The only case for trial under 'Sati Prevention Act' during 1998, resulted in acquittal. No case remained pending for trial at the end of the year.

Note: * *Disposal of Police is taken as cases investigated by Police + cases where investigation was refused.*

** *Disposal by Courts is taken as cases tried + cases compounded & withdrawn.*

2

Basic Issues

The last decades focused much attention on one specific group i.e. women. The group is a majority one, we can say that more than half of the world population comprises of women. Inspite of this dominant majority, the irony of fate lies here. The pathetic condition of women in society is itself an indicator of the low value set on women's lives, and their suffering is very well in tune with the social system and life pattern. Women have various problems which are centuries old, they suffer much oppressions all over the world and solution of their problems are also not easy.

A sound conceptual approach to the issue of violence and women is the need of the time. Though it is a much discussed topic, still various types of misconceptions persist, the role of men and women in society are analysed still millions of women both in rural and urban settings are facing violence and its various manifestations like a routine affair.

The condition of Indian women are very much shocking.

There are certain special limitations due to India's cultural and familial background - the social, economical, and political conditions are also responsible for women's oppressions.

They are the victim of the circumstances which have been created due to gender discrimination which persist in India from cradle to grave. This phenomenon, however takes its rise from the decline of the Hindus, reaches its apex during the Muslim rule, but gradually tends to loosen its grip during British rule. Even in Independent India this situation persists, although much efforts have been directed by men and women reformers, the activists, and other self-less persons to bring the situation under control.

Defining Violence

Before we proceed further on the subject of violence on women, it will be proper to define and describe violence or crime. A German mystic philosopher considered crime as the lacking of a stitch in a man's make-up. That may become a Sociological concept by a stretch of imagination. Criminologists have, however, defined crime in different ways because their training is different.

In simple words crime is merely an anti-social behaviour. One European Criminologist says that "Because a collective system has social validity in the eyes of each and all of those who share in it, because it is endowed with a special dignity which merely individual system lack altogether, individual behaviour which endangers a collective system and threatens to harm any of its elements.... It is only a harmful act, an objectively evil act, a violation of social validity, an offence against the superior dignity of this collective system."

But the social scientist forgets to consider the case of a collective group harming an individual i.e. a women forced to be a Sati by the whole community. As such Sutherland's definition of crime "as a legal description of an act as socially injurious and having legal provision of penalty for the act," seems more tenable although the emphasis is on legal aspect. Legal or illegal covering of an act is always under discussion while individual may continue to suffer in different ways as the women in India, Nepal and Sri Lanka.

When we look into the various activities that are socially injurious, we find innumerable examples of these which are particularly directed at women. For example, the cases of rape and gang-rape; sexual exploitation and harassment and abuse as in prostitution; physical and mental torture and humiliations as in police stations, prisons, after-care homes and other private and public institutions; vulgar exploitation of women figures in advertisement of all sorts including modelling and commercial films; sexual and mental harassment in streets and work places; domestic violence and unwilling motherhood; and the recent happenings of our times the tremendous rise in killing and burning of young brides for non-fulfillment or insufficient offering as dowry. "Murdered for not bringing in adequate dowry is shocking! It may shock a Westerner, but it no longer shocks us Indians. Dowry deaths have become quite a regular feature in the Newspaper these days." Of course, all the dowry deaths do not result in burning alone.

There are cases of strangulation, poisoning, injury inflicted by heavy weapon, falling down from high places as a result of being pushed to death, being compelled to commit suicide and so on. The barbaric custom of Sati or self-immolation of widows on the funeral pyres of their husbands is another example which was used to be given religious cover. But nowhere do the Hindu Scriptures permit Sati.

The support that 18 year old Roop Kanwar's form of death in Deorala village of Rajasthan, drew from the local population is an eye-opener. Their total approval and even glorification of the act asserted their belief that Sati is an integral part of Rajput culture and Hindu Dharma. Thousands watched approvingly while the young girl burnt herself to death. It is most surprising that so far no Brahmin, no Kayastha and no Vaish have been Sati in Rajasthan. "If the widespread, implicit acceptance of wife murder in our society today expresses the low value set on women's lives, the public burning to death of a woman is an open endorsement of that devaluation." The life of widowhood is self-explanatory of violence against women which is centuries old.

The same social process support female infanticide and foeticide. Cases of desertion and separation on filthy grounds and for false vanity are also increasing. Women become victim of these for no fault of their own. Lastly we must not miss the latest type of violence with the help of science, i.e. Amniocentesis test which determine the sex before birth. Parental preference for sons is, of course nothing new, nor indeed a feature peculiar to India. There are thousand of incidents where women are terrorised and even killed for being unable to produce a male child.

Parental preference for sons give rise to female foeticide. It has shocked everyone right from planners and policy makers to the academicians, social thinkers and activists no doubt, but after sex determination test in our country female foeticide are mostly aborted. J.B.DSouza reports that of 8000 abortions that followed sex - determination tests only one involved a male foetus i.e. 7999:1 ratio. These are all frightening indicators of a deep-seated social malaise, whereby it seems all right for a male dominated society to victimise powerless women. These and many more are the violence in latent and manifest forms against women rampant even at the close of the 20th century. "It has been distressing experience all over the world that in any conflict, a war, civil strife, communal riots or disturbances women and children became the unfortunate of violence and atrocities victims. Children are orphaned and women are not only widowed but also become victims of rape."

The root cause behind all these criminal incidents, is the concept of Patriarchy. Let us examine it in some detail to serve our purpose. "The term 'Patriarchate' suggests the inclusive powers of the family's father.... The power of the patriarch over his children, young or adult was often almost unlimited. In ancient Palestine he could sell his daughter into servitude; in ancient Rome the "Patria Potestas" meant the power of life and death. In principle, almost complete social subordination marked the position of the wife. She could not own property in her own right; she had no standing before the law over her husband. Among the Jews, the early Romans and the Chinese, for example, she should be divorced on certain grounds at the will of her husband, though of course, she had no reciprocal right." Many features of it survived into the 20th century, traces of it still remain especially in the less-developed regions. India is no exception to this. The patriarchal ideology and joint form of family exist as a cultural norm.

The patriarchal family is here also patrilocal and patrilineal and male possessiveness and women subordination is accepted as a social norm. "It is not surprising therefore, that women have a low position in this society which is reflected in lower life expectancy, lack of access to education, health and employment opportunities, widespread practice of female neglect and abuse, such as wife-beating, leading to female suicide and bride-burning as the ultimate fate for the hundreds of powerless women every year."

The prevalence of female infanticide and female suicide may be associated with hypergamy. Practices like pre-puberty marriages, ban on widow-remarriage and the practice of Sati are means of rigid control over women within the caste and the family fold. Here the women is considered the property of man not the individual, they have only responsibilities while men have power. Women worth is measured in terms of her ability to produce male children through whom the patrilineality is perpetuated. She has no right in decision making process in the patriarchal family they have principal obligation to arrange, observe, and continue the local traditions and rites pertaining to welfare of sons and husbands.

The entire process of socialisation of female is to internalise the concept of dependency. "More often than not women are seen as object of change rather than agents of change, imitators rather than initiators, bystanders rather than full participants. Despite legal and constitutional privileges marked inequalities persist between men and women." This pattern is found all over the country and even among other religious groups such as Muslim, Christian etc. One can assert that Muslim women, under the Islamic injunctions, are provided better status compared to other religious groups but this is only in theory. In practice, even the Muslim women face many handicaps such as polygamy, unilateral divorce, lack of support in the event of a dissolution of marriage etc.

Cultural Criterion

The patriarchal ideology as a cultural norm enforces gender construction which is oriented towards hierarchic relations between the sexes. We find that gender identity is created spontaneously; in the family and the household, continually recreated and endorsed and modified through a series of ideological representations. Women are divided by gender and class with men, hence this class gender conflict is most problematic. Socialisation for gender differentiation and sex inequality starts early in a girl's life. Most of the things we associate with being male or female are cultural they are socially determined. From before birth to the death a person is supposed to be inextricably and forever male or female.

The whole range of social apparatus-names, clothes, toys, beliefs, behaviours and values are nothing but a complex process of labelling which begins when a child is born. "Young men and women grow up labelled by their names, clothes and their languages either male or female. The way they grow up will depend almost entirely on the beliefs about appropriate behaviour for men and women in the subculture in which they live and it is their biology that is, their sex."

It is worth noting here that the socialisation process, patriarchy and the related subjugation of women-all are interlinked and determined essentially by a male hierarchical order, that enjoys both economic and political power. This ideology affects the position of women as well as determines it irrespective of whether the women are in the domestic fold or function are outside of it. The most oppressed under patriarchal values are the middle class educated women. It is the patriarchal organisation, not class structure that defines women's position in the power hierarchy.

This system is perpetuated through marriage and the family. Patriarchy then is a sexual system of power. This exist everywhere "Patriarchy is cross-cultural and cross-national, existing differently in different societies through the institutionalisation of sexual hierarchy." Thus patriarchal system in society is the root of male hierarchical order, power is enjoyed by them only and as violence accompanies power, it is committed to feel a sense of power. Violence against women takes many forms as mentioned earlier, but what is near universal is that male violence exceeds female violence.

A word of caution, however, our present agony should not lead us to believe that the plight of women was always bad in India. There is not one verse, not even a word indicating a slighting humiliation or an insult for women in the Vedas. Instead, women are friends in life's journey, creator, menter, guide and partners in all fields. The very word Mahila is made up of the root with which means the repository of greatness and goodness. There is no such word as Mahila in any language European or Asian. Marking ahead, we find even the Gita calling women as the symbol of sweet speech, intellect, memory, patience and forbearance.

The Upanishad has stories of very chaste women, but if compulsion of circumstances had made her fall, neither she nor her child will be denigrated. Let us remember the case of Swetketu's mother and his entry into a *Gurukul* with utmost dignity. (The name of Satyakama's, Swetaketu's mother was Jawala). A woman like Draupadi who has suffered ignominy at the hands of the Kauravas in the very face of Bhima and Bhisma, is indomitable. She is the fountain of inspiration, the great spur to lead the Pandavas to battle. Let us listen to her speech in Kiratarjunium addressed to Yudhishtra in exile:

> " He is a fool who does not employ trickery with the tricky enemies. That man is worshipped by all who punishes defaulters with his anger, but if one is not competent to punish even his friends ridicule him - what then to say about the enemies".

Decidedly, the women could fight back with violence as in the Mahabharata or with non-violence as Sita does in the Ramayana. But she never reconciled with evil as our women do today in the name of modesty or modernisation. Even Buddhism gave equal status to women after a little debate in the Mahasangha. But time changed very fast. Invasions by the Sakas, Huns, Tartarians, and Kushans from Central Asia via the Hindukush mountain range brought out the necessity of changes in the Grihasutras and Dharmasutras in order to protect the honour of the ladies. Hence Apastamba, Vishnu and Narada Smirities made rigorous laws for the purity of the harem.

It is rightly mentioned by Shakuntala Rao Shastri "when Hindu culture came into clash with a culture far different from its own, the leaders of society began to frame rules and laws to safeguard their interest - specially the position of women. Rigorous restrictions were imposed on them. But even while restricting the freedom, the law-givers did not forget to make provision to welcome the abducted women back to their homes."

With the coming of the Pathans, the house seemed more unsafe. Due to the lustful proposal of Alauddin Khilji, Rani Padmavati with about 700 Rajput committed themselves to flames which came to be known as 'Jauhar Vrata'. Gradually child marriages were preferred in the society and the death of a widow was welcome news as she would not fall into evil hands. A woman in Hindu society has always been considered an appendage to her husband, she has no life apart from him. Consequently, on her husband's death, there was no reason for her to live on. Also the husband was her sole protector. Once he was gone, who would protect her? During foreign invasions by the Turks, Muslims and others when their menfolk were killed, the widows were very naturally expected to commit Sati.

Hence immolation of widows and the killing of girl child - infanticide, started in a large number. The catholicity and humanism of the Hindu law thus perished out of fear of molestation by 'Malechhas'. Such willful violence came to be called a curse of the Hindu society, but historically it is wrong because these atrocities were attempts of fencing the Hindu women against the long hands of the Muslim and foreign settlers in India.

Convention enters a culture through the process of meeting a necessity. Child marriage, girl-killing, widow burning all come to stay with the dignity of a convention in Hindu society because the Hindus were destined to remain slaves for about thirteen centuries. Even the Muslims were not spared this fate when they became subjugated by the white rulers of England. They developed purdah, illiteracy, disease, legal discrimination and handicaps, restrictions in owning land, wealth and many other encumberances. But the worst part of their fate is the male dominance in their society and their century old dumbness. Rationalisms is smothered by hard-core traditions that have taken the shape of religious injunctions. The Muslim divines have to look into what is really religious and what is an imposition.

As stated herein, conventions die hard. Instead, they make a home in the social structure and fight for their ownership rights. As time passes, they take on different shapes and forms and make a durable crust of the society. If males turn sadists under the intoxication of power over female, the females turn masochists and pride over their suffering as if God has willed it. Illiteracy, the mother of economic dependence, plays havoc in the lives of women for they are left without any knowledge of the radical changes in law whether it is labour law or social law. While the government offers equal opportunities, equal wages to the woman as compared with males, while the Hindu Marriage Act, Divorce Act, Maintenance Act, offer plenty of help to the women; the women would not like to utilise them because the question of earning social stigma is too deeply ingrained in them. Such a situation persists even today, that is 58 years after Independence. Let us have a peep into the sphere of labour, "since 94 per cent of the women workers are engaged in the unorganised sector of the economy (81 per cent in agriculture), but they are unaffected by the protection afforded by the Labour Laws, and are victims of low productivity, unemployment and under-employment, object of poverty and exploitation by intermediaries.

According to estimates of various Expert Committees women constitute the larger share of both the unemployed and the underemployed in India." If such situation continue to stay, let us think, who is to blame, not the government, nor the male people but we ourselves - the women especially the educated women whose duty is to enlighten the sisters living in darkness. Tradition has always been invoked to buttress arguments for the continued suppression of women. We, the educated one can very well assume that many aspects of tradition are no longer valid today, therefore we should choose that which suits our present needs and neglect those which are worthless. Gandhiji had shown us the light even in those early days of freedom struggle. "Women have been suppressed under custom and law for which man was responsible and in the shaping of which she has no hand....Women has as much right to shape her destiny as man has to shape his. It is up to men to see that they enable them to realise their full status and play their part as equal of men."

All-pervasive Threat

The life of women in India is still surrounded by violence neglect and exploitation what is the price fixed for a women's services night and day within the household? Love is the reward, it is said; where is the reward if the husband and the in-laws do not appreciate the bride's services? Perhaps nowhere, except the fire on her clothes and her body. This is happening everywhere in our country these days and the number is increasing alarmingly. Even the educated urban and well informed women are exposed to such events.

The committee on the status of women in India rightly concluded therefore. "The entire exercise of our committees has indicated that in certain important areas and for certain sections of the female population there has been regression from the normative attitudes developed during the freedom movement. Large section of women have suffered a decline of economic status.... Even after the promulgation of these laws (legal measures), the protection enjoyed by the large masses of women from exploitation and injustice is negligible.

Though women do not numerically constitute a minority, they are beginning to acquire the features of a minority community by three recognised dimensions of inequality of class (economic situation), status (social position) and political power.... The chasm between the values of a new social order proclaimed by the constitution and the realities of contemporary Indian society as far as women's rights are concerned remains as great as at the time of independence."

Therefore, the pious labours of all the discussions on women and violence will be profitably rewarded if we search for remedial measures to eradicate violence on women in our society. After we have developed a concept and a proper perspective of the task before us, we are in a position to discover certain remedies. There are two basic questions which require our attention (1) to ease the constraints of man woman relationship and (2) to make efforts for women's development, the former demands fundamental changes in our value system and process of socialisation and the latter can only be possible in a social structure that would ensure gender justice.

Such social structure can be visualised only when women be recognised as 'individual in their own right' and not as moveable property as they are considered. Women should have full participation in every walk of life. Gandhiji gave us right advice in dealing with the question of social injustice to women. He opined "She has the right to participate in the minute details of the activities of man and she has the same right of freedom and liberty as he. She is entitled to a supreme place in her own sphere of activity as man is in his."

Laudable Act

Women organisations are doing commendable work in our country in helping women with their manifold problems. Women activists with their various organisations have demystified the sources of women's oppression. Their services vary from counselling, free legal-aid, professional training for women, campaigning against dowry, organising morchas and processions, and holding seminars, workshops etc. highlighting the problems of the women and pin-pointing the recommendations.

It is the increasing impact of the women's efforts to act as the single most important factor in changing the terms of the public debate on issues like rape, domestic violence, Sati, women's employment and social justice and numerous such topics, bringing them on surface and making them national issues. But women organisations are mainly city-based. We cannot overlook the fact that the problems are prevalent in the rural areas too. Hence such women organisations should be prepared to take the movements to the villages. We find, social workers are trained who are from generally the educated middle class urbanities and hence do not care to go and live in the villages and work. A team of grass root social workers are required to accept the challenge and work in the village.

Some preventive measures and remedies are also important. To be brief, we would propose to begin with spreading education among the women masses - more so in rural areas. This will naturally lead to a social awakening towards their labours contributed in fields, industry and houses. Women should be made self sufficient economically and given training in self-defence methods to protect themselves from exploitation. Participation in administration, in legislatures, should be made easier for women. Complete reorientation of social norms and values, a rethinking for evaluation of changing situations and women conditions therein should be started. Changes are required not only in the social codes, but in legal codes also. Law should be strong enough to protect women's fundamental rights. Even the Muslim women should examine what is really Islamic in personal law and what is sheer imposition by later men.

They too should join the fray for a rational society or perish with unjust laws. We should be clear in our mind that crime against women should not be treated as part of other crimes in the society. We must apply special criteria to examine women's plight and also apply special means to solve them. A programme for total emancipation of women should be drawn up, vigorously perused and if in the process, certain walls have to be demolished, let them be demolished - and no regrets for them. From the last decades violence have become a part of our life, whether it is morning news or the late night news they start with its reporting. Our peace efforts are seldom highlighted, Good work done by ordinary people' never comes to light. There is always a small group of good people in every society, their services can be utilised. A brighter tomorrow is ahead, if we remove the cobwebs from our medows, violence on women shall be an unheard story if the women light up the torch of social revolution.

Victims of Violence

The fact that violence against women should have attracted so much attention in recent years may speak for a greater sensitivity to human suffering, a keener sense demands justice in our society. But that such violence should persist, even increase as a backlash as the women's movement gains strength, would indicate that matters are much more complicated. To combat this violence one must first understand it. Here the breakthrough has come with the feminist movement which has been able to conceptualize violence in terms of an inevitable manifestation of the patriarchal system, a system resting on and vesting in the subordination and exploitation of women, a system that is age-old, worldwide and is only beginning to be challenged. One reason why violence against women is so difficult to eradicate is precisely because it is socially sanctioned to some degree. Even today the wife and mother roles are seen as women's primary roles. Thus patriarchy legitimizes women's oppression.

Criminal Deeds of Varied Types

How pervasive and how brutal the violence is proved by the fact that 50 per cent of Canadian women have experienced at least one instance of violence since the age of 16. Around three quarters of the women killed annually in Canada are by the very men they are living with. Many of these killings are of an exceptionally brutal nature and are accompanied by sexual assault, also brutal. Six women are burnt every day on an average in Gujarat. Studies of the violence that is prostitution indicate that it has taken on the dimensions of an industry. It is estimated, for instance, that 2 lakh Nepali women are working in Indian brothels, the largest number of them belonging to the age group of 10 to 14 years. There are numerous instances of the extreme brutality to which young wives are routinely subjected, such as being locked up without food, light or air, being made to stand on one foot, being made to stand with a grind-stone on the head.

The vulnerability of children to sexual abuse and violence also co-exists in society. No place is safe, not the home, the campus, the work-place or the street. No age is safe: infants, old women, paraplegics can all be victims of rape. Several of the victims of rape are children. There are instances of child brides who develop a horror of sex, leading to their abandonment by their much older husbands. It is devastating to note the vulnerability of children in flesh trade.

Exposed to infection and violence at the pre-natal stage, forced to sleep at night under the cot of the mother who is presented herself with a chain of clients, they are, if girls, soon forced into the trade and are constantly exposed to the danger of rape. Lori Haskell cites figures demonstrating the revictimization of women abused in childhood, while Julie Lee stress the utter isolation of such a girl child, whom no one believes and whom her own mother will not protect. Jaya Sagade points to some of the factors such as superstition that prompt men to rape a child.

Mass violence against the weaker sections of society, whether on the basis of class, caste, race, religion or gender, frequently takes the form of mass rapes and gang rapes of the women of the targeted group. This amply bears out our contention that violence is a means of asserting power. The dishonouring of the women of the other group is a blow directed at the men, a violation of their property and it is noteworthy how the upper castes, the upper classes and the state machinery act in collusion in the mass rapes of lower class and caste women whenever their community struggles for its rights, whether it be the right to own the lands they till, or the state's decision in favour of positive discrimination in their favour in matters of education and employment. Police harassment of the poor is a routine, which in time of stress, leads to the targeting of one particular community. It is important to draw attention to a recent tendency that is particularly dangerous to the women's movement, the tendency of women themselves to become polarized in terms of community, setting up a dichotomy between 'our' women who are sacred and 'their' women who are fit targets for attack.

International Concern

Another issue which is of concern is the violence in the form of racial discrimination that is directed against women of colour in Canada along with their men. These women are assigned ill-paid jobs in the unorganized sector which are not commensurate with their qualifications. Women's organizations working with women of colour are reluctant to recommend mandatory arrest for male offenders, since they are keenly aware that the justice system will deal with them much more harshly than with white offenders.

The machinery of the State — the law, the police, the judiciary— has an important role to play in the eradication of violence. There was a mandate given to the Women's Commission recently set up in Maharashtra State to ensure that the Fundamental Rights and Directive Principles of the Indian Constitution which stipulate equality before the law and prohibit discrimination are effectively implemented. The Commission recommends legislation, monitors the implementation of existing laws and frames schemes for more effective implementation. It is privileged authority to investigate complaints and to inspect detention and custodial centres. The Committee has recommended the setting up of vigilance committees and of police cells among other measures.

The Government of Canada has become increasingly conscious of the demands of gender justice, while recent reports revealing the magnitude of violence against women have spurred the consideration of a national action plan aimed at its eradication. Equal opportunity guidelines and policies on affirmative action have already been formulated. The Provincial Government of Ontario has set up the Ontario Women's Directorate under a minister responsible for women's issues. The Directorate has been able to provide funds for support services such as Rape Crisis Centres and a criminalization strategy has been enforced whereby the laying of charges for wife assault becomes mandatory. One goal of the Directorate is the creation of public awareness along with a programme of sensitization of those responsible for law enforcement for which seminars are being organized for crown attorneys and for the judiciary.

The situation in Alberta where a minister for women's issues who totally lacked a feminist perspective went so far as to say that there are no women's issues left and where appointments to commissions are patronage appointments shows clearly the importance of a feminist perspective. Institutionalized power generally perpetuates violence against women, even in services such as health and education. And within this general scenario there is marked discrimination against non-whites and lower classes. There have been instances of bitter experience of the reluctance of the government machinery to fund support services.

Disillusionment with regard to the law, the police and the judiciary is widespread among victims and activists. Studies and statistics show how few cases are reported to the police, an activist who studied law in order to be of greater use to women victims, now advises them to avoid going to court. The reasons for this failure of the machinery of redressal are several. In the first place there are lacunae in the law itself. A glaring instance is the rape law in India. In the law, as it stands, a woman has to prove that consent was withheld and the criteria for this are so framed that it becomes virtually impossible for her to prove that her passive submission was not consent. Then again women are ignorant of legal provisions. Hence they do not know that the law offers them protection. Thus, majority of women do not avail themselves of the law regarding maintenance. Nor do they know that certain necessary measures must be taken in time. The medical report required in cases of rape is an instance.

It is reported that the legal system in the case of women represents further victimization, sentences being light and discriminatory, depending on the race of the perpetrator. The system apparently views crimes against property as more serious than crimes against persons, particularly female persons. The humiliation of rape victims in court and the social stigma that is attached to the victim are reasons for the reluctance of girls and women to appeal for justice. There is evidence corroborating the fact that child victims are disbelieved and are humiliated on interrogation. The poor are subjected to persecution by the police which is why they distrust the machinery of the law. The pressure by local bureaucrats and politicians is particularly unchecked in rural areas and small towns and bribes are freely given so that the woman victim ends by finding herself put in the wrong. Similar discriminatory treatment, in the case of non-whites, is observed in Canada.

Several case studies reveal, the reluctance of victims of domestic violence in their dying declarations to implicate their husbands reasons being: The woman often fears retaliation against her children and her parental family in the event of her accusing her husband or in-laws. She also pathetically clings to the notion of a family honour that must be protected. In the absence of clear evidence it is often difficult to establish that a death by burning is a case of homicide and not a suicide or accident as claimed by the culprits.

The police and judiciary are all the products of the same patriarchal system that subordinates women. Their attitudes to the victims as well as the perpetrators of violence are shaped by patriarchal beliefs. It is small wonder that there is delay in bringing cases to trial and that the accused get away with light sentences. Activists have therefore come to see the need to lianise with the police, while at the same time striving to bring about a change in their attitudes. An attempt in this direction is being made by the cell run by the Tata Institute of Social Sciences at the police headquarters in Mumbai.

Since members of the cell are available to assist victims in registering complaints and obtaining legal aid, victims feel assured of competent advice and a following up of the case. As it is backed with the support of police, the cell in its turn carries more weight. The police have collaborated in rushing emergency aid in crisis, in recovering *stridhan* (the wealth given by the parental family to the bride, which is to be treated as her property, not that of her husband) and in obtaining custody of children. Training for police personnel has also been organized in which they are given information regarding the law as well as trained in sympathetic interviewing and investigation. Ultimately it is only a strong women's movement that can galvanize the state machinery into action, change deeply-entrenched social attitudes and provides a safe space and redressal for individual victims.

Such a movement gathers strength through organizing study circles to create feminist awareness among women, pressing for changes in legislation, banding women together in mass campaigns imparting awareness in society through pamphlets, posters, songs, street plays and films. The play "A Girl Child is Born", produced by Sharada Sathe's organization, was enacted before large audiences of women all over Maharashtra and sharply brought home to them that the many instances of denial and oppression they had lived through were part of the lot of the girl child in patriarchy.

Research has proved that small determined groups can, in the face of the discouragement and hostility, step by step, build up their services so as to provide a centre for counselling and redressal, a crisis line, access to a safe space. During the worst communal riots in Ahmedabad, it was a women's organization which protested arrests, registered cases, set up night vigilance committees, nursed the injured. In a rare demonstration of courage, a group of women could intervene in a case of rape by accosting the perpetrator. Demonstrations in support of individual victims have been able at least in some cases to press for justice for victims of rape and domestic violence in rural Gujarat and this gives them encouragement. The home for prostitute's children in Pune run by Vijaya Lavate's organization has given these most vulnerable children a chance to have a normal childhood.

Counselling services also provide a great support to victims of violence. All of them stress that a sympathetic hearing brings immense relief to a woman who has hitherto been disbelieved and belittled. Even centres which lack trained workers, such as the student centre at McGill University in Montreal can offer this service, while directing the women to other centres which are staffed by experienced professional counsellors.

The stages through which counselling must proceed if it is to lead to resocialization are: in the beginning women learn to identify controlling behaviour and to understand the impact of violence on themselves and their children. Later they are led to question the patriarchal system itself, which represents a challenge to deeply-embedded cultural and social beliefs. They also undertake the counselling of perpetrators of violence. The object is to make them realize that an act of violence is a conscious choice made by themselves, that they cannot push away the responsibility.

The counselling of children is again skilled task, whether they are themselves victims or are witnesses to violence directed against their mothers.

Activists are acutely aware that without a shelter where women are safe from their persecutors, what they can achieve for these women will always be limited. For want of a shelter there is often no alternative but to work for a compromise and run the risk of sending the woman to her death.

There are two major drawbacks of the existing shelters run by government or by charitable organizations lacking a feminist perspective. These will generally not accept children above a certain age and they also confine the women to the premises. Hence many women who can make no alternative arrangement for the children and who must work to support themselves cannot avail themselves of their facilities.

Women in India, however, can draw encouragement from the fact that it was only after a long struggle and much disappointment that these shelters could be established and similarly their own efforts too will, in time, bear fruit. One notes also what can be done even in the absence of a full-time shelter. When the shelter in Kenora (Canada) had to close down for a length of time for lack of funds, members sheltered women in their own homes, accompanied them to the police, the courts and hospitals and operated a crisis line.

Dilemmas and differences of approach do exist even among feminist workers struggling to combat violence. There is a tendency among some to avoid involvement with the police and courts, whereas others take the view that these too serve a purpose. Sharp differences of opinion exist on whether an organization should clearly declare that it is feminist in aims and outlook or should refrain from doing so to avoid alienating some sections of women. For instance, there are several diametrically opposed attitudes to prostitution. Among feminists there are those who see it as a choice of profession by the individual woman which must be respected, while others stress the fact that large numbers of women are not only forced through poverty to turn to prostitution but are literally forced into it, having been sold or abducted. They are then faced with a dilemma: how can they reconcile their support for these women in their struggle for better treatment without condoning prostitution as an institution?

In spite of such differences, their commitment to the cause of women has led women's organizations to network and to fight shoulder to shoulder on issues of common concern. But not all these organizations have a specifically feminist commitment. It is only such a commitment that can take them beyond individual issues and lead them to challenge patriarchy as a system for reaching the desired results.

3

Crimes in Practice

A definition of aggression, acceptable to most social psychologists says "Aggression is any form of behaviour directed towards the goal of harming or injuring another living being who is motivated to avoid such treatment" (Baron, 1977). However, the concept of intentionality is important in separating aggressive behaviour from other forms of behaviour that might lead to some harm. Wrightsman and Deaux (1981) argue that the definition of aggression does not limit aggression to physical harm. Verbal insults, and even the refusal to give a person something that he or she needs can be considered a form of aggression.

Study of Specific Features

Inflicting and experiencing violence in many subtle forms, causing and suffering mental pain in day to day life, being and becoming insensitive to such violent everyday happenings has become ways of our world in interpersonal relationships. "The ways of cruelty are many and subtle... We kill peoples' reputation with a word or a gesture; we wipe people out through gossip, contempt and defamation. The cruelty, the hate that exist in ourselves is expressed in the exploitation of the weak by the powerful and the cunning..." (Krishnamurthi, 1977; p. 166). Home is no safe place when it comes to aggressive behaviour. Fitz and Gerstenzang (1978) observe that episodes of verbal or physical aggression were most likely to occur in the home, and the relatives (such as parents, offspring and spouses) were the most frequent targets of aggression. Steinmetz and Straus (1973) described the family as "cradle of violence". Straus (1975) drawing from incidences of violence between spouses called "the marriage license as a hitting license".

"Women experience both structural and behavioural violence more sharply than men because social definitions of their biological equipment assign them to a special secondary descriptor (female) as a limitation to their social status at every level in a given social hierarchy" (Boulding, 1975; p. 239). According to Boulding (1975) the concept of structural violence"... refers to the organized institutionalized and structural patterning of the family and the economic cultural and political systems that determine that some individuals shall be victimized through a withholding of society's benefits and rendered more vulnerable to suffering and death than others"(p. 240). The structural patterning also determine the socialization practices that induce individuals to inflict or to endure according to their role.

Purpose : Recently, in a study were interviewed some 30 women from upper, middle and lower classes with the aim (a) to have some idea of the painful, and psychologically damaging experiences of these women in their day to day family life. (b) The intention was to understand violence in its subtle or manifest form as prevalent in interpersonal relationships and everyday routine interaction among close family members. (c) The intention was to derive some conclusions regarding the differential nature of violence in the different groups if any and finally. (d) It was proposed for psychologists to intervene in presenting the psychological truth behind aggressive behaviour. The resolution lay in understanding the problem itself.

Sample : Our sample consisted of thirty women, ten from each upper, middle and lower classes. The upper and middle class women were educated and at least graduates. The lower class women had no formal education. All the upper class and lower class women were married. However, out of ten middle class women five were unmarried. The age range for the total sample was from 25 years to 50 years. The sample was selected without any bias, and the women were interviewed with the help of a semi-structured interview schedule.

WOMEN OF UPPER LAYER

Our first respondent was brought up in a liberal parental home. She was motivated to have high aspirations in life and achieve excellence in whatever she aspired for. She was encouraged to have skill in fine arts, success in studies and self independence. However, she was married into a rich business class family where her husband and in-laws perceived her education, attributes and talent only as a matter of pride for enhancing the social status of the family. In a materialistically charged home environment her love for education personal growth and self-independence through job, etc. were totally ignored. She was not allowed to join a central school teaching job which she desired but was asked to enhance her attractiveness by visiting beauty parlours and keeping herself out of boredom by engaging into meaningless pursuits like shopping and seeing video films. Her apparently loving and caring in-laws and husband were insensitive towards her likings and interest and made her feel like a puppet in their hands. The interview ended up on a pessimistic note our respondent saying that she has given up her aspirations for a job or realising her worth otherwise. However, she felt that she might suffocate in this atmosphere which was extremely incapacitating for a woman who looked for her own identity. She said there was adjustment in her life but no satisfaction.

In this case violence lay in the sure and steady messages regarding proper and improper behaviour for this women. The family members in so many subtle ways contradicted all the things that she valued. There was negation of her existence beyond a daughter-in-law of a rich business class family, and her resources like education and talent were considered commodities for raising the social status of the family. Another woman under similar circumstances said that she could retain her mental peace and santity in an atmosphere which apparently appeared to be non-aggressive but in fact asked for lots of adjustment on her part, only through compromises and adjustments. As a wife, daughter-in-law, sister-in-law, and mother she found little scope for realising her personal aspirations like appearing for UPSC exams, studying more, or doing a job. Like the first woman her need for personal growth and achievement was not appreciated nor she was expected to "step-out" of her prescribed social roles. She thought of herself as another "show-piece" in the family.

The kind of mental suffering women are likely to experience in joint families come from the fact that the family members take them for granted. Most of the time the hurt is caused by the intentional avoidance of recognition due to their services and a non-sympathetic attitude towards their domestic and professional labour. We talked to at least three women under this kind of situation. In general, the family members of working women blame them for saving their energy for their work outside home.

Our first respondent in this category told us that her family members did not help her in completing domestic chores, nor they seemed to be pleased with what ever she did for them. Her mother-in-law particularly and her sister-in-law in general were jealous of her. At times her father-in-law and brother-in-laws would make comments for hurting her. For example, they would ask what keeps her working in a college which was not yet constituent, or how she was not able to complete her Ph.D. Their pain inflicting strategies were simple as a word, as a gesture or a comment, but they were capable of insulting the woman and killing her personal dignity and self-respect

Another working woman had similar story. She was criticised for minor mistakes and was miserable because no body felt obliged with all the work she did. Her family members non-cooperation and unsympathetic attitude was almost revengeful towards her. Her mother-in-law and sister-in-laws did not approve of her working outside home. Both the above mentioned women's husbands worked elsewhere and they were dependent on their husband's family for boarding and lodging. In such circumstances what they might be looking for would be companionship, sympathy and understanding, as they accomplished their dual roles of housemakers and professional women.

However, what they did experience was a net work of expectations and duties whose fulfillment never seemed to oblige anybody. The pain inflicted on the woman here was intentional; specially, when other female family members become part of violent practices it shows their own frustration and revengeful attitude towards a person whom they consider some what more privileged than themselves (as a working woman) and in whose shoes they would like to step in.

A major reason for undergoing lots of mental agony for women was their husband's infidelity. We could note at least four out of ten women who suffered due to this. One of them aged 50 disclosed how her extremely contended married life only six years back had turned sour due to her husband's attachment with a woman much younger in age. Her husband was now a changed person. The other women was allowed to stay with him day or night and went around with him on his professional trips. People came and told her about all this and she herself had seen them together on many occasions. To add insult to the injury her husband has been spending money on some quack "tantrik" to use some mystical means to make her sick and die. The wife was quite sick now. She vomitted blood occasionally, but the husband did not seem to care.

A woman whose husband gets involved into extramarital relations undergoes deep psychological trauma due to several reasons. First, she is deprived of the love and companionship of which she has the legitimate right. Secondly, her husband's indifference proves her to be an inadequate martial partner whom he does not find interesting anymore. This is a severe blow to a women's self-esteem as a woman and as a life-partner. Infidelity shatters a women's confidence in herself and grinds her in spate of self criticism and self-doubts. Moreover, she has to take up the additional responsibility of a parent whose children should not be affected by the husband and wife's marital discord. The woman has to keep her sanity intact amidst her own personal agony and the demands of the family. The sole responsibility for maintaining family peace and social status lies with the woman.

Our next respondent had other reasons too in addition to a disloyal husband to feel victimized. Her husband was suspended from his job for bungling a sizeable amount of money and loved drinking. Father of six children he was a man of easy virtue. His wife was deeply hurt when she saw him going around with woman right in front of her eyes and she knew at least about one woman with whom he was going steady for quite sometime. To his wife he was critical for the food she cooked and got mad if she wanted to discuss their marital problem. He thought his wife was dumb and unsophisticated. He was not concerned even about his children and made no efforts to look for a match for his elder daughter.

One of our respondents otherwise satisfied in her relations with her husband was hurt by discovering some love letters while arranging his old books. Still another one suffered because she suspected her husband to be more attentive towards her younger sister than to herself.

Some Indian women have to undergo acute mental distress because they cannot bear children. The family members very often add to their suffering. One of the issueless respondents now married for fifteen years told us that no body in the family gave her any respect for the reason beyond her control. Her husband was often advised to get remarried. Her husband besides being blind to her feelings distrusted her specially on money matters.

She was not allowed to spend even a rupee without his consent nor she had freedom to buy things she wanted to. She was immensely hurt when her husband left her at her mother's home and did not ask her to come back to him for two, three years. This woman admits having feeling of inferiority and apprehension. She was afraid that her husband might desert her anytime.

This particular case is an example of the psychological damage done to a women's personality and self-esteem for reasons beyond her control. It also depicts almost cruel attitude of family members towards one of them. This woman had to be in a situation where she was living her days in and days out in a psychologically crippling atmosphere.

At times children hurt their mothers by insulting them, not obeying them and not reciprocating their love and care as they should. Many times their misconduct and misbehaviour cause deep psychological discomfort and put the mother into a spate of self-criticism. At least two women in our upper class sample under went distress and anxiety with their children's behaviour.

Women of Mid Layer

Our first middle class respondent talked about the prison which was her own home, and where her husband forced her to remain confined. Her suspicious husband did not allow her to meet or socialise with family members or relatives. Her parents and siblings were not allowed to come and meet her either. She was not trusted by her husband and had to be under his close supervision always and everywhere. At times he took leave from his work to be around and keep a watch on her. Once she was physically dragged away from her sister's home where she had gone without his permission. She was mother of six children and her husband did not care if she had more. The woman felt that restrictions on her physical movement and mental freedom had gone to maddening limits. However, she had succumbed to her circumstances and was afraid of her husband. Her husband did not think of her more than a show piece which remained at its place and looked pretty. To add to her miseries he allowed himself to go around with other females occasionally. The mental suffering for a woman in such circumstances can be immense. The husband appeared almost a sadist whose love for his wife if any, was only carnal and lacked depth of feeling.

Our second respondent was a middle aged woman who found herself victim of her husband's wrath and anger for reasons not quite understandable to her. The husband wanted to be treated like an important guest in his own home and asked to be obeyed. He behaved in an authoritarian manner and disregarded the wishes and feelings of his wife. The important decisions in family matters were taken by him or his mother and sisters. His decision to marry their daughter in a particular family landed her into an unsuitable marriage, the wife's consent was not asked for. The husband's irritable nature, short temper, whims and autocratic ways of heading the family was a constant source of tension and disturbance for the wife. Our next respondent had problems with her husband's inflated ego. Her husband did not want her to be respected for the higher education she had or for any other matter. He thought that acknowledging his wife's qualities would automatically make him appear inferior to her. He made it clear to her that he had all the reasons to dominate her and she had to remain in her limits. The woman was not allowed to move around freely nor buy things of her liking. The husband was an extremely conservative and rigid kind of person who thought that he was always right. The woman was now fed up with him and even thought of separation. However, with a daughter it seemed almost impossible.

A similar story was disclosed by another respondent who experienced lots of mental stress due to extremely inconsiderate husband and in-laws. Her family members apprehended that an educated daughter in-law could dominate them by her superior qualities. Their strategy was to engage into petty cruelities and insulting behaviour aimed at lowering the woman's self esteem and confidence. Even her husband's younger brother got mad at her and once attempted to hit her. All that they cared for her was for the things she brought in her dowry. The woman felt like revolting against their crude nature and behaviour.

In both the above cases we came across husbands or family members who have their self-esteem problems and inferiority-complexes. Both the cases speak of people who look at relationships not for its quality and potentialities for happiness, but are defensive for reasons that point out towards their own inner problems.

Next we came across a woman who was fairly ambitious and educated, but had an unemployed husband, she was living at her parental home and was teaching in a school. Some what contrary to what we expected this woman was continuously insulted, defamed and taunted for being dependent on her mother's family. Her brothers had gone so far as to throw out her belongings on the street and her mother was particularly cruel to her. She asked her to go to her in-laws who were in a village. At times she was beaten up by her brothers. Moreover, her husband's attitude was also extremely conservative and unsympathetic towards her. He believed that women ought to remain at home and bear children. For him a women's ambition ought to be limited to serving her husband only. He was not concerned about looking for a job for himself either. Our respondent's unwillingness to leave her parents home was linked to her need to be independent which she thought was not possible in a village. This is the story of a woman who was fighting her battle alone, unloved and un-cared and at the cost of her self-respect.

We interviewed five unmarried middle class females who were graduate and postgraduate students. Their problems were somewhat different than the married ones and they were by and large satisfied in their surroundings. Nevertheless, the first respondent complained that she had no freedom to move around on her own, go to films with friends or any clothes and books, etc. of her own choice. Her father was very strict and scolded her if she did not cook well.

Our next subject thought that her family was conservative in its attitude towards the likings, wishes and education of a young girl. Her brothers resented her talking to boys and once strongly reprimanded her for taking help from a male classmate for her exams. Her mother wanted her to do and learn domestic work. In general the family members disregarded her existence as an adult and considered her to be an irresponsible child.

Another student who stayed away from her parents with her uncle and aunt felt that no one was really interested in her education. Her uncle and aunt expected her to do all the cooking and house work even at the cost of her study. They did not want her to go out, wear good clothes or do good in studies. She was very upset when although an examinee, she was asked to nurse her sick brother and complete the domestic chores.

She said that her relatives were very conservative and did not care whether girls were educated and became self-independent.

Women of Lower Strata

Most of the lower class women were victims of serious mental and physical violence specially in the hands of their husbands who gambled, were drug or alcohol addicts and battered their wives.

We talked to a vegetable vendor, whose husband was a rickshaw puller and instead of supporting his family spent his earnings in gambling and liquor. He also physically assaulted her when drunk. Further more he sold his house and land for gambling and drinking and made his family homeless. The respondent now lived with her parents with their two daughters.

Another respondent had almost identical story. She worked as part time domestic help while her husband pulled rickshaw. She had four children but the husband unconcerned with his family responsibility drank and battered his wife. He also accused her of being loose charactered and went on as far as to saying that the children were not his. He himself however, was of doubtful character. Another respondent again a part time maid and wife of a rickshaw puller had additional problem besides being a victim of wife battering. Her husband was involved with his younger brother's wife who lived in his village home. He sent all the money, home utensils, bed and bedding for his beloved while his wife and children slept on floor. His first wife, tried to win him back by showing and giving him food, money and clothes that she got from her employer, but nothing seemed to please him. Earlier he used to beat her also because she had three daughters and no sons. Now he had a son, but there was no change in her story of miseries.

Our next respondent again a domestic women and rickshaw puller's wife, was deserted by her husband for another woman with whom he lived now. He deserted her with two children. His second wife had a daughter too. When his wife resented his involvement with another woman she was severely beaten up. While interviewing the lower class women we observed that five out of ten were victims of wife battering and irresponsible husbands. However, there were at least two women who were put to pain by their relatives. In one case an arrogant daughter-in-law intentionally hurt her mother-in-law who was our respondent. She did not invite her to her grandson's marriage which took place in the same house in which the respondent lived. Another respondent was beaten up by her mother-in-law and was kept hungry for some action her mother-in-law did not approve of.

We came across a middle aged pan shop keeper woman, whose husband had deserted her and gone to Delhi. She was mother of seven children. The reason for desertion was her husband's suspicious nature. He listened to his neighbours who talked against his wife. The wife however, resented that he never believed or trusted her. After her husband left her she went to stay with her in-laws but had to face more hardships. Her mother-in-law made her do all the housework and kept her half-fed. Her sons were married and the daughter-in-laws did not care for her feelings. She was now a middle aged lonely woman who wanted her husband to come back to her. We came across at least two young women who were very poor and were victims of their husband's indifferent attitude towards family planning. Both of them had five or six children, but their husbands were neither concerned about limiting their family nor took responsibility of the children. One of the respondents disclosed that if she resented her husband's careless attitude towards family planning she was beaten up. The women worked as part time maids to support their families.

INJURIES OF SPECIFIC TYPES

The upper class women were by and large victims of mental violence and suffered in the hands of their husbands and close relatives. One of their major painful experiences referred to the husband's infidelity and indifference. Another source of violence had reference to structural violence against women. Such violence lay in the attitude and conditioning of family members and spouse who would not accept that a woman may wish to "step-out" of her prescribed social roles, to realise her worth and self identity or want to have self-independence. Similarly, women looking for recognition of their worth and services were ignored or taken for granted. Violence took new heights when a barren women's mental agony was ignored while she was looked down and insulted for being childless.

The middle class married women were by and large victims of some or the other kind of mental torture in the hands of their suspicious, controlling, dominating, whimsical and autocratic husbands or close relatives. In fact, they felt victims to the ego problems and frustrations of the victimizer on many occasions. The unmarried girls were looking for more freedom and liberal guardians and wanted to be considered responsible adults.

The lower class women were perhaps the most disadvantaged class as they were victims of wife battering, infidelity, insecure future, and poverty. Their unfortunate circumstances added to their painful experience of physical violence and mental tortures in the hands of their irresponsible husbands in most of the cases.

Views of Psychologists

As a psychologists one must attempt to bare the psychological truth behind violence and its manifestation in every day life. The reality is somewhat as follows.

(a) People derive pleasure out of inflicting pain on others. They do not give it up because the pleasure however superficial out weighs the pain that violence manifest at subtle levels and is capable of providing.

(b) People are infested by their own frustrations, ego problems, of personality, and self-esteem, etc. Violence is used as a copying-strategy to acclaim and prove one's superiority.

(c) By being possessive and acquisitive we are seeking power or a position of authority. One has to see and be free from every form of antagonism, and from the desire for power to be non-violent in the real sense (Krishnamurti, 1977, p. 116).

(d) People look at interpersonal relationships with expectations and demands. They desire to possess the person in relationship and feel jealous and apprehensive if threatened. All this some times, some where becomes instrumental in precipitating violent behaviour.

(e) People lack the quality of empathising with others. They lack the feeling for the victim. In general people are insensitive towards others, even if the other person is a very close relative.

We would like to conclude by saying that violence on women or for that matter on any one, is part of a total problem. It is the problem of man's cruelty, brutality, hate and insensitivity. The resolution lies in complete action against the total problem and not only its part (like cruelty on women, cruelty on animal or cruelty on children, etc.)".

Encountering Violence

Women are victimized in many ways through overwork, undernourishment and ill treatment, having no say in any matter. It is for us to investigate into the attitude of indifference prevailing in our society and ensure justice and equitable status for them.

Factors which attribute this indifference are: Lack of awareness of seriousness of the problem, general acceptance of man's superiority over woman being the reason why violence against women was not viewed as violent or deviant, and the denial of violence by women themselves owing to their religious values and socio-cultural attitudes. As the cases of wife-battering, rapes, kidnappings and abductions, intra-familial murders, dowry-deaths, eve-teasing, molestation, etc., have been more frequently reported since the late 1960s and early 1970s, the issue of violence against women has been transformed from a private issue into a public problem.

Fundamental Problems

We should focus our study on interpersonal relations and the social context in which violence is committed or atrocities are inflicted on women and in which the victim recovers and adjusts. All these issues have to be examined and assessed with a sociological perspective. The present study presents not only the conceptual perspectives with which to understand the problem but also analyses the socio-cultural and interpersonal determinants of violence, shock, and recovery.

It may be true that the incidence of violence by men towards women is not identical in all groups and communities, and that moral and social beliefs and family arrangements differ from group to group, yet instead of looking into these group differences and analyzing the subcultural and socio-ethical beliefs of these groups, we should concentrate on violence against women as perceived in general terms. There is no woman who has not suffered at one time or another the harassment, humiliation, exploitation and violence that shadows her sex. A woman life swings between pleasure at one end and danger at the other end. In daily life, women are routinely defined by sex, and even if not all men are potential kidnappers, rapists, batterers, molesters and torturers of women, all women are potential victims.

WOMEN'S STATUS

Women in India are way ahead of their counterparts elsewhere in the matter of social legislation. However, in matters of implementation of laws granting rights to women we have been lagging far behind. Women are discriminated against at work and are denied their due in every field. At home, they are ever worse off, being reduced to slavish drudges and maltreated in a hundred different ways. Constantly rebuked and mocked at, frequently bullied, sometimes assaulted, and occasionally burnt to death, they remain victims in every role. Indian women, thus, have been described as the underdogs of society where, in theory the law of equality exists, and women are considered to be on a par with their male counterparts, but in reality, men remain all powerful and thrive at the expense of women. While in the West, women's problem/issue is mostly one of identity, job equality, and sexual roles, in India, the question is simply one of stark survival.

The Constitution of India guarantees equality, freedom, opportunity and protection to women, and various social legislations give them several exclusive rights. Yet, they enjoy an unequal status. This may be due to the social conditions in our society like illiteracy, poverty, social customs, ignorance, and lack of awareness of rights, while others relate it with their personality characteristics like feeling of helplessness, inferiority complex, poor self-image, lack of self-confidence, self-reliance, and resourcefulness. Added to these is their unrecognized output in domestic chores and help to male family members in their economic pursuits.

Recently, incidents of aggressive violence against women are reported to be escalating alarmingly in our country, and this in itself is a sufficient cause for growing concern, and on the other hand, awareness of rights among women has increased, leading to the rise of feminist movement, resulting in a new sensitivity to all forms of subjugation of women by men. Rise in the rate of crimes against women have been reported in all types of crimes—ranging from eve-teasing to abduction and killing. Such trend has been seen in other crimes too. The number of registered cases having spiralled alarmingly in the past few years, the actual number of cases reported is estimated to be many times more than the number registered. In cases like rape, it may be even 15 to 20 times more— large number of rape, assault, and battering cases being marginalized due to social pressures.

Criminal Record

Let us first have a glance at the background material for general issues in some important categories of violence against women.

Strangely, no statistics on crimes against women were collected separately by the Ministry of Home Affairs or the Police Research Bureau till 1988. It was only in 1989 that data relating to crimes against women began to be collected. These data relate to: (a) incidence of crimes committed, (b) number of persons arrested, (c) cases disposed of by the police/courts, and (d) social background of victims.

Various Types

Crimes against women are broadly classified under two categories:

(A) crimes identified under the Indian Penal Code (IPC) and

(B) crimes identified under the special laws (SL).

The crimes under the former category include eight types:

(i) rape (section 376 IPC),

(ii) kidnapping and abduction (section 363 and 373),

(iii) dowry homicides (section 302 and 304B),

(iv) torture—physical and mental (section 498A),

(v) molestation (section 354),

(vi) eve-teasing or sexual harassment (section 509),

(vii) importation of girls (section 366B), and

(viii) murder (other than dowry homicides) (section 302).

The crimes under the last category includes four types:

(a) immoral trafficking (1956 Act),

(b) demanding dowry (1961 Act),

(c) commission of *sati* (1987 Act), and

(d) indecent representation of women (1986 Act).

Statistics of Women's Crimes under Law : On the total crimes committed in India under the IPC every year, about 6 per cent are crimes against women. In 1995, of the total crimes committed under the IPC (16.95 lakhs), 6.3 per cent were crimes against women (*Crime in India,* 1995: 223). Taking the total crimes against women recorded under the IPC and the SL, 8 per cent were Local and Special Laws cases and 92 per cent were IPC cases.

The statistics collected point out that the total number of crimes against women (under the IPC and the SL) (excluding murders) increased from 68,000 in 1990 to 74,000 in 1991, 79,000 in 1992, 84,000 in 1993, 99,000 in 1994 and 106,000 in 1995 (*Crime in India,* 1995: 223). Thus, in five years (between 1991 and 1995), crimes against women increased by 45 per cent.

Break-up : Of the crimes against women committed in 1995 under the IPC and the SL (1,06,471), about 29 per cent are torture cases, 27 per cent are molestation cases, 13 per cent are kidnapping and abduction cases, 13 per cent are rape cases, 4.5 per cent are sexual harassment cases, 8 per cent are immoral traffic cases, 5 per cent are dowry-homicide cases, and 0.5 per cent are other cases (*Ibid:* 222). Broadly speaking, every year, under the IPC, there are about 31,000 torture cases (cruelty by husband and other relatives), 28,000 molestation cases, 14,000 kidnapping and abduction cases, 14,000 rape cases, 5,000 eve-teasing cases, and 5,000 dowry-homicide cases (*Ibid:* 222). Likewise under the SL, there are about 7,500 cases of woman trafficking, 2,800 cases of dowry harassment, 400 cases of indecent representation of women, and 170 cases of importing of girls, and one or two *sati* cases.

All India Ranking of Crime : The highest recorded cases of crime are from Maharashtra (15.3%) followed by Madhya Pradesh (14.4%), Uttar Pradesh (11.2%), Rajasthan (8.8%), Andhra Pradesh (8.5%), Tamil Nadu (8.2%) and West Bengal (6%). Of the 1,06,471 recorded cases in 1995 (under IPC and SL) in the country.

Rajasthan: In Rajasthan, the incidence of crimes against women has sharply increased since 1994. Many committed by influential and moneyed people who could manipulate things in their favour namely — the Shalini Sharma sex scandal of Alwar; the throwing of acid on Shivani Jadeja in Jaipur; the J.C. Bose (Rajasthan University) Hostel gang rape of a girl by seven persons (including the nephew of a minister, an advocate and a police officer); the alleged rape of a woman in Jalore district by a Jain monk who later committed suicide; and the Chomu firing case over the issue of a woman's rape are some of the more serious examples of increasing crime. A point worth noting is that in all these cases, the women involved were blamed and held responsible through manipulation. Rajasthan thus being designated as Rapisthan.

Orissa: In Orissa also, atrocities on women have been similarly on the rise since 1991. Rape cases have registered an alarming increase of about 33 per cent every year. While in 1991, 309 rape cases were registered, their number had gone up to 372 in 1995 and 617 in 1996. Dowry-homicides in the state rose from 98 in 1991 to 169 in 1995 and 354 in 1996, and dowry torture cases from 214 in 1991 to 710 in 1996. The torture of women (not for dowry) was also on the rise with such cases increasing from 183 in 1991 to 361 in 1995 and 405 in 1996. The kidnapping of women increased from 209 in 1991 to 221 in 1995 (*The Hindustan Times,* March 11, 1997).

Delhi: The Delhi figures of crimes against women, as revealed in the latest data issued by the Delhi State Commission for Women are simply shocking wherein *Situation of Girls and Women in Delhi*, Delhi's record in rape cases was twice as bad as that of all the three metropolitan cities (Mumbai, Chennai and Kolkata) put together. That the rate of crimes against women in the capital was far higher than that of the national average (34.1 per lakh of population against 9.5) represented one part of the problem. The alarming aspect was that minor girls were particularly targeted as victims. The incidence of rape cases involving girls below 10 years of age in Delhi was four times higher than that of the rest of the country. What was even more shocking, was the fact that crime in 88 per cent of the cases was committed by relatives or acquaintances, and in 89 per cent of the cases, it was committed at home. The problem thus goes out of the control of police or law and order. It underlines a psychopathic condition (*The Hindustan Times,* March 5, 1997).

There are six categories of violence: sexual violence, kidnapping and abduction, dowry deaths, murder, wife-battering, and a few other specific categories of violence like torture, molestation, etc. These have been discussed in the following pages:

Sexual Violence

Rape : Virginity is valued by man, yet it is man who violates it and commits rape. The important factors in rape are: age, consent (including implied consent and obtaining consent under fraudulent pretext of marriage), duress, state of mind and resistance. Section 376 of the Indian Penal Code describes rape as sex with a woman against her will, or without her consent, or with her consent when the man knows that he is not her husband but she believes him as her husband, or with or without her consent when she is under sixteen years of age. Statistics on rape worldwide show that in the United States, the annual rate of rape offences is about 26, in Canada 8, and in the UK 5.4 per one lakh of total population against 1.38 in India, 3.62 in China and 1.29 in Japan.

There are fewer cases of rape in India as compared to the West. The number of rape cases per one lakh population in 1993 was only 0.5. However, in the last decade, rape cases were more than doubled. Of the 13,754 rape victims reported in 1995, 5.4 per cent were below 10 years, 24.1 per cent between 10 and 16 years, 56.3 per cent between 16 and 30 years, and 14.2 per cent were 30 years and above (*Ibid:* 226). The highest number of rape cases in 1995 was reported from Madhya Pradesh (22.7%), followed by Uttar Pradesh (13.1%), Maharashtra (9.9%), Bihar (9.5%), Rajasthan (7.5%), Andhra Pradesh (6.2%), West Bengal (5.7%), Assam (4.3%) and 21.1 per cent from other states and union territories (*Ibid:* 237).

Causes of Escalation : Though it is difficult to indicate the causes of increase in the incidence of this crime, some factors which appear to have an impact on the conservative social morals and on the increasing rate of rape could be identified as :

(i) urbanization and urbanism;

(ii) industrialization and the growth of slums;

(iii) better reporting by the police;

(iv) co-education and co-work;

(v) movies, obscene and pornographic literature;

(vi) changing attitudes towards women;

(vii) decreasing religious restrictions;

(viii) fall in moral values; and

(ix) emergence of the neo-rich people.

It should be clear that these figures do not reveal the true picture. A high percentage of rape cases go unreported either because the victim does not dare to face the shame and humiliation being heaped on her by society, or because of the disgrace it will bring to her family, or because of the police harassment, or threats and consequences by the rapist. Many cases are put behind the action. It is not only the illiterate and the poor but also the educated and the socially advanced victims of rape who are rejected by their own families, and at times forced to take up the oldest profession. Some victims even commit suicide. Social values turn them into outcastes, a disgrace to their family, and unfit to marry. No wonder, therefore, most victims choose to conceal the fact of having been victims of forcible criminal assault.

Instances : Shamim (real name concealed), a Muslim girl of seven years, was brutally assaulted in Jandhera village near Meerut in 1994 by a 20-year-old truck-driver, a Dalit from the same village. Shamim's mother, accompanied by two policemen, took the traumatized girl to a hospital in Meerut. The little girl had to be operated upon because of which the doctors said, she would never be able to conceive.

The case was brought to the notice of a women's organization—Disha—which got her admitted to a hospital in Saharanpur. The rapist was arrested but soon released on bail. He has since been boasting that "in a state where the Dalits reign supreme (Mayawati at that time was the Chief Minister), no one can touch him". He even went to the extent of taunting Shamim's mother: "Shamim is like the *ber* fruit that can be eaten when it is unripe or when it has ripened." The district magistrate had assured a home to Shamim's homeless family but the assurance remained only on paper. For obvious reasons, the villagers dared not throw the rapist out of the village.

Another instance is, a five-year-old girl who was raped in Pehalwan village in Rajasthan by a shop-owner and his servant. The mother was so traumatized by the incident that she became insane and the father committed suicide. The little girl, who was the butt of cruel jokes and taunts in the village, was moved to an *ashram* in Jaipur.

There is a case of two school teachers, 57 and 52 years old, were suspended and arrested for rape/molestation of three school girls of 12, 13 and 14 years in May 1997 in Uttar Pradesh. They were released on bail by the sessions court which maintained that the medical records did not show rape. It so happened that the teachers had taken the girls to school for coaching in view of the forthcoming school examination. They stayed overnight in the school building. Each child was given five tablets in the night. As fate would have it one child did not take any tablet but the other two took two to three tablets. Two girls were found unconscious in the morning and one was bleeding. They were rushed to a doctor, the husband of an 'anganwadi' worker informed the incident to the parents. The villagers beat up the teachers and rushed the children to a hospital in Saharanpur. After the intervention of the National Commission for Women, the teachers were arrested and suspended. The teachers brought to bear tremendous pressure on the parents to take back the cases. Are these girls to become 'Phoolans' to take revenge?

The Vulnerable Sections : The girls belonging to socially deprived classes are not only inclined to be raped, the women employees belonging to socially advanced classes are sexually humiliated and exploited by their employers and thus are equally under the category of possible victims. Similar treatment is meted out to the inmates by the superintendents of hostels, to patients by hospital personnel, to maid-servants by their masters, and to wage-earners by contractors and middlemen. Even the deaf and dumb, lunatics, blind women and beggars are not spared. Women who come from the lower-middle class and who are the main supporters of their families bear sexual abuse silently as a part of life. The reason makes the incidents of rape increase. As culprits are not punished.

At times it is felt that the stories of rape are exaggerated. Women have to deal with these opinions and attitudes as well as with the age-old myths, such as, "a woman cannot be raped unless she wants it". These myths have been coined and propagated by men, for every woman knows that none of these are true, as in India rape is tantamount to death.

The victims are socially ostracized facing disgrace and suffer serious guilt-pangs and personality disorders as a consequence. When pregnancies result from forced rape, all the outraged sentiments of the community are vented on the women. Children are also stigmatized unless their parents marry, or they are fortunate enough to be adopted into homes sanctified by marriage.

What is the character of rapists? Are they abnormal sexual perverts or ordinary normal men found in all walks of life? Social scientists' contend that by and large they are normal men. A large number of rapes are situational rapes. Criminal assault is instrumental for men either to exploit women or to take revenge. In villages, it is a tool in the hands of the landlords to terrorize their agricultural labourers. One survey on prostitution has revealed that 80 per cent of the prostitutes took up the profession after becoming victims of rape.

Protection by Law for Women at Work : Sexual harassment of women at the workplace is also becoming a serious problem day by day. Public interest petitions were filed in the Supreme Court in 1997 by social activists and NGOs to ensure that women be allowed to work freely and with dignity. The Supreme Court directed the centre and the state governments to enforce twelve guidelines to protect women from harassment at the workplace under which it shall be the duty of the employer or other responsible persons in workplaces to prevent the commission of acts of sexual harassment and provide procedures for the resolution, settlement or prosecution of acts of sexual harassment by taking all relevant steps.

Sexual harassment in workplaces, according to the Supreme Court, includes (*Sunday,* September 28-October 4, 1997):

(i) physical intimacy and advances;

(ii) a demand or request for sexual favours;

(iii) sexually tainted remarks;

(iv) showing porn material to women employees; and

(v) any verbal or non-verbal conduct of sexual nature.

Complaints and Redressals : There has been a great increase in harassment incidence with more women coming out to work. Between 1992 and 1997, of the total complaints (1817) received by the National Commission for Women, as many as 49 were of sexual harassment at the workplace. A sample survey done by the Delhi-based NGO—Sakshi—among women in the private sector has revealed that 60 per cent of the respondents had at some time or other been victims of sexual harassment and that in almost half the cases, a superior was responsible for the harassment (*The Hindustan Times,* September 21, 1997).

Most working women have come to regard sexual harassment as an 'occupational hazard' and society in general believes it is 'normal male behaviour'. In its milder form, sexual harassment is generally abstract and therefore hard to prove. There is no evidence, for instance, of a whispered remark, an obscene sound, or just plain ogling, can be provided unless it is persistent and repeated and witnesses are available. The humiliation can be as intimidating, embarassing and annoying as being pinched, shoved or solicited by a stranger. In a survey conducted by Sakshi, 46 per cent of the victims chose to do nothing about it because they feared they would not be believed or because of the worry that by complaining they would invite allegations of "taking revenge on male colleagues for relationships besmirched"

Myra Dias who was secretary to the Regional Manager (Western region) of Vayudoot Ltd. was subjected to sexual harassment by the Regional Manager and when she did not yield to his advances, he ensured that she was superseded by her juniors. Myra refused to be cowed down. She appealed to the National Commission for Women who took up the issue and after a six-month battle she was upgraded. Myra's case was an exception. She was brave enough to take up the issue and what is more important is that she won. Less fortunate was Ela Chaudhary, a commercial artist in the Government Directorate of Employment and Training: Ela was molested by her immediate boss. Her complaints to the Director General were of no avail. Counter allegations were made against her like having tampered with the attendance register, etc. Ela took the case to the courts and after an eight-year battle, the remarks in her confidential file were expunged. But it was only after her boss retired that she got justice and her stand was vindicated. Somehow the department delayed the procedure because they wanted him to retire with a clean record (*The Hindustan Times,* September 2, 1997).

The Unorganized Sector : Providing protection against sexual harassment may be possible in the organized sector, both in private and government offices, but what about women in unorganized sectors and in rural areas? For example, take the case of domestic female workers or maid-servants or female labourers tilling the land. These women are extremely vulnerable to advances and, having little power to fight such attempts, end up being sexually abused. Caste factor poses another threat. When employees belonging to lower castes are harassed more than those belonging to other castes. In villages, the power structure is controlled by the dominant class. The nexus between the political head of a village and the moneyed gentry is impregnable. Any attempt to quash its stranglehold over the villagers finds with strong resistance.

The court directives to create awareness among women may be used by NGOs. But what about the harassment which female volunteers with NGOs themselves face carrying out their work? Bhanwari Devi, a Sathin in Rajasthan, displeased many upper caste people for trying to prevent child marriage in her village. She was raped as a punishment. And, of course, her rapists were acquitted by the court.

Eventhough the Supreme Court directives on sexual harassment of women in their workplaces may be well intentioned, they do not appear to be practical. Unless the socio-economic ethos undergoes change, unless women themselves show courage, social legislation is likely to fail to make a difference to the life of those who face the danger of sexual harassment. Trade unions can play a significant role by encouraging women to report cases of sexual harassment and then standing by them. Men should also be sensitized and re-educated. Most of men appreciate and recognize the need for laws and change. Men must be subjected to introspection and to look at the problem in their own context as husbands, employers and colleagues. There is also the tendency to dismiss it as a Western input even though it is very much a part of our own male dominated system.The whole matter should be looked at in the Indian context.

Kidnapping and Abduction

Definitions (under IPC) : Kidnapping (under section 363 of IPC) is taking away or enticing a minor—a female of less than 18 years and a male of less than 16 years of age—without the consent of the lawful guardian.

Abduction (under section 363 of IPC) is forcibly, fraudulently or deceitfully taking away a woman with the intent of seducing her to illicit sex or compelling her to marry a person against her will. Thus 'abduction' differs from 'kidnapping' whereas the latter is committed only in respect of a minor, the former is committed in respect of any person. In kidnapping, the victim's consent is immaterial but in abduction, the victim's free and voluntary consent condones the crime. In kidnapping, the offenders' intent is irrelevant but in abduction, it is an all-important factor. Thus, a girl of 18 and above could only be abducted and not kidnapped; but if she is under 18, she could be kidnapped as well as abducted.

Statistics : The incidents of kidnapping and abduction like rape have been increasing in our country by leaps and bounds. The total number of cases recorded in 1990 was 11,699 which increased to 14,063 in 1995 (*Crime in India*, 1995:237). The highest number of kidnapping and abduction cases in 1995 was found in Rajasthan (2,579 out of 14,063 or 18.3%) followed by Uttar Pradesh (16.6%), Assam (7.9%), Madhya Pradesh (7.3%), Gujarat (6.9%), West Bengal (5.8%), Maharashtra (5.6%), Andhra Pradesh (4.8%), and Tamil Nadu (4.7%) (*Ibid:* 237). The rate of this crime per one lakh of population is 2 in our country.

Reports of poor girls being abducted and sold either as wives to rich Arabs or as potential prostitutes to pimps are not unknown. A broker is reported to get from Rs. 5,000 to Rs. 10,000 per girl/woman, and sometimes even more if he caters to every whim and fancy of the prospective customer depending on his economic status. A large number of liaison men and agents are reported operating in big cities. Significantly, the Report of the UN Human Rights Panel has pointed out that the phenomenon—child/girl/woman prostitution—has taken an uglier form in India. The sale of unsuspecting innocent children/girls/women brought from remote tribal areas and villages feeding the big metropolises and other towns and cities has increased.

The number of abducted girls and women rescued is woefully small. Some rescued ones are siphoned into the Protection and Correctional Homes. The conditions at Delhi and Agra Nari Niketans which were pursuing flesh trade within their compounds were exposed by the Supreme Court.

Dowry Deaths : The Dowry Prohibition Act, 1961 has banned the practice of dowry, but in reality all that the law has done is to recognize that the problem exists. It is not often that we hear of a husband or his family being sued for insisting on taking a dowry. If anything, the demands for dowry have escalated over the years along with dowry-deaths.

All India Statistics : At a modest estimate, the figure for deaths in India that occur due to non-payment or partial payment of dowry could be placed around 5,000 for one year. The total number of deaths was 4,836 in 1990, 5,817 in 1993, 4,935 in 1994, and 5,092 in 1995 (Ibid: 222). The highest number of cases in 1995 was found in Uttar Pradesh (36.3 per cent), followed by

Maharashtra (9.2 per cent), Bihar (7.5 per cent), Rajasthan (7.2 per cent), Andhra Pradesh (7.1 per cent), Haryana (4.3 per cent), Karnataka (4 per cent) and West Bengal (1.7 per cent) (*Ibid:* 237). Under the Dowry Prohibition Act (SL), the number of cases registered in 1990 was 2,155 which increased to 2,679 in 1993 and 2,814 in 1995. Bulk of cases in 1995 were reported from Bihar (982), Uttar Pradesh (653) and Karnataka (337) (*Ibid:* 230).

The Dowry Act, 1961 states that dowry is a bailable and non-cognizable offence and ceases to be recognized if demands are made or met one year after marriage. Most dowry-homicides occur in the privacy of the husband's house and with the collusion of the family members. The inability to convict anyone for lack of proof is therefore a natural concomitant. Sometimes, the police are so callous in conducting investigations that even the courts cast a serious reflection on the efficiency and integrity of the police authorities.

The figures of dowry deaths assuming a large number of unreported deaths are as it is unnerving — leave alone if all figures were included. Having their origins in social, economic and psychological factors, too deep-rooted to be tackled by amending the law. Their genesis lies in the tension created by persistent demands, accompanied by torture, for dowry. The greed for money, the aggressiveness increased by resistance and the ease with which the weaker sex can be exploited, all combine to encourage family members to take the bride's life.

Murders of Women : Though all-India figures pertaining to murders and their victims on the basis of sex are unavailable, it is well known that the number of female victims of homicides in comparison to male victims is low. Whereas in the United States, female victims comprise between 20 per cent and 25 per cent of the total victims of homicides (about 25,000 to 30,000 every year), in India of about 38,000 murders committed every year, women constitute about 10 per cent to 15 per cent of the total victims.

Reasons : Being inspired by many factors, such as illicit relations, petty quarrels, feeling of revenge, the desire to get rid of a person who is to get a share in the property, and so forth, many murders may be disguised as suicides and some are even called 'accidents', as if they are natural deaths in some epidemic.

At times, the victim is believed to be a major contributor to the criminal act. She perpetrates the murder either by her habit of constant nagging, or her illicit relations with some other male, or by completely ignoring her husband's or her in-laws' advice, and so forth. The victim may provoke a person into attack, and though the provocation may be slight, if perceived by an egoistic attacker, it may be sufficient to result in homicide. The analysis of the victim-offender relationship in such homicides is, therefore, considered necessary in criminological literature.

Redressals : The inability of the kith and kin of the victim to get redressal through courts is a common occurrence. This is due to notoriously long-winded legal procedures and the offender's social and economic status prevents it.

Women's organizations have been galvanized with the rising curve of murders and other crimes against women. The realization has come amongst women that the individual protests are not strong enough to enable them to fight against their collective oppression. They have started forming forums and associations.

Moreover the government also keeps on amending the social laws pertaining to marriage and family from time to time. But will the women's voluntary organizations and the government's legislative measures reduce women's oppression. Solving the problem of violence against women is a matter of introspection. What social measures need to be adopted to tackle this problem? These are some of the issues that need our immediate attention.

Victimisation of Women

There can be nothing more shattering for a woman than being battered by a husband who is supposed to love her and look after her and whom she trusted the most. Ranging from slaps, kick to breaking of bones this includes violence, torture, attempted murder, and even murder itself. The violence may be related to drunkenesss sometimes but not always. It may also be related to demands for sex, a refusal to obey the husband's commands, extravagance, habit of using vile and disgusting language, and so forth. Battering being occasional or frequent. It may be as frequent as once or twice a week, once or twice a month, or three to four times in a year. In some marital relationships, battering may begin soon after the marriage while, in others it may begin one or two years after marriage. Some wives are held captive by the husbands who insist on controlling their every movement, and knowing every detail of their lives.

Redressals : The Indian cultural system rarely gives examples of a wife reporting to the police of having been battered by her husband. Preferring to suffer humiliation in silence, she takes it as her destiny and does not revolt, due to the fear that her own parents would refuse to accept her in their house permanently after the marriage. It is not always the poor and the illiterate who are battered but even the rich and highly educated are similarly undergone to these sort of ordeal by their husbands. Likewise, even those women who earn and are economically independent also face violence.

Male violence crosses class boundaries and has no association with poverty or lack of education. The common public image of the battering husband is of a working-class male. As wife battering is concealed from the public eye, it is difficult to estimate its extent in society. Since divorce cases in the courts are not always related to marital violence, the extent of divorce also does not reveal the nature and extent of wife battering in society. The battered victims and the indignation they face pose a serious problem for society. There is great need to create an awareness for the scientific study of the problem of domestic violence for ascertaining its intensity.

Victims of Other Category

Torture : Torture of women includes cruelty by husband, in-laws, parents, siblings and relatives. Among crimes reported against women in India, incidence of torture is the highest. Of the total crimes against women (1,06,471) reported in 1995, 29.2 per cent were cases of torture (*Crime in India*, 1995: 222). In a survey, Maharashtra had the highest number of torture cases (28.1 per cent), followed by West Bengal (10.7 per cent), Rajasthan (10.3 per cent), Uttar Pradesh (10.2 per cent), Andhra Pradesh (9.1 per cent), Madhya Pradesh (8.5 per cent) and Gujarat (6.2 per cent) (*Ibid:* 237). Generally, husbands and in-laws are more accused of torture cases, but an exceptional case from Rajasthan in October 1997 shows that brothers and fathers also torture their sisters and daughters. Here, a girl of 22 years was locked in a dark room by her brother for more than two years for her refusal to live with her husband after the marriage. When ultimately the case was reported by a neighbour to the police, she was rescued and admitted to a hospital in Jaipur. The brother and the father of the victim were not arrested till two months after detecting the case.

Molestation : Molestation after torture, is another major crime against women. This constitutes 25 per cent of the total crimes committed against women in our country. While the total number of molestation cases in 1990, 1991, 1992 and 1993 ranged between 20,000 and 21,000, the number increased to 24,117 in 1994 and 28,475 in 1995. The rate of this crime in 1995 was the highest in Madhya Pradesh (25.8 per cent), followed by Maharashtra (12.2 per cent), Andhra Pradesh (9.4 per cent), Uttar Pradesh (9.2 per cent), Rajasthan (7.4 per cent), and West Bengal (4.6 per cent) (*Ibid:* 238) thus accounting for about 70 per cent of the reported cases.

Eve Teasing : Eve teasing or sexual harassment is widely prevalent in India. While the total number of these cases was 8,620 in 1990, their number increased to 12,009 in 1993 but decreased to 10,496 in 1994 and 4,756 in 1995. The highest crime rate in 1995 was reported from Tamil Nadu (22.7 per cent), followed by Maharashtra (17 per cent), Andhra Pradesh (16.2 per cent) and Madhya Pradesh (16.1 per cent) (*Ibid:* 238).

Importation of Girls : Importation of girls is an insignificant crime in our country. Only 167 cases were reported in 1994 and 191 in 1995. Still the police has to be concerned about this crime. About 80 per cent of the total cases of this crime occurred in the following six states—Andhra Pradesh (33.5 per cent), Punjab (14.1 per cent), Gujarat (11 per cent), Madhya Pradesh (8.9 per cent), Maharashtra (6.8 per cent), and West Bengal (6.3 per cent).

Violence, Concept and Definition : An aspect of power dynamics of social situations 'violence' is not simply aggression or injury committed by one individual (man) against another (woman); it is more precisely the abuse of power; it is a behaviour in which a more powerful person takes advantage of and abuses a less powerful one.

This relationship of power differential is clear in sexual violence against women (rape), in their kidnapping and abduction, in physical battering of wives, as well as in dowry deaths and murder of women. In rape, either a man in authority/position victimizes a girl in a subordinate position or a male takes advantage of his physical power and assaults a female. In wife battering, a similar principle of the stronger victimizing the weaker operates. High risk category include women who have less power by virtue of not being an earning member, by virtue of being excluded from participation in decision-making, because of being considered socially immature, and by virtue of having no education or less education than her husband. This underlies the need for research in the dynamics of power and how it operates in and outside family.

Violence; Consequences : Violence has been defined as "injurious and destructive behaviour which damages the victim physically, mentally and/or financially". The three consequences of 'violent behaviour' are: (a) pain to victim, (b) social disapproval and public concern, and (c) realising the need for enacting legislation. That violence against women generally occurs in the privacy of the home or in the privacy of the working places or in the institutions away from the public eye sharply reduces the likelihood of a complaint.

Crime Against Women : 'Crime against women' refers to crimes in which a woman becomes victim. The phrase contains two terms, viz., 'crime' and 'against women'. While the latter term refers only to those crimes in which the victim is female, the former term is meant by the acts which are legally forbidden, intentionally committed and punishable by courts. If we use the definition of crime as "conduct which incurs the formal punitive pronouncements of the courts", or that crime is "the violation of conduct norms of the normative groups", the scope (of crime) becomes broader and more meaningful vis-a-vis violence against women.

Aggression : 'Aggression' refers to injurious behaviour. BUSS (*The Psychology of Aggression*, 1961) defines it as "a response that delivers noxious stimuli to another person". Berkowitz used the term to denote "behaviour aimed at the injury of some object". Many issues cloud the definition of aggression.

Intention : Injury to the victim is the goal of the perpetrator, or such injury is a by-product of some other goal-seeking behaviour? This issue of intention centres on two things:

(a) whether the perpetrator had a reasonable expectation that his behaviour would injure the victim, and

(b) whether such injury was in fact desired by the offender.

Kaufmann (*Aggression and Altruism*, 1970) opine that unless the person performing, he/she had some expectation that the behaviour would deliver noxious stimulation to the recipient the act would not be considered aggressive. Berkowitz maintained that for an act to be considered aggressive, the injury to the victim had to be reinforcing.

Injury : Another issue is, whether the injury need be only physical or whether there can be psychological injury too. Those definitions which limit aggression to acts that physically injure the victims have the advantage of being precise and operational. Psychological injury refers to disparagement, scolding, coercion, harassment, and a variety of other non-physical agonistic behaviour.

Buss distinguished 'angry aggression' behaviour that is reinforced by pain or injury to the victim, from 'instrumental aggression' in which aggression is a means to an end. Delivery of electric shock or verbal criticism are two milder forms of instrumental aggression.

Aggression Vs. Violence : The term 'violence' may be used for more extreme forms of aggressive behaviour that are likely to cause significant injuries to the victim. Although violence refers to physical aggression, it is also applied to psychological stress that causes suffering or trauma. Broadly, the term 'violence' has been applied to the narrow issue of physically striking an individual (Kempe, 1982) and causing injury (Gil, 1970), to the act of striking a person with the intent of causing harm or injury but not actually causing it (Gelles and Strauss, 1979), to the act where there is the high potential of causing injury, and to the act where there is no actual hitting at all, such as verbal abuse or psychological and emotional violence.

Megargee (1982) has defined violence as the "overtly threatened or overtly accomplished application of force which results in the injury or destruction of persons or property or reputation".

Where does one draw the line between aggression and violence? The rapist, for example, uses coercion to obtain sexual advantage over a non-consenting victim. When that coercion involves the overt or threatened use of physical force, it clearly constitutes violence. But what of psychological coercion? A husband may pressurize his wife to submit to sexual relations. This constitutes sexual harassment. Some writers, however, feel that sexual harassment by husband is not an act of violence whereas some others attempt to resolve the issue by making a distinction between 'force' and 'violence'. Hofstadter (1970) defined acts of force as "those which inhibit the normal free action of movement of other persons, or which inhibit them through the threat of violence". Luckenbill and Sanders (1977) have maintained that some actions, for instance rape, are considered violent yet may involve only force. This would exclude acts like kidnapping from the roster of violent crimes, unless the victim is injured.

Thus, if we wish to use the term 'violence' to denote an observable reality, it (violence) must be recognized as a specifically human phenomenon in as much as it consists of the freedom of one person to encroach upon the freedom of another.

4

Easy Targets

Women in India through the ages have been victimised, humiliated, tortured and exploited as long as history can tell. There have been incidents of murder, rape, abduction and torture from time immemorial. In spite of such a dark past, violence against women has not been given much attention, more so, no attempt was made on the issue of why such a socially relevant theme has been left neglected and ignored.

Living in a country which is the world's largest democracy, a sovereign, socialist republic with a comprehensive charter of rights written into its constitution, a signatory to most treaties for struggle against colonialism, imperialism and racism is a matter of great pride for all of us. However, underneath this impressive veneer and national pride about our three thousand-years-old civilization lies a history of systematic violation of basic civil, democratic, and human rights of large sections of our population, such as women. Ironically in a country where womenhood has been put on a pedestal for worship, incidents of wife battering, molestation of women in various forms like rape, eve-teasing, abduction and bride burning keep on increasing year after year. Women find no security be it home, where they are ill-treated by husbands and in-laws, or the streets and work place where they are vulnerable and fall prey to antisocials, moneylenders and men-colleagues, bosses and are subjected to innumerable indignities, perhaps in higher frequency than in most of the civilized societies world over. The general perception today is that the crime against women has increased to such a great extent that women cannot move freely and participate in the community. There is no safe territory left for women not even in their "*mohallas*". Apart from being widely harassed but women are also being assaulted and raped before the eyes of their family members, be— they single or married. Significantly, female victims of violence have not been given due attention in the literature on social problems or in that of criminal violence. Nor any attempt was made to explain why both the public and the scientific communities ignored for so long the varied instances where women were being greatly exploited in our society.

This attitude of constant indifference and negligence can be attributed to three factors: (1) a lack of awareness of the seriousness of the problem, (2) the general acceptance of man's superiority over woman because of which violent acts against women were not viewed as violent or deviant, and (3) the denial of violence by women themselves due to their religious values and social attitudes which leaves no recourse.

Victimization of women in India starts from the time of their birth. Boys are preferred to girls. In most of the cases the birth of a girl child does not make happy even the parents of the child, not to speak about other members of the family. On the contrary, the birth of a son is enthusiastically celebrated with blessings showered on the couple by all the members of the family, friends and neighbours alike. If a woman accidentally gives birth to two or three daughters, she is made to hang her head in shame. She is subjected to abuses and all sort of ill-treatment specially by in-laws. Many women have committed suicide being fed up with torture by mother-in-laws and husbands for being unable to give birth to a son for the family.

There are innumerable instances where the parents leave the female babies at the door-steps of some orphanage or hospital or in parks and say goodbye to the child for ever. A couple from village Tatigharia under Bishungarh police station of Hazaribagh fled the hospital after throwing the baby in the bushes closer to the hospital compound wall. In the meantime a sweeper of the hospital found the baby while cleaning the campus. She brought the baby to her house and started looking after her. Later the police arrested the couple and released them only after executing a bond that both the husband and wife would look after the baby properly.

Dowry Issue : There are cases where the parents kill their young daughters because of their inability to fulfil the demands of dowry and sometimes young girls commit suicide due to their fathers' meagre income sources to fulfil the demands of dowry.

Leading newspapers of India almost daily publish as banner news, crimes against women in various manifestations, i.e., bride burning, rape, abduction, eve-teasing, wife battering both in rural and urban areas of India. This is a news item which is generally noticed, keenly read, and attracts our attention. The issue of crimes committed against women has been a topic of discussion in various forums of public opinion. Press reports reveal that crime against women has increased manifold. The problem of crime against women is not new. Women in Indian society have been victims of humiliation, torture and exploitation for as long as we have had written records of social organisation and family life. There are many records of episodes like rape, abduction, battering, and so forth of women.

Violence is present everywhere though the incidence of violence by men towards women is not identical in all groups and communities, the type, frequency, intensity and control of crime against women may vary from time to time, community to community, or place to place.

No woman who has escaped at one time or another the

harassment, humiliation, exploitation and violence that shadows her sex. A woman's life swings between pleasure at one end and danger at other end. Daily women are being defined by sex and even if not all men are potential rapists, kidnappers, eve-teasers and wife batterers, all women are potential victims.

Protector's Avatar of Law

There have been scores of amendments and inclusion of various laws in the statute book to check the victimization of women. The Dowry Prohibition Act 1961 was amended twice to make its provisions more punitive. The Indian Penal Code, the Criminal Procedure Code and the Indian Evidence Act have also been amended simultaneously to deal effectively not only with dowry deaths but also cases of cruelty to married women. Similarly, the law against rape was also modified to remove some of its drawbacks. But all these changes cannot reduce the volume of the crime at all. One reason why crime against women continues to increase being that the laws are not deterrent enough. So, the culprits feel that they can easily get away with anything.

Their Implementation : Women in India are way ahead of from women of elsewhere in the matter of social legislation. But the implementation of laws granting rights to women are inversely related being slow, lopsided and haphazard that socially, economically and politically women are kept far behind the men. Even today, many decades after independence, women are suffering from various kinds of discrimination, exploitation and torture, mental and physical in society and within the four walls of the family. In a male-dominated patriarchal society, women are protected by the family from other men, but may be unsafe in their own families.

Incidents may occur in the family, offices, agricultural fields, industries, and even public places for which women have to pay the price. Indian women thus can be described as the underdogs of a society where theoretically, the law of equality is supposed to practise and women are considered to be on a par with their male counterparts, but in practice the men remain powerful and thrive at the expense of the women.

The issue of crime against women has been graduated from a private issue to public issue. The large scale reporting on incidents of crime against women by the mass media has brought the ugliness of such crime right inside our homes and makes us realize that the existing efforts have been hardly able to create even a dent in the structure responsible for such crimes.

Lately, Indian women have started rising against their victimisation and there is a growing understanding of the pathetic condition of woman in our society. However, something substantial is yet to be done. Crime against women is one such problem that now offers a challenge. The problems faced by Indian women and specially the crime committed against them need to be realized and checkmated at the earliest, so that no more time may be lost before the situation deteriorates. This study is meant to contribute something concretely to this understanding.

Norms of behaviour exist in every society and any deviation attracts censure from those who are authorised to enforce these norms. Where the behaviour is intentional and harms another person or property, it amounts to punishable by law. There are numerous acts which have been declared offences under the various laws by the Central and State Governments from time to time which are applicable both to men and women. In this study we confine ourselves to a discussion of crimes against women.

Ascertaining the Crime

The phrase "crime against women" refers to those the crimes involving violence against female. Defining the term in parts: (i) "Crime", (ii) "against women". The latter terms refers only to those crimes in which the victim is a female. The former term refers to those acts which are legally forbidden, intentionally committed, and punishable by courts.

Human violence includes any aggressive behaviour of a person or persons hurting body or positive regard or both of another person or persons. Further analysis reveals:

(a) Aggressive behaviour means vigorous behaviour or action.

(b) A person means victimiser either a male or a female.

(c) Hurting body means inflicting physical injury.

(d) 'Positive regard' means need to be level or accepted.

(e) Another person means the victim. Keeping in view this definition, certain misconceptions regarding crime against women may be removed.

Misconceptions

1. Men alone are involved in crime against women and it is a battle of sexes in the general belief. But crime against women is both an inter-sex and intra-sex problem as the victimiser may be a male or a female or both. In bride burning, the husband alone or with the in-laws, male or female, may be the victimiser. The mother herself discriminates between a male and a female child in rearing practices. In sexual crimes, males are the victimisers. Mostly men are the victimisers. But in many cases of domestic violence, females also play their roles in victimising women.
2. Violent behaviour is misconceived to be only on physical level. It is not so. Crime may be expressed in physical torture like wife battering, killing, it is also expressed on verbal level in the form of abuse, rebuke, threat or teasing and also in its talent or indirect forms like all sorts of deprivations, discriminations and obstructions imposed upon women in achieving their goals. These latent forms of crime psychologically hurt women.
3. Crime always results in physical injury. This is not so, criminal behaviour of the victimiser may results in physical or psychological injury but both to the victim. When a

woman is raped or abducted or battered or burnt, she is not only physically injured, but also psychologically hurt.

Categories : Crime against women may be classified into three broad categories viz., (i) Sexual offences, (ii) Offences for gain, and (iii) Customary laws and customs.

Offences of sexual character may be divided further into those which have a predatory element and those which are non-predatory. Predatory element is violence. In an offence in the first category there is a deliberate injury to the victim such as rape or molestation.

The second category includes prostitution, here the victim is a willing participant. The case of rape constituted by sexual intercourse with a girl below the statutory minimum age, stands on a special footing and may not strictly fit in with the above classification. Reverting to the two broad categories contemplated by the dichotomy, it may be mentioned that crimes in the nature of obscenity and bigamy stand midway between them. There is no coercion here and no physical injury and the 'victim' may or may not be a consenting party. The real damage is to the morale of society and such damage is present even though the parties involved in the act give their implied consent. Bigamy where there is full knowledge of both the parties, involve no fraud in contrast to bigamy, where one of the parties may not be aware of the existence of the previous marriage. Crimes indicated by the impersonal desire for gain do not themselves constitute 'crimes against women'. Robbery, burglary, theft (and even some cases of assault), may occur between persons of two sexes but they cut across several lines. Such crimes are intended to enrich the thief and not to express personal hatred or passion towards the victim.

Offences under customary laws and customs are generally peculiar to a particular society. As the customary laws and values are intricately woven in our society through which violence is perpetrated against women, there is need for fundamental changes in the patriarchal values. Else such violence is bound to continue in its familiar forms and newer guises.

Soft Targets

The resurgence of women's liberation movement in India has been accompanied by endeavours at research and action which analyze nature and forms of violence against women. The purpose of this paper is to consider the increased violence against women and the maintenance of the mechanism that perpetrates such violence. The paper also intends to show how social and ideological practices which are often located within the family and the social structures construct male and female subjects with differential powers to act as fully independent beings in relation to others. There is an extreme manifestation of unequal social relations between men and women within the family and the organization of economy; the state legitimizes the inequality and fails to transform the existing social relations based on dependence, oppression and exploitation. What has been the attitude of the family and the role of the state towards the countless numbers who experienced violent martial and non-martial lives? How the feminist activists and scholars have viewed the social origins of the women's degradation and the specificity of violence against women?

A narrow concept of violence may suggest an act of illegal, criminal use of physical force, but it also includes exploitation, discrimination, upholding of an unequal economic and social structure, the creation of an atmosphere of terror, a situation of threat reprisal, and other forms of political violence.

While these concepts of violence are interrelated, the specificity of violence related to the situation of women demands a closer and critical look of the aspects of structural violence i.e. acts of violence that are exercised on the part of the family and society. The state not only tends to overlook these forms of violence, but perpetrates them in the name of the cultural legitimacy and the maintenance of 'law and order'. Recently at a meeting on 'Women and Violence', organized by the South Gujarat University and Centre for Women's Development Studies, we summed up the specificity of violence against women:

> The specificity of the gender dimension lies in the fact that while violence against women perceived as a structural phenomenon is indeed part of the general violence against oppressed classes, the forms of control and coercion exercised in the case of women are gender specific and arise out of a hierarchical gender relationship, where men are dominant and women are subordinate. The forms of control exercised over women cover essentially three areas: sexuality, fertility, and labour. Secondly, women become instruments through which the social system reproduces itself and through which systemic inequality is maintained. This is achieved through rules of legitimacy of offspring, through controlling sexual access to women (as for example, in caste-endogamy rules) and in general through the establishment of possessional rights over women which men have as husbands or fathers or older male relations, such possessional rights include promise of protection (whether actually fulfilled or not in reality) in return for submission and exclusive use. This is further strengthened and maintained over time by the socialisation process that embeds women strongly within the familial structure and hierarchic gender relations such that they have little or no independent status and transgressions outside the family and male authority expose them to swift retributions and confirm their vulnerability.

Violence against women, like all other historical phenomena of violence, must be seen in a socio-economic and political context of power relations. It is produced within a class-caste, gendered society in which the male power dominates. For example, women from landless, agricultural wage labour families, particularly from the scheduled castes and tribes, are most vulnerable to violence. Mass rapes are used by the ruling class men for the repression of the poor peasants and landless labourers whenever they get organized and demonstrate militancy for higher wages or for the implementation of land for the implementation of land reforms. Violence against women in such cases is the result of an attempt to grind women and their men down into submission, as form of social political control and which is ideologically supported in a variety of different ways by the state. However, as discussed above, the specificity of violence against women involves an analysis of gender and its centrality to the family which has gender inequalities at its heart, the state provides the legitimizing ideology of the family-centred male dominance. In other words, the state in India has not attempted to effectively outland the subordination of women to men or to change the relations of dependence within the family.

Women under Constant Trouble

Over the past few years, the phenomenon of women burning and rapes has registered a sharp increase throughout India. In Delhi on an average in 2002, two women died of burns everyday. In Bombay, a survey from two police stations indicated that in a period of 8 months in 2000, one woman was burnt to death every five days. In Bangalore, suicides and 'dowry deaths' nearly doubled in 2001 as compared to the previous years. According to police reports, on an average two women committed suicides every day in 2000. In Madhya Pradesh, records from the biggest hospital showed that one woman died of burn injuries every five days. According to various women's organizations an equal number of burning/suicide cases go unreported. Mostly this is on account of the refusal of the police to register the cases or when they do register, they tend to minimise the offence. For example, over 90 per cent of the cases of women burnt in Delhi were registered as accidents, only five per cent were noted down as murders and five per cent as suicides.

The dowry witch-hunt has taken its heaviest toll in the middle class urban areas, but the burning of women for more money and domestic goods in the form of dowry is quite widespread in the slums and rural areas. Investigations have indicated that women burning is prevalent all over the country, it is most acute in Delhi, Haryana, Punjab, the Western Uttar Pradesh and the Saurashtra region in Gujarat.

In the early 1984, serious concern was expressed by the members in Lok sabha at the increasing cases of criminal assaults on women, gang rapes, molestation, sale of women and kidnapping of female children for the purposes of prostitution. In 1983, United News of India reported 811 cases of eve-teasing (sexual harassment), 68 cases of molestation, and in the first half of 2002, there were 324 cases of sexual harassment and 28 cases of molestation. It was further reported that nearly 5,000 women were made Devdasis every year. According to the figures given by the Bureau of Police Research and Development, New Delhi in 1999 there were 2,562 cases of rape reported all over India. In 2001, the number of cases increased to 3,283 and in 2002 to 3,899. Nearly 435 of the rapes committed in the rural and tribal areas in 1982 were by government officers. Besides, it is a matter of common knowledge that the majority of rapists are set free for the want of adequate evidence.

In Delhi in 2000, there were 202 cases of rape registered with the police and a large number of such coses were left unreported. Of these only 27 were convicted. There is much more to it than crime statistics. They are a manifestation of political malaise in India and malady in the organization of our socio-economic system. The atrocities committed against women within families have often been hidden from the public eye by a social attitude which is mix of apathy towards woman and an inexplicable sense of privacy. To understand the nature of violence against women in India today, it is necessary to look at women's subordination in the structure of material production. To what extent present institutions of family in India is responsible for creating and maintaining structures and ideologies of subordination, structures that inherently resist the participation of women in decision-making and ideologies created by a sex/gender system to maintain existing power relations and forms of exploitations?

Role of Women in Family

Violence runs along the lines of power in the sex/gender system. Family with its basic axis of the sexual division of labour is the principle institution that underlies the sex/gender system. The violence of women burning in the privacy of home has to be examined with regard to its systemic relevance. Details of violence and crimes meted out to women are not necessary in the present context. The focus is on the impact of these types of act on women.

As stated above, there is need to look at the familial authority relations according to which the dowry violence is organized and of property relations which this authority structure realises and maintains. Socio-economic arrangements of sex/gender based disparity e.g. lower wages for women, their under reporting in the labour force, and the disadvantaged position of women in health and education have been justified on the assumption that women's employment and physical existence is secondary to that of men. Therefore, there is, a close connection between the family and the organisation of politico-economic system. In other words, the family approach legitimizes the subordination of women in the policy making and the organisation of economy.

The Constitution of India declared the equality of sex as a guiding principle and thereby acknowledged that a family should basically be an equalitarian unit founded on equal rights and willing choice by both the individuals who form a family. In practice, however, the subordination of women to men and junior to senior pervades family life in all classes and castes in India.

The ideology of subordination is required by the material structure of production. Women are subordinate to men (and thereby dependent too) because men may own land and hold tenancies while women by and large do not. Customary practices preclude women from inheriting land as daughters, except in the absence of male heirs. This is wrongly justified that women receive their share of patrimony at the time of marriage in the form of dowry.

Hindu laws of property and ownership of the means of production give women negligible rights as independent entities, to family income, assets and property. The Hindu Succession Act which has put the daughters on an equal footing with the sons in regard to the succession to the parental property and the Dowry Prohibition Act are not a dead letter by any means but they can be appealed to in certain circumstances—in cases of disputes among families or where land ceiling legal provision makes it expedient for large land holdings to be divided 'on paper' waive male and female heirs.

In most of the cases, daughters waive their land rights in favour of their brothers. Otherwise, they would be denounced as 'selfish' sisters and would risk alienation or severance of the ties with the natal families. Women's effective exclusion from the possession and control of land is largely the basis of their subordination and dependence on men in the rural India. The dowry witch-hunt in India stems from women's subordination in the structure of material production, the organisation of marriage and family and the sexual division of labour; these create gender-specific personalities where as men tend to value their role as the principal one in the national economy and 'bread winners' and supporters of the family while women are excessively undervalued for their dependence, ignorance of outside world and preoccupation with children and household chores.

It is important to point out at this point, that it would be wrong to assume that women in India are passively groaning under an ever increasing oppression within and outside the family. Rape and women burning emerged to the fore-front of the women's movement. The judgement of the Supreme Court on Mathura case drew the country-wide attention to the efficacy of rape laws.

This was followed by a number of forums against rape and atrocities against women in several parts of India. The initial protest in the form of a big demonstration against harassment and killing/ burning of women because of inadequate dowry came in June 1979. Ever since, women's organizations have been demanding from the government more stringent, deterrant measures to check crimes against women. Women have organized to protest the rapes, the sexual harassments and the killing/ burning of women.

Demonstrations and meetings are organized throughout the country to protest against direct and structural violence on women. For the past few years in Delhi and other major cities in the country, women's organizations and housewives have had sproadic demonstrations against the husbands, in-laws, lawyers and police officers involved in the cases of women burning/killing by other means. In the early August 1982, thirty women's organizations in Delhi, under the name of *Dahej Virodhi Chetna Manch* and Dowry Consciousness-raising Forum jointly organized a protest march against dowry, and they were joined by several hundred ordinary women and men, including the "parents of dowry victims".

They questioned police in action and tardiness of investigation, highlighting Government's lethargy towards this problem. They demanded to ostracise the bride-burners/killers and pleaded to legal pundits and legislators to suggest some system of summary trials for such crimes against women.

These demonstrations on the one hand have acted as checks on the husbands and in-laws by exposing the real nature of violence or crime (i.e.,protracted harassment and battering of the women followed by killing and/or burning her) and thereby disallowing an easy escape through a facade of suicide or accidental death. On the other hand, they have pressed for effective change and implementation of laws, tightening of the loopholes in the legal procedures and giving due considerations for women's unspoken experiences of harassment, torture and molestation through proposals for reorganization of arrangement for police enquiries. Further, these demonstrations have opened the areas of female subordination and domestic violence to public attention, bringing in a culture of 'speak bitterness' — empowering harassed wives and rape victims to speak out. The victim's knew ability to describe their plight merged with a resurgence of feminist consciousness raising efforts and led to its consideration by other. Moreover, these groups have particularly suggested critical scrutiny of the family and role of the state in reinforcing the familial structure of domination.

Women's organized efforts could no longer be ignored and the government responded by amending the laws related to rape, criminal procedure and dowry as well as by setting up anti-dowry cell in Delhi and other cities while these laws did seek to improve the existing legal situation related to the women, they failed to question women's subordination and dependency on men within the institution of marriage and family, the state still continued to create structure and legislate for the demonstration of women. The construction of socio-economic dependence of one partner on the other is at the core of legal treatments of husband/wife statues. Strangely enough, the woman cop in charge of Delhi Anti-Dowry Cell, in a recent interview said:

> "It is very difficult to decide whether a burn case is suicide or murder. In both cases the victim is doused from head to toe in kerosene and severely burnt. We feel that 80 per cent of the cases which are brought to our notice are suicides. The husbands and in-laws are certainly culpable because it is their harassment which drives the person to this act".

The social awakening implied by a number of neighbourhood action committees, the emergence of women's wings and front organizations of various political parties, including the increased attention to the women's question in some radical Marxist-feminist organizations, and by the non-party political association, trade unions and profession groups has been a welcome trend. Conscious women activists have been organizing Padyatra (long-march) made skits, plays and movies on the oppression and exploitation of women, launched protests and set up women's centres, where women in distress could be helped and could get help, support and legal aid.

Feminist magazines and network bulletins have reported on both the problems of women and their attempts at resistance. Some feminist academics have questioned the limitations of social sciences in the study of demographic patterns and the female roles in economic production in their own society. A landmark was the report *Towards Equality* pointing out the national neglect of women in development programmes for women in the the fields of employment, health and education. Feminist researchers have been involved in studies of women's roles in the protest movements and their participation in the nation building. These studies have further pointed out the existing inequalities in the socio-economic, political system, and how women's studies offer a new perspective which enables researchers and students to make an attempt to build a legalitarian social structure, within the family and community.

The women's protest through their studies and demonstrations has made this violent crime of women burning visible as a serious social problem. It has opened a whole new vista by calling attention to the oppression, conflict and violence hidden behind the superficial portrait of love, support and nurturance in the family. Nevertheless, it would be simplistic, to say that we are on a brink of profound change in the social structure in the direction of equality and justice and we agree with William J Goode that "we must never under-estimate the cunning or the staying power of those in charge".

Besides, there is, however absence of satisfactory theorizing in the women's movement in India. Family in India has been explained in purely functionalist terms or in terms of the distinctive cultural features of the sub-continent. Social Scientists have been engaged in debate on: (i) nuclearisation of joint-family structure is taking place in India; and (ii) nuclearisation of joint-family structure is not taking place. A few of them concentrated on studies to know the extent of nuclearity or jointness in urban and rural families. They did not question the complex power relations between gender and generation that underline the family, the ideology and structure of dependence and sexual division of labour that strengthen the patterns of inequality and the oppression of women and children.

In recent years, however, the family has emerged as a political issue in India. The Government has formulated policies to further strengthen the family, while the women's movement raised questions about family boundaries. The women organizations pointed out the proposed planning with its women in the family approach would not lead to greater equality in society but to an increased polarisation between the sexes. As a result of pressure from women activists and scholars, a concession was made by incorporating a chapter on "Women and Development" in the Sixth Five Year Plan. The chapter admits that women are "the most vulnerable members of the family" and will continue to be so "for some time in future". It further promises to give "special attention" to the interests of the 'vulnerable members'. Nevertheless, the Sixth Five Year Plan insists that "the family is the unit for programmes for poverty eradication".

The problem of the repression of women in the family was acknowledged, but the family as the basic unit of economic development was maintained, and thereby preventing a constructive analysis.

Status and Role of Women in State Affairs

The state in India never set out to fundamentally restructure relations of authority within the family or to enable women to have an access to property and other resources. Through its construction of the family-centred programme, in its assignments of productive and reproductive functions, and above all in its land/property holding and technology control functions to the (male) heads of the households, the state seems likely to erode even further the rights which women earlier enjoyed. However, for many political and intellectual reasons the specificity of women's oppression and exploitation and the role of the state remains substantially unexamined.

Historically speaking during the nationalist period under the leadership of Mahatma Gandhi, there emerged a distinct approach to the role of women in society. The leadership realized that women were "condemned to domestic slavery" and therefore sought to liberalize the family to expand women's activities in the public sphere within politically acceptable limits. Women were urged to participate in the struggle for freedom of the country. Gandhiji viewed women's oppression as historic and nearly universal.

He lamented over their non-participation in social, political affairs, women's sexual subjection into their role as "man's plaything". In Gandhi's view, the qualities of courage endurance and moral strength made women the natural leaders' of a non-violent struggle against injust socio-political system. He wanted to 'feminize politics' because women had the potential to give a blow to established socio-political power structure and could be vanguards of a non-violent struggle for a just and non-exploitative socio-political order.

This seemed a radical stance but the kernel of women's oppression— the sexual division of labour and thereby her subordination in the structure of material production were neither fundamentally questioned nor altered. "She is essentially mistress of the house. He is the bread-winner, she is the keeper and distributor of the bread". Women supplement the meagre resources of the family, but man remains the bread-winner.

The traditional glorification of women's role as guardian of Hindu morality and spirituality and their self-sacrifice and endurance are central to the concept of non-violence advocated by Gandhi, while he has frequently referred to women in their domestic roles. He was oblivious of the violence done to women in the notion of chastity. For instance, he believed in moral appeals to the rapist and, failing that, suicide as the only course left to a women. One must admit though that there simply has not been enough research to do justice to Gandhi's views on women's historic role. The dominant trend however, is, the ambivalence on women's role.

In the thirties and forties, there was an uneasy alliance between feminism and nationalism. While women's organisations accepted a subordinate and complementary role in politics they repeatedly came in conflict with the Congress when it threatened women's issues and alienated women members. At the initial exclusion of women from the Dandi March in 1930, the Women's Indian Association protested against the Congress leadership: "This division of sexes in a non-violent campaign seems to us unnatural and against all the awakened consciousness of modern women". The Association demanded, that "no demonstration organised for the welfare of India should prohibit women from a share in them".

In the following years, the three basic components of the strategy of planning in India i.e. land reforms, cooperative farming and community development in the fifties and sixties were ridden with class, caste and gender relations. Protagonists of rural development worked to help rural women become "a good wife, and a wise mother" and totally disregarded women's work in the rural economy, specifically their contribution to agriculture and side-line production e.g, cattle-rearing, fishing, weaving etc. Most of these wife, mother, improvement programmes have proved a failure because they are irrelevant to the needs of women in subsistence agriculture and were unable to augment women's income in any way.

Women constitute 48 per cent of the population, while the percentage of women in the total work is only 20 per cent. Approximately thus every fifth woman is a worker, as against every second man. Among the 'marginal workers' (those who are engaged in work for less than six months), 84 per cent are women as against 16 per cent men, while of the non-workers, more than 61 per cent are women.

Moreover, work opportunities and participation of women has been declining over the last several decades. It was observed in a earlier study that Green Revolution technology on the one hand denies women employment opportunities otherwise available to them, on the other hand stereotypes all those jobs which pay less and require less skill, forcing women to take up jobs which come to be regarded as purely female tasks. As a consequence, the invisibility of women as producers of economy is enhanced and they increasingly lose ground in the traditional economic and decision-making roles. There was no attempt to redefine the roles of women; perhaps most important, the division of labour within the family retained all its force. In a report on rights of women: *Inside the Family,* conducted by people's Union for Democratic Rights, it was stated:

> "The treating of family as a private area governed by religious and social customs, regarding of women a peripheral to economic development by the state, the inability of the legal system to recognize their unique unequal status, the bias of the police and courts in relations to crimes against women, are all part of these social values".

However, while a number of legislative measures were adopted to guarantee legal equality to women, in practice there are hardly any opportunity provided for women to learn their new roles; the process of revolutionary transformation in the social position of women came to an end of being submitted to an anti-participatory, elitist bureaucratic structure of exclusion and manipulation. Attempts to legislate, reform and enforce laws have tended to build on the assumption that society is against such phenomenon, so law enforcement would reduce or delegitimize them.

The state initiatives were accordingly directed towards making its executive functionaries more sensitive, judiciary more receptive and the law, in words, less sexist. This may create an illusion of progress or improvement, but now it has empowered women to halt the increasing violence and destruction of their lives. We need to know what the state has done to transform its class-caste and gender construction. Has it changed its formal and legal norms for professional right of men over women, the rules of legitimacy of offsprings, which denigrate and limit women as sexual, subhuman objects? Has it effectively de-legitimized processes which are in agreement with the advocacy and interest of the ruling class and gendered social structure and made substantive policies for the development and liberation of women? Is the liberation of women crucial to the development of a society?

Women involved in the liberation movement have increasingly realized that the phenomenon of violence against women will not be challenged without a struggle to end the subordination of women to transform unequal social relations based on oppression and exploitation. The need of the hour is a radical transformation in the organization of economy along with a radical change in the structure of family, including reordering of peoples most personal and intimate relations.

5

Factors at Work

People have always been deeply disturbed about violence against women, but they have never quite understood what makes the sense of pain conveyed by the term violence more painful than any other pain, the sense of fear more awesome and the terror more terrifying than any other. Women suffer and are made to suffer in many ways. In behavioural terms, violence against women ranges from simple suppression to abuse, aggression, exploitation and severe oppression.

We know it as female infanticide, the abortion of the female foetus, the neglect and undernourishment of the girl child, denial of education to girls, rape, pre-puberty marriage, wife beating, the harassment of a bride leading to her suicide or murder. Each of these is more awesome than comparable or even greater pain or fear experienced in other contexts. For instance childbirth can be extremely painful, but one never refers to the pain of childbirth as violence, no matter how severe it is. The fear of death in a situation of terminal illness, can be extremely terrifying but one does not refer to it as violence.

In an effort to try and identify the element that makes violence different, an attempt has been made here to define violence. A recent Indian report of a study on Women and Violence sponsored in India and in Korea by UNESCO, Bangkok, looked promising in terms of providing a lead. This report, edited by Dr. Krishnaraj, has been prepared by the SNDT University's Research Centre for Women's Studies.

It is based on an analysis of violence against women reported in Gujarati, Marathi and English language journals and newspapers and on findings from some case studies specially undertaken for the purpose. It also offers a review of Enactments on Violence against Women made in the decade of the eighties (1980-1990) and discuss women's action groups and the State machinery against women.

The Notions

According to the above report:

> Violence, in general, is a coercive mechanism to impose one's will over another, in order to prove or feel a sense of power. It can be perpetuated by those in power against the powerless, or by the powerless in retaliation against coercion by others, to deny their powerlessness. Any hierarchical system of social organization, where there are categories of dominant groups and subordinate groups, is inevitably accompanied by the victimization of the latter through various means — subtle pressure through the power of ideology, through mechanisms of socialization that reward compliance and punish noncompliance and also through open force. Usually, the last form is resorted to when other methods fail. In fact, it is often not even necessary to actually use physical force or inflict severe injury, for the mere threat to do so is enough to subdue the subordinate person or group.

> Any individual or group facing the threat of coercion or being disciplined to act in a manner serving the interests of another individual or group, is subject to violence. This is not necessarily confined to physical violence but the creation of an atmosphere of terror, a situation of threat and reprisal..... A hierarchical social structure has violence built into it.

Impressive as it is this statement on violence leaves one feeling more inadequate about the understanding of the concept. To start with the very first line, describing "Violence as a coercive mechanism to assert one's will over another to prove a sense of power" leaves one wondering about where one would place punitive action considered socially legitimate.

For instance, the State legitimately uses coercive mechanisms to assert its power over deviants. Whether it does so to "prove" its power or to "assert" the power legitimately given to it is a matter of semantics. What matters here is that this coercion and exercise of power are socially accepted as a legitimate means of resolving a problematic situation.

One of the core elements of violence seems to be that the coercion involved is neither legitimate nor socially acceptable. The statement does not make this point. On the contrary, by saying that "any individual or group facing the threat of coercion or being disciplined to act in a manner serving the interests of another individual or group is subject to violence", it reduces all coercion, legitimate or otherwise, to violence.

There are other problems with the definition. For instance, the sixth line talks of "Any hierarchical system of social organization where there are categories of dominant groups and subordinate groups, etc." The "Any" in this sentence suggests that hierarchy is not a universal feature of social systems and that there may be some social systems without hierarchy.

This is not true. All societies, even those that are supposed to be egalitarian, have distinctive hierarchies. Not surprisingly the author of the introduction to the report, who makes this statement on violence, seems, herself, to find it too broad to be of any use. She says, "If we accept this very wide definition of violence, it is difficult to know where to draw the line" and decides to go on with her project with a relatively limited definition of violence against women as sexual harassment and sexual violation.

Among other definitions of the term, Collins dictionary defines violence as :

(i) "Behaviour which is meant to hurt or kill people";

(ii) "a great deal of energy used in doing something — usually because you are very angry";

(iii) "words, actions or other forms of expression which are critical or destructive".

The Oxford dictionary defines violence as :

(1) "the quality of being violent";

(2) "violent conduct or treatment, outrage, injury";

(3) "the unlawful exercise of physical force; (3b) "intimidation by the exhibition of this".

The Thesaurus adds a few additional dimensions to the concept offered by the two dictionaries. It indicates that the noun violence connotes vehemence, impetuosity, vigorousness, excess, destructiveness, vandalism, turbulence, turmoil, roughness, severity, brute force, brutality, savagery, mercilessness, exacerbation, explosion. The adjective 'violent' is explained among other terms by the terms aggressive, charging, disorderly, turbulent, stormy, anarchistic, nihilistic, intemperate, immoderate.

Thus, at the end of the exercise of consulting the dictionaries and the Thesaurus, the connotation of the term violence comes across as coercive, destructive behaviour, with a great deal of powerful, aggressive energy and force, destroying in a merciless manner what it is directed at and disorderly, anarchist, turbulent, outrageous and unlawful in its functioning.

Area of Concern

This concept is further elucidated in a television series entitled *Maharashtratil Stree Muktichya Paulkhuna* (Footprints of the Movement for Liberation of Women in Maharashtra). Depicting the emergence of new values, a new self-image, self concept and consciousness among the women of Maharashtra during the course of the nineteenth and early twentieth centuries, it depicts how values pertaining to the rights, the status and the situation of women, steadily changed in this part of the country under the influence of Christianity and European Liberalism. History indicates that the change first occurred among Western educated men, who, inspired by these values, were stimulated to social reform. It occurred somewhat later among women.

The series also conveys the fact of the gradual change in values very cleverly. It picks characters, events and scenes from novels, plays, biographies and autobiographies from during a century between 1840 and 1940 and uses the dialogues, soliloquies and events from these literary sources to illustrate how awareness perceptions, and values steadily changed in those times. The core element of this change was a gradual transformation in notions of right and wrong. Practices like child marriage and the denial of the right of re-marriage to widows which, were the social norm of yesteryears, came to be considered oppressive.

Shaving the heads of widows in particular, a routine practice among Brahmins and other upper caste Maharashtrians, came to be seen as an outrageous violation of the helpless widow. There was something terribly wrong about a situation wherein both the parental family of the woman as well as the family of her husband, responsible for protecting her in her widowed state inflicted such torture on one who was an important member of the family, loved and cared by all. She was disfigured as soon as her husband was gone with no consideration that widows subjected to this practice were often no more that ten or twelve years old did not seem to matter. As change occurred, this fact made the practice seem even more cruel and heinous bringing about protests and movements against such an oppressive custom.

With the unfolding of episodes to reveal how the reactions of the women to some of the traditional practices steadily changed, it was obvious that not only did these practices gradually come to be seen as wrong but the sentiments that they evoked also changed. What was once accepted and respected as religious customs and generated sentiments of pity, sadness and even horror accompanied by a feeling of the inevitability of destiny, a deep sense of awe, and a commitment to surrender to the authority of religion transformed into sense of outrage and injustice, a feeling that what was being done was enormously inhuman and wrong and must be stopped. Initially this was only felt by the reformers.

The reaction of the others, including the women subjected to the practices, was that the practices were extremely painful, but virtuous. Steadily this changed. The women themselves started to question these practices and began defying them. In essence, reform thus consisted of a transformation wherein what was earlier acknowledged to be painful but accepted with reverence as something required by religion, now came to be seen as aggressive and inhuman. The religious norms and beliefs that legitimized this aggression were seriously questioned.

Fresh Developments

Significantly the forces that led to this change came from outside the Hinduism. The change occurred because Christian values and European Liberalism had established their hold, first on the consciousness of the Western educated reformers and then on women. Hindu men and women had acquired a new sense of humanism influenced by these new values. A new notion of the dignity of the self, of the sanctity of personhood and of the obligation to protect the helpless was introduced. Seen from the vantage point of these new values, the earlier practices were a transgression and violation of humanism. What was earlier only seen as painful and sad, now appear to be inhuman and therefore violent. This then seems to be the essence of violence — a feeling of violation, of the transgression of what is considered to be human.

Corollaries of 'Violence' : Thus conceived, the concept of violence has several important corollaries. For instance transgression implies a transgressor. Thus violence is something that a transgressor inflicts upon a victim. Violence in a manner is socially unacceptable. This corollary to the concept of violence fits in very well with the definition of the verb "violate" defined in the Oxford dictionary as: (A) "to disregard, fail to comply with (an oath, treaty, law, etc.)" (B) "to treat profanely or with disrespect" (C) "to break in upon: disturb (privacy etc.)" (D) "to assault sexually, rape etc."

Behaviour viewed as violence in one society may not be so in another is another interesting corollary to the concept of violence, defined as violation, transgression or socially unacceptable infliction of pain. This is so because what is unacceptable in one society may be acceptable in another. There are many examples of this. For instance, female circumcision, routinely practised in some African countries, is viewed as violence by those of us who do not belong to the African culture.

A related corollary is that practices that are not perceived as violence in a society at one point of time may be considered to be so in the same society due to transformation of values. For example, the fact that practices such as child marriage or the denial of the right of remarriage to widows, which were acceptable within our society only three or four generations ago, are now considered to be violent by all of us is by far the best example. The change in values that occurred with respect to traditional practices governing the lives of women in our society has been highly uneven, thus generating serious turmoil and unrest, this turmoil has often been channelized into constructive movements for social reform and change.

Finally, practices and behaviour that may not be considered to be violent by a person at one point of time may be considered violent by the same person as his/her values or awareness change. This can lead to deep personal conflict, anomie and even complete breakdown if the person experiencing the change is unable to contain or manage the fluctuating values.

An example of the last two corollaries is the transformation in the awareness of Black Americans after the Second World War. Discrimination on the basis of colour resented by the Black population of the United States of America had been broadly accepted until the Second World War where the Black soldiers fought shoulder to shoulder with White, with equal courage and patriotism. On their return from the War these soldiers resented the racial discrimination they had earlier subjected to. They saw it as a serious violation of the equality promised by the Constitution of their country.

So did many White Americans. Those who had acquired a new awareness of equality suffered deep resentment and personal conflict when they faced racial discrimination. But this new awareness of equality was not evenly shared in our country. And this led to the strong movements against racial discrimination that rocked American society in the decades of the fifties, sixties and seventies. As the change continues to be uneven, the feeling of violation persists. This is a source of continuing personal and social conflict in the USA. There is no denying the fact that the people may undergo deep personal conflicts and upheavals due to this.

Women all over the world have started to resent the discrimination they suffer in different spheres of life. This has been channelled into constructive activism towards the empowerment of women, and towards legal measures and structural reforms aimed at improving their status and situation in life. However, some of it has given way for angry feminism, and resulted in deep personal conflict, even breakdown, among women who have been unable to cope with their resentment against gender discrimination.

In keeping with the trend of Women Empowerment, SNDT University launched a foundation course entitled Women in a Changing India. The objective of this course is to make the students aware of their situation as women, to help them to look critically and analytically at their status in life, to recognize the restrictions that women face because of gender discrimination. The course also aims at enabling students to recognize their strengths and to inform them about the Constitutional provisions ensuring them equality. It attempts to introduce them to the range of new provisions and opportunities now available for their advance.

This course has been enormously well received. The feedback from those who teach the course indicates that students are eager, alert, receptive and full of questions. Many of the students at SNDT University come from very orthodox families. As expected, the feedback reveals that exposed to the course, they have started to question the discipline and the traditional values within their families. They have started, questioning traditional role expectations which they had earlier accepted with ease.

Many of them now consider some of these expectations to be a violation of their personal dignity and individual freedom. Some of them are able to cope with this sense of violation and advance towards greater autonomy and independence. But many face deep personal conflicts in striking a balance between what they have been raised to believe and what they now determine on their own. This conflict is part of the process of their empowerment. It is part of their advance towards autonomy, freedom, and the new rights and opportunities available to them.

But it is difficult to handle. The challenge for the University committed to the empowerment of its students, is to help them to resolve this conflict and to advance without allowing their new awareness and sense of violation to seriously damage their personalities or destroy their relationships within their families. It may not be easy but surely there will be a way out some day.

Social Crisis

Two points are sought to be made here :

> First, that India has always been the land of contrasts and that a wide spectrum of value systems, from the extremely "traditional" to the extremely "modern" exist side by side.

Second, that Indian society remains firmly rooted in the patriarchal ideology which is premised upon male supremacy and a legitimization of women's oppression. Because this basic ideology remains largely unchallenged and unchanged, violence against women is also perpetuated, sometimes in the old forms and sometimes in different and newer guises.

The concept of tradition and modernity is debatable as indeed the factors for classification are based on tradition and culture which are largely followed in underdeveloped countries. There is the additional need to distinguish between "modernization" and "Westernization". However, we can bypass these complexities by simply employing the term "tradition" to mean age-old customs and "modernity" to mean partly Westernized social practices thus focusing primarily on the multiple forms of violence against women which remain an oppressive reality.

Menace of Patriarchical System

Patriarchy as prevalent in India a hundred years ago was premised upon the male predominance authority, power and female subordination and subservience, the woman's wife-mother role as her *raison d'être*, and her status as the legal, economic and sexual property of her husband. This was sacralized through the ancient Hindu socio-legal treatises. The most authoritative of these, the *Manusmriti*, stipulated that a woman had to be under the protection and control of her father in childhood, her husband in youth and her sons in her widowed old age, and furthermore that a woman does not deserve independence.

This dictate was translated into practice with ease given the practices of universal and early marriage for women (always before puberty in the upper castes and usually so in other castes and also among other religions), immediate post-pubertal consummation of marriage, early and frequent pregnancies and physical and verbal violence in the marital home. Thus, the traditions were legitimized due to sanctions from treatises.

A woman's life revolved around the extended family which was a small community in itself, finely graded along the triple axes of sex, age and degree of relationship with the head of the family. The extended family spanned several generations and comprised the patriarch and his younger brothers with their families, all the married sons with their families, all the unmarried sons and daughters and sometimes widowed or deserted daughters who returned to the parental home.

The source of power was the patriarch who designed the chief economic resource of the family, its immoveable property and ancestral wealth, to be held in common by all the males born into the family, as coparceners: so that the daughters were not entitled to a share in this indivisible property and were therefore compensated at marriage with a smaller share of the moveable property, especially jewellery, clothes and household articles. This bridal portion was intended to be treated strictly as her "woman's wealth" solely under her control but was eventually transmuted into "dowry" to which her husband and marital family laid claim. The economic dependence caused by this loss of assets was considerably aggravated in those regions where women were largely economically inactive. Directly or indirectly man controlled all the wealth and made woman a puppet to their whims and fancies.

Male Monopoly : The male monopoly of domestic authority and decision-making powers increased women's dependence on their husbands and grown-up sons through whom alone they could access power.

Whereas a son would remain within the family, carry on the family name, care for his parents in their old age, and perform the necessary rituals after their death, a daughter would marry and leave the parental home and was thus in effect "a stranger's wealth" — to be nurtured and trained only to be given away at the great expense of a suitable dowry. The preference for a son and undesirability of daughters stemmed from this situation, as did the mother's possessive love for her son/s as her future protector/s and provider/s. Such values relegated women to a low value premium in the family.

Mother-in-law Syndrome : A bride entered her husband's family after marriage according to the practice of patrilocal residence as the junior-most and most vulnerable member. A strong bond between her and her husband was prevented from developing by his mother who wished to monopolize his affections in the interests of her own survival. Thus the institutionalized harassment of the bride or the "mother-in-law" syndrome came into being. Whereas all the brothers grew up and continued to live together in an atmosphere conducive to male bonding, a parallel female bonding was effectively prevented by the fact that all daughters-in-law were unrelated outsiders in competition with each other for a better share in the common resources for themselves and their children and that the mothers-in-law were in competition with their daughters-in-law.

Thus patriarchy effectively pitted the women against one another and revealed the divisive potential of the extended family as far as women were concerned. The pattern thus cultivated was a well calculated move and developed through well-motivated ideals.

Female Undesirability Deprivation : This normative structure has resulted in the traditional institutionalization of violence where violence against women started almost at birth, its most extreme form being the culturally legitimized femicide through female infanticide. Limited to parts of Rajasthan and Gujarat (and was forbidden by British legislation introduced in 1877 specifically in these areas), a girl was usually made to feel unwelcome and undesirable as well as inferior to her brothers and to all men in general.

Physical chastisement, sometimes in quite severe forms, was meted out to her by her mother who was solely entrusted with the task of socializing and disciplining her for her future wifely role— thus sometimes obstructing a warm mother-daughter relationship from developing. Given her burden some share in the household duties, a girl experienced only daughterhood and was deprived of a carefree childhood which was reserved for boys. The denial of education to girls even among the traditionally literate upper castes which provided mandatory education for boys was another discrimination largely aimed at keeping females submissive and ill informed about their rights.

The Criteria

Early Marriage : Marriage well before the age of puberty, the girl was sent to her husband's house as soon as she came of age, and the marriage was consummated immediately usually with appropriate ceremonies. The early start of married life followed by early motherhood — sometimes in the early teens and always by the midteens — was physically traumatic, debilitating and injurious upto the point of death. Failure on the wife's part to produce a child— and sometimes failure to produce a son — could jeopardize her position in the marital family and could lead to her being deserted by her husband making it even worse for the women.

Widowhood : Widowhood in some parts of India (notably Bengal and Rajasthan) lead to the widow's immolation on the funeral pyre of her husband until stopped by British legislation in 1829. In other regions of India and in the castes which did not practise widow immolation, a widow still suffered a social death. Having outlived her main sexual and reproductive function in life, she was made to live a life of sufferance by renouncing all forms of enjoyment and wear drab clothes. She was sometimes physically disfigured (for example, by shaving off her head as in Maharashtra) considered inauspicious and treated as a household drudge. Upper caste widows were forbidden by religion to remarry, even though they were widowed in childhood and even after the Widow Remarriage Act of 1856 made it legally valid, while widowers were encouraged to remarry at once.

Types of Crimes

The large bulk of the population living in rural areas has not changed much during the last hundred years and still follows some of the customs outlined above. There are occasional female infanticides in small rural pockets in Tamil Nadu and Rajasthan, frequent early marriages (sometimes below the minimum legal limit), early motherhood, inadequate information about the access to family planning methods. Dowry demands and related harassment, as well as wife-battering are rampant. A few incidents of widow immolation have also been reported in the recent past from rural Rajasthan.

Other forms of violence which are passive include inadequate nutrition and health care for girls and women. Many demographers claim that the unbalanced sex ratio in India, showing a female deficit is due to higher mortality among women caused by health neglect. It is alarming that the general proportion of women in the total population is not only unbalanced but also declining consistently, at the Census of 1901 there were 972 females per 1000 males, while in 1991 there was a further drop to 929 females per 1000 males.

Current Status

At the other extreme is a very small progressive segment in urban upper class Westernized areas where the situation has changed radically and where women enjoy the benefits of education, careers, economic independence and occasionally of political power, although true gender equality still remains an elusive dream.

Somewhere in the middle lies the urban, educated, relatively well-off and partly conventional section of society where the value system is less harshly patriarchal than before, but where gender discrimination and oppression still continue. The undesirability of daughters still remains deeply entrenched in the Indian psyche, and a new form of eliminating girl babies through female foeticide is becoming prevalent through the diagnostic technique of amniocentesis — basically designed for detecting foetal abnormalities — to determine the sex of the foetus, followed by the selective abortion of female foetuses.

The practice continues despite the recent legislation to prevent sex-determination and sex-preselection — a telling example of misuse of science. Having enjoyed a childhood relatively free from cares or household duties, the girls are psychologically always being made aware that marriage is their primary career and educational achievements or job-oriented careers are of secondary importance. Marriage takes place after (usually soon after) the age of 18, the minimum legal age at marriage for women, and still tends to be universal. Though now with education and awareness, girls do not want to join the bandwagon of lifelong drudgery. They would rather settle for an identity of their own through entering into an occupation of their choice and stand on their own feet.

Dowry demands are on the rise whether due to increase in registration or in reality is a matter to be studied. Torture of the bride for extorting more money and consumer goods resulting sometimes in death (either through suicide or outright murder by burning camouflaged as an accident while cooking), continue on a large scale in spite of relataively stringent legal provisions. The culprits are rarely arrested more so, rarely convicted.

The chief attribute which earns a woman true respect is

motherhood. The pressure to produce sons remains unabated. The wife/mother has to submit to the decisions of her husband or mother-in-law rarely having any say. Even when families are planned and limited, the chief responsibility for contraception rests with the woman, and usually takes the form of sterilization through surgical procedure.

The man takes the back seat — not ready to face any inconvenience — all at the woman's expense. A widow can rarely claim her rightful share in her marital property and continues to be economically dependent.

Sex Factor

The ever-present threat of sexual violence, by far the most common type of violence against women, similar in all societies covers a wide range. The least serious is "sexual harassment" or Eve-teasing in India (and the offenders labelled indulgently as "Roadside Romeos" and glamorized in Hindi movies) though it remains a very humiliating experience for women. It is encountered in public places and on the streets, in the form of wolf whistles, touching, pushing or pawing. In the workplace it may lead to sexual demands from superiors, in rural areas it is village headmen or other powerful men who exert such pressure.

More serious is sexual assault which does not technically amount to rape and does not carry a severe penalty. Rape is legally defined in India as involving penetration of the vagina by the penis, thereby revealing the underlying patriarchal assumption that the offence consists in the violation not of the woman's body and personhood but of another man's sexual property. Another way of holding the man on the helm. A male chauvenistic viewpoint.

Other than the physical trauma, there are several frightening aspects related to sexual assault and rape. The stigma attached to the victim rather than the culprit, even when the cultprit is apprehended (which is well-nigh impossible because of the private nature of the offence and the difficulty of proving lack of consent on the woman's part when her own testimony is not considered sufficient) being one aspect. The second aspect is that the victims are not necessarily adult women of a sexually active age group, but can be small babies or old women, a proof that the crime is directed against the entire sex and stems from a view of women *per se* as sex objects.

If a woman is viewed primarily as her husband's property, an effective way of penalizing him is to snatch away or violate his property, that is, his wife. An increasingly common phenomenon in India today is the large-scale violation of women, with rape used as an instrument of revenge upon men, this has been widely experienced in situations of ethnic violence.

Indian society is a mixture of traditional and modern values. On the one hand, we have the belief that women must get education, employment, better health care and more freedom of choice; we also accept their entry into the professions and positions of power (including the prime ministership, the highest office in the country). On the other hand, the basic view of women as inferior and subordinate remains unchanged. Again, the improvement in their status is usually, though not always, more apparent than real and modern technological knowledge and health facilities are sometimes used to the detriment of women. This is the nature of society — a strange blend of tradition and modernity.

The Vulnerability

Without changing the basic view of women as inferior, servile, self-sacrificing and as essentially instruments of sexual gratification and reproduction, the problem of violence cannot be resolved. The mass media of entertainment is largely responsible for this image. One powerful influence on public opinion is exerted through movies. In a country which is largely poor and illiterate, movies are inevitably an important source of entertainment; and they provide a skillful combination of the woman's traditional role model as the submissive, self-sacrificing, all-forgiving, nurturing wife-mother and the liberated girl who flaunts her bodily attractions to satisfy the common male fantasies. An additional obnoxious feature of popular movies is the depiction of rape as entertainment.

To resolve the problem of women therefore needs a revolutionary change in values, else the problem will continue in their usual and even newer forms.

LITERARY WORKS ON THE TOPIC

Elise Boudling in her paper on 'Women and Social Violence'(1988) clearly points out that social violence against women are primarily based on :

(a) *Social or institutional structure* of the patriarchal order perpetuating all kinds of discrimination and oppressions against women which result into,

(b) *Behavioural violence.* In general, she reports that because women are 'easy' victims, they experience a great deal of direct behavioural violence in every society.

Of the most common expressions of behavioural violence against themselves women as victims find involved in rape, wife-beating and prostitution all over the world.

Boulding under structural or institutional violence lists all kinds of discriminations and oppressions perpetuated against women in the socio-economic fields, in political participation as citizens with equal rights and at home. She thinks that the 'patriarchal ethics' brings in different kinds of socialization practices for the male and female in the family which ultimately lead to turn the male child into an 'oppressor' and the female child into a 'victim' when they become adults. At the root of such oppressions against women is the reality that women are taken as 'objects' of both discriminations and violence by men.

Only of late, it is now being realized that women's fight against oppressions is to emphasize that they exist as "persons" and not as a "property" or "sex-objects"of men. To quote her:

> "No matter how victimized, human beings are subjects as well as objects, and help to maintain the very structures that victimize them . Thus women in their roles as wives and mothers give vital reinforcement to military structures by socializing battle-ready sons and docile daughters. Since boys spend much of their prepubertal life with their mothers it is impossible to minimize the role of mothers in creating the aggressive, fight-happy, rape-ready male. By forcing male children to repress tears and expressions of emotions and of pain , mothers directly contribute to the emotional infantaism of the adult male, who has grown without adequate techniques for working through his feelings"
>
> (Boulding, 1988; 341)

In order to understand the roots of violence against women, Niroj Sinha (1987), in a recent paper presented at a workshop at Patna Women's College, held the patriarchal social order responsible for discriminations and violence against women where they have no rights on landownership, they are taken to be 'non-persons' and as 'sex-objects', the dowry system denegrated womanhood, scriptual writings are against women including Manu's laws, socialization processes for girls aim at turning them into "ideal wives" and nothing else, prostitution is even practiced in places like Delhi and Bombay, caste structure leads to many a time rural violence in which women and female children are the worst victims etc. She held men and the patriarchal system responsible for all the ills and firmly believed that unless men and their attitudes changed, violence and discriminations against women will continue to exist.

If importance for the present concern is her attempt to define violence against women. To her, violence may include specially in relation to females both the *physical violence* against women and *exploitations* of all kinds. But she does not feel satisfied with such a definition. To her, any group of persons may be identified as "victims of violence" if they are shown the threat of use of force against them if they do not act as per the desires of the group of persons identified as oppressors.

In short, it will not only include all kinds of physical violence against women but will broadly also include the *contexts and particular situations* under which such "threats of use of force" are indicated. No doubt, Niroj Sinha's attempt to define violence against women is a good one, nevertheless, like all definitions has a few limitations i.e. it does not operationally define the *contexts and situations* under which use of force becomes violence. For example, Richard J. Gelles (1972) in his empirical study of conjugal violence as also child-abuse separates "violence" from "force":

> "Defining 'violence' to mean one individual hitting, striking, battering, assaulting, or throwing an object at another person is questionable when dealing with violence in families. While there is probably agreement that a wife who slaps her husband has committed a violent act, there is little agreement as to whether a parent slapping a child's hands is being violent. One possible solution to the rather broad conceptualization of violence would be to separate 'violence' from 'force'. Violence could be thought of as acts that society views as non-normative, while force could be those acts that fall within society's definition of legitimate behaviour such as disciplining children by spanking or slapping them..," (p.26).

Here also a question remains who decides which acts are legitimate and which are illegitimate. Niroj Sinha is probably correct then she indicates that "threat of use of force" against female forcing her unwillingly to do a thing in a particular situation that she would not do is an indicator of violence against her. This may be a sensitive definition if all the indicators of situational oppressions are clarified.

For the time-being, we would consider "illegitimate use of force" as customarily revealed in social customs, traditions and laws as violence in critical areas of choice for female e.g. vocation selection of life partner (marriage), sex behaviour, search for self-identity, participation in public life etc. to name a few. Gelles (1972), to make things clear, categorised family violence into three varieties e.g. :

(a) *normal violence* (routine, normative and necessary)

(b) *secondary violence* (when the use of violence to resolve a conflict is contrary to family norms, it creates additional conflict over violence which produces further violence) and

(c) *volcanic violence* (occurs when the offender has reached the end of line - has run out of patience; it is illegitimate violence that is explained as arising out of the building of stress and frustration) - the stress builds up to the point where the offender "erupts" into violence.

Fundamental Instincts

Considering the fact that violence is a primary instinct of all creatures for survival in the hostile environment and its ubiquitous nature, social scientists like Coser (1964), Gurr (1970),Daniels (1970), (Mannah Arendt, 1966), Casfield (1970), Mackenzie (1975) etc. have considered some amount of violence as natural and functional and only when it becomes volatile the destructive aspects of violence are recognized.

The arguments run as follows: violence in itself is neither beastly nor irrational (H. Arendt, 1966); violence in its occurance and form is socially structured as a part of human communication—as an area of achievement, a danger signal and a catalyst, as a mechanism of serving social structure for conflict resolution then established authority fails to accommodate demands of new groups for hearing; the aim of conflict is *to neutralize, injure or eliminate* their rivals (and thus is not always pathological); some violence (e.g., political, familial) is a normal phenomenon and is a 'self-adjusting conflict' situation, contributing to the eventual maintenance of social equilibrium.

Probably, all these led in the contributions to *Encyclopaedia of the Social Sciences* (1935:265) to define violence in the social context as the "...illegal employment of methods of physical coercion for personal or group ends... which is distinct from force or power", a purely physical concept. It goes beyond the dictionary meaning of the term 'violence' as merely the exercise of physical force so as to inflict injury or damage to persons or property - both spiritual and non-spiritual.

The "illegality" and "illegitimacy" of social violence, as stated earlier will differ on situational norms and social context. The present author understands the overlap between 'force' and 'violence', 'legitimate' and 'illegal' violence, between 'violence' on the one hand and 'discriminations' and 'oppressions' perpetuated on the femalefolks as a group. For all these reasons 'social violence' is roughly defined here as the illegal use of physical, mental and social coercion or use of threats for personal or group ends reflected broadly in our traditional social structure and present day developmental processes. Here the 'coercive' aspects (physical, psychological and social), 'threats' for harm (battering, killing, insulting, isolating, molestation and rape, eve-teasing) and the 'discriminating' and 'oppressive' aspects (subjugation in different walks of life i.e. child-rearing and child-bearing, employment, low wages, education, health, denial of opportunities for dissent etc.) are included.

Given the definition of social violence as illegal use of force, or, threats for use of such force by the patriarchal social order and their agents (e.g., men) against womenfolks in general for perpetuating the goals of that group (e.g.men) for subjugating women physically, socially and psychologically, our next step could be to identify the underlying assumptions of the older paradigm under which womenfolks do operate:

1. It is the patriarchal social order which subjugates womenfolks to a second-class or even third-class citizenship or even denial of this right.
2. It is the men who oppress women physically, psychologically, socially and spiritually.
3. Women are bound by the limitations of their body, specially their physical structure and thus they are easy prey or targets of men's aggression, hostility and violence and suffer molestation, rape, battering, burning, prostitution etc. and the mass media (print, electronic) have added fuel to the fire by adding to the list of their miseries by creating 'pornographic market (e.g., 42 street in New York, Sonagachi in Calcutta, pepshows, magazines like "Penthouse' and 'Playboys', video cassettes and movie film rated as 'XXX' etc.) have defiled the image of the women.
4. It is men who are violent and de-humanize women and it is 'they' and 'their social order', which ought to change, if the status of women have to change and improve. The 'mentality of men must change'.
5. As a serendipidity one could add: it is women who are nice, peaceful, decent and for all these reasons they are subjugated, although all humanity could not exist without them.

In brief, the old paradigm is nicely presented by Leela Dube (1986) in her paper on 'Seed and Earth'. The Symbolism of Biological Reproduction and Sexual Relations of Production' (of Leela Dube, Elenor Leacock & Shirley Ardener (eds.) *Visibility and Power: Essays on Women in Society and Development,* Delhi: Oxford, pp. 22-53). The importance of 'seed' (semen) over 'earth'/ 'field' (female body) has long been debated from patriarchal and matriarchal angles, showing the priorities of either seed or earth reaching to no conclusions at all. A large amount of data could be presented regarding the social inequality and social injustice done to women down the ages in matters concerning discrimination, oppression, physical torture etc. (e.g., data concerning sex-ratio, health, education, participation in labour force, payment of wages and promotion in work employment status of graduates in different fields, illiteracy rate, sex-test for legal termination of pregnancies) especially in India.

One could also rally facts concerning the aftereffects of such discrimination and oppression, e.g. feminine psyche and character (Venkatarayappa, 1966; Kakar, 1978; Sr. Margaret Mary, A.C., 1981), Sex stereotypes across thirty nation (Williams & Best, 1982), women in inter-caste marriage (Deshpande, 1972) and job (Fiona McNally, 1979), in case of marital violence and child-abuse (Johnson, 1985; Gelles, 1972), differences between being males and females (Wiseman, 1976) and in working as 'female eunuch' and portraying philosophies concerning 'sex and destiny' (Germaine Greer, 1984), Ms. Germaine Greer (1982) went to the extent of saying that females have to stop dancing on the tunes of their male partners (e.g. spouses) to act, as if, as 'female eunuchs' to earn their living and livelihood and must become militant to demand carving out their identies. She surprisingly said that in western societies neither of the parents desire and love their children and they have their progenies, as if, to man the future manpower requirements. Similarly, the concept of 'chastity is a form of birth control' practiced by different societies and it is for this reason that anthropologists in different cultures have found that free sexuality between a boy and girl is accepted till the period they are not able to produce.

Elements of Patriarchy

Whatever be the patriarchal reasons for social and physical violence against women and their aftereffects, the present author, following Marlyn Ferguson's (1980). *The Acquarian Conspiracy,*

Personal and Social Transformations in the 1980s (Granada, London) (p.452), considers the patriarchal bogey as a 'power paradigm' which needs to be replaced by a 'peace paradigm'.

Briefly, the earlier paradigm was essentially a de-humanizing paradigm and data presented concerning the feminine psyche and biology in the next paragraphs are only to suggest a shift in paradigm i.e. of having the 'seed' and 'earth' go together. Patricia Mische in a recent congress on the role of women in world peace wrote of 'the transformation already slowly in process among individuals and groups who, in a deep probing of their own humanness, are discovering the bonds they have with people everywhere'. The quality mark of the feminine psyche is their 'humanness' and their 'sensitivities' and similarly the 'male psyche' is dominated by 'adventure' and 'exploration' which make them serve as aggressive agents in society. A confluence of the two energies was the genius of Indian concept of "Ardha-narishwar' or present-day concern with 'androgyny' in the west. Although, as a counterpoint, we can really points as mentioned below:

1. Neera Desai (1986) in trying to analyse women's movement in India during the period of freedom struggle and subsequently after independence clearly pointed out that the 'women's issues' were taken for granted during the freedom struggle and it almost became a non-issue after independence i.e. there is hardly any concerted action toward achieving the goal of "equality". Women are involved in the present-day context with concern for nutrition, maternal health care, child-care, employment etc. as per the government programme. To a great extent the middle-class women have become agents for the delivery of such social welfare programmes where women are taken as "beneficiaries' and not "partners in the development process". This time one section of women have become oppressors against poor women they are doing the violence.

2. Hardly 5% of women representatives exists in our Parliament and State legislatures. They are very unequal in terms of political power.
3. Women during the 8-day period of menstural cycle (before-during-and after) remain quite energetic and are aggressive in orientation. In England, premenstural Syndrome (PMS) is now legally argued in the courts as defence in criminal cases (Verma UR, 1987), certain hormones (testosterone) and chemicals (amines) are concerned with violence and if females are administered these substances, they case qually be aggressive.'

The purpose of paradigm shift from 'men only' or women only' hypotheses to accumulation of facts of behavioural aspects of men and women can lead us to a androgy aspects of behaving i.e both male and female elements are within our behaviour and that it is the feminine sensitivity which can offer hypotheses to bring in a new world. Let's do that.

6

Victims of Crime

There are a variety of social, economic, legal, and psychological forms of victimization against women. We live in a society in which men are in hold of the majority of institutions. Economically, women are discriminated against in the job market. Sex role stereotyping has victimized and "imprisoned" a number of women, often women have been victimized by the institution of marriage, in which, although they are no longer identified as property, they are still repressed by implied and covert socio-cultural practices.

In some cases in the course of a marital relationship, women have been exploited physically, emotionally, and sexually by their husbands. Mental as well as physical "injury" has been inflicted on women by the health profession. Until recently women did not have the right to decide whether they could continue a pregnancy or terminate it. Number of women have suffered through months and years of psychotherapy by therapists whose attempts are being objective all too often fall short of that goal, resulting in the perpetuation of a value system that feeds the sexist social structure. The fact that the Equal Rights Amendment remains unratified is perhaps the most apparent indicator of the victimization of women.

Crime as a Subject Matter

The study of victims has emerged as a recent development in the field of criminology, criminology itself that is a discipline is not more than a century old. Victimology as a branch of criminology developed first in the United Kingdom, West Germany, France, the Scandinavian countries, Canada, Australia, New Zealand, and the United States. Indian scholars are also focusing their attention on the victimology to understand the importance of victim in criminal justice system.

The dynamics of victimology could be useful tools within the criminal system for administration and policy makers.

Victims of Various Hues

The term "Victimology" and its parameters of the subject, are not yet well defined. The concept "Victimology" was coined by a French jurist named Benjamin Mendelsohn, who is now a citizen of Israel. He states that victims are of five types:

(a) Completely innocent victims such as children and people who are victims of crime when unconscious;

(b) Victims with minor guilt and victims of ignorance, such as pregnant women who got to quacks for miscarriage;

(c) Voluntary victims, such as the ones who commit suicide or are killed by euthansia;

(d) Victims who are more guilty than the offenders, such as persons who provoke others to commit crime; and

(e) The most guilty type of victims who commit offences against others and get killed by the victim in self-defence (Mendelsohn: 1963).

A more popular categorisation is the triple alliterative pattern, which describes victims as provocative, precipitative and participating. Another recent and fairly authoritative view, as provided by the classification of Abdel Fattah of Canada as follows:

(a) the non-participating,

(b) the latent,

(c) the provocative,

(d) the participating, and

(e) the defiant.

Victimology is basically a study of crime from the point of view of the victim, of persons suffering from injury or destruction by the action of another single person or group of persons. Dadrian (1976:42) has broadly described this field as "the study of the social processes through which individuals and groups are maltreated in such a way that social problems are created." This encompasses two areas of concern: "the social context in which victimization occurs, and the social consequences of such victimization."

In this study we will look at the social context of female victimization, its social consequences though organizing a discussion of the social context of female victimization is difficult as the problem has historical, cross-cultural, and inter-disciplinary dimensions. The fact that most men are physically stronger than most women, so that when it comes to fight, women are more often losers is the simplest explanation of male-female maladjustment. To add to this is their vulnerability by their child-bearing function (Chapman and Gates, 1978:10-11).

Distinctive Character

Aggression and victimization are correlated, be it physical or verbal. Men are socialized to be aggressive and women to be victims. Support for the theory that aggressive behaviour is instinctual comes from:

(1) ethologists such as Desmond Morris, Conrad Lorens and Robert Ardrey;

(2) research on electrical and chemical brain stimulation;

(3) psychoanalytic theory.

The ethologists propose that our animal ancestors were instinctively violent beings and that our violent behaviours are products of these inherited instinctual drives. However, this is not always the case—some research (Binford, 1972) confirms that certain animals are not aggressive at all, and humans do not always pattern themselves on other primates' behaviour because of their more complex nervous system. An intriguing theory is that violence is not an instinctual behaviour but a learned one, resulting from the same matrix whereby we learn to speak, dress, and socialize. The expression of such learned aggression may be varied as the environments in which it is learned. Freud and his contemporaries held that aggression is instinctive. Coldstein (1975:19) viewing aggression as a learned behaviour, proposes that there are long-term and situational factors that facilitate either aggressive or non-aggressive behaviour. Long-term factors include the process of socialization, we undergo as children; for example, the values, norms, attitudes, beliefs and expectations that our parents, teachers, and peers instill the selectively reinforce, situational factors facilitating aggression include familiar environments, the presence of a alcohol, or the presence of relatives or peers with whom aggression is associated.

Situations place even the most violent people as non-aggressive and vice versa. Therefore, the factors that facilitate non-aggression are notable. Goldstein (1975) believes that there are certain environments and individuals that do not elicit or facilitate aggression. Inappropriate locations for aggression include churches or theatres, and inappropriate targets are hypothesized to include children and the aged. Psychological experiments demonstrate that aggressive behaviour is learned or acquired (Kagan and Moss, 1962; Loew, 1967). Interestingly, several of these studies find that males are more prone to aggression than females. Kegan and Moss (1962) found that aggressive behaviour learned in childhood persist through adulthood, especially for males. Loew (1967) and Green and Pigg (1970) found this if parents positively reinforce verbal or nonverbal aggressive responses in their children's behaviour.

Theoretical Explanations : Erich Fromm's (1973) analysis of human aggression clearly defines the errors and limitations of both the instinctive and behavioural schools of psychology in explaining the causes and origins of human violence and destruction. Extensive studies of violence as innate and instinctive in origin, as opposed to being learned through the socialization process (nature versus nurture), have ignored the question of observable difference between the levels of male/female human aggression. Regardless of which theory predominates at a given time, it would be logical that the theory hold true for all members of the species, regardless of sex. Fromm specifically includes women in his definition of mankind as it relates to human destructiveness. It will be wrong to assume that the male is innately more violent than the female. There are certain prevailing cultural and psychological conditions which encourage male aggression as its own reward and encourage acceptance of female passivity as its own reward.

There is a little evidence to explain female victimization beyond the shadow of culturally conditioned gender-biases. The major explanations which seem to evidence certain degree of objectivity in their treatment of the subject put the problem of female victimization in a socio-economic, legal and cultural context. Srivastav (1989: 33-37) views female victimization as a product of socio-economic factors including the status, role, right of women in general. The explanations discover the genesis of female victimization in the institutions of marriage and family, in the different sex-role socialization, etc.

Classifications of Theories : Various scholars namely, Gelles and Strauss (1979), Steinmetz (1974), Strauss (1974), Wolfgang and Weiner (1982) etc. have given different explanations to violence. After a detailed study of these writings Ahuja (1987: 166-185) identifies fourteen theories for understanding violence committed by an individual. Theories range from intrapsychic theories to macro-sociological theories. He divides these theories on the basis of three (theoretical) levels of analysis:

(1) psychiatric or psycho-pathological analysis;

(2) socio-psychological analysis; and

(3) sociological or socio-cultural analysis.

The Psycho-pathological Model : This focuses on the offender personality characteristics as the chief determinants of criminal violence. This model includes analysis that links mental analysis (i.e., a very small portion of mentally ill persons are violent), alcohol (i.e., what one does under the influence of alcohol and violence).

The Socio-psychological Model : This assumes that criminal violence can best be understood by a careful examination of the external environmental factors that exercise an impact on the individual offender. This model also examines the types of every-day interactions, patterns, etc., which are precursors to violence. Theories such as the Frustration-Aggression Theory, the Perversion Theory, the Self-Attitude Theory and the Motive Attribution Theory approach criminal violence from a socio-psychological level of analysis.

The Sociological or Socio-cultural Model : This provides a macro-level analysis of criminal violence. This model examines criminal violence in terms of socially structured inequality and social and cultural attitudes and norms regarding anti-social behaviour and interpersonal relations. Besides the two well-known theories, viz., the structural-functional theory and the theory of sub-culture of violence, the learning theory, the exchange theory, the anomic theory, and the resource theory, etc., also come under a socio-cultural analysis (Ahuja, 1987: 166-167).

Ahuja (1987) examines his own Social Bond Theory to explain crime against women. In view of these theoretical approaches, he calls this a "middle range theoretical proposition" based on the phenomenological approach. This has been borrowed by certain concepts from sociologists and criminologists like Hirschi (1976), Schutz (1964), etc. Social

Bond Theory based on adjustment, commitment and attachment and the relative feeling of deprivation is different from the Frustration Aggression Theory in the sense that status frustration as the consequences of interpersonal relations and the functioning of sub-system in the society. Hence, Ahuja (1987) claims his theory has a sociological orientation.

Various explanations have thus been advanced to account for crimes against women discovering the genesis of female victimization in the history, literature and culture of different societies. The dominant view holds that female victimization is a complex phenomenon having deep roots in the male dominated socio-economic, legal and political order. It is an expression of imbalance in the power structure that relegates women to a secondary social position, thereby making them vulnerable to various forms of oppression, exploitation and abuse.

Categorisation of the Victims

Ill-treatment of women takes several forms. Singh (1990:104) categories the oppression of Indian women into three manolateralistic forms. All these three take the form of victimization, namely:

(i) *Patriarchal Victimization* (inter-gender: man *v* woman) : Here men are responsible for crimes like sexual harassment, wife beating, rape, dowry murders, and setting in processes like patriarchisation, genderisation (a process of social differentiation based on gender) (Singh, 1989:1).

(ii) *Patriarchally Propelled Self-victimisation* (extra-intra person) : Here the present suicide committed by four girls of Kanpur (three sisters and the other drawing cue from the former) and the suicides committed by brides figure. In the former case it is the patriarchal forces which compelled the three sisters to commit suicide notwithstanding their being educated.

(iii) *Victim-propelled Victimization* (intra-gender; women and women) : Here the publicly celebrated rift between mother-in-law/ sister-in-law versus daughter-in-law to discredit women as oppressor of her own sex figures.

Ashish Nandy notes that "...even man's cruelty toward women is not match for the cruelty of women toward women." "Indeed", observes A.R. Wadia that "the greatest enemy and the only one that ultimately counts-of women's 'Emancipation' is women herself'. To Renuka Singh "the worse deprivation of the 'deprived class' takes place when the women vs woman battle begins resulting in the loss of support of women for the cause of their own liberation." K.L. Sharma observes, "it has been observed that it is women who obstruct the path of other women even more than men do; as is the case with mothers-in-law and colleagues at work." And a more shocking aspect is that "women are murdered by women themselves" (Taneja: 1987:4). However, it is unjust to say that behind every crime or injustice against a woman there is a woman.

Categories of Crime : Atray (1988:33-34) classifies crime, into three categories. The first category consists of individual acts which stop short of death of the victims like eve-teasing, wife beating, etc. The second category of crimes which is the most common and the least appreciated is the consequences which visit women as a result of enforcement by the society of its own rules and regulations. In the third category would fall cases of outright homicide whether it is intentional murder or forcing a woman to take her own life by committing suicide. In these categories of crimes, the first category of cases are to be treated more as social failing bordering on crime while the second category is out and out criminal. The third category raises certain basic issues concerning the society's own code of conduct and the blame is squarely on the society as a whole.

Mishra and Arora (1982: 5) classify crimes into three broad categories viz., (i) sexual offences, (ii) offences for gain, and (iii) customary laws and customs. Offences of sexual character may be further divided into those which have predatory element, and those which are non-predatory. Predatory element means the element of violence. In an offence is the first category that is a deliberate injury to the victim such as rape or other physical molestation. In an offence in the second category such as prostitution, the 'victim' is a participant who is willing. Rajan (1981: 84) identifies the following categories of offences against women:

(i) Wolf-whistling, ogling, winking, passing lewd remarks, sometimes openly, and at other times behind the anonymity of the telephone.

(ii) Bottom-pinching and forcing physical intimacy on board public transport, in bus queues, on festivals or on other occasions when large concourses of people together.

(iii) Molestation and rape.

(iv) Harassment at home leading to suicide and murder of young brides.

(v) Immoral trafficking, exploitation of women, and commercialization of sex.

The IPC classifies women related crimes in six categories as follows: Offences against women's bodily interest; offences against women's proprietory interest; offences relating to marriage; offences relating to criminal intimidation, insult and annoyance; suppression of Immoral Traffic in Women and Girls Act; and Dowry Act.

Deshpande (1984:71) classifies crimes against women into three categories which are as follows:

(i) Crime against personal liberty which may be sub-divided into kidnapping and abduction of minors and majors who are mostly women;

(ii) Crime against marriage which includes bigamy, attacks on monogamy, fraud, decoit etc.;

(iii) Crime against persons which includes harm to both body and mind. The two interact on each other and harm done to one affects the other also.

Verma (1990) enumerates crimes against women in two categories, namely physical torture and mental cruelties. These are further divided as follows:

Physical Torture : Medical termination of pregnancy, abortion of female foetus (if it found that it is a female child, the pregnancy is terminated), malnutrition of female child, female infanticide, eve-teasing, molestation, abduction and kidnapping, wife beating, wrongful confinement, fraudulent marriage, adultry-enticement of married women, cruelties on married women, rape, outraging the modesty of women, defaming young girls, prostitution, indescent representation of women, etc.

Mental Cruelties : Discrimination in male and female child, married women debarred of employment in several organizations, female generally having no say in her marriage, no equal remunerations, wife having no title in her husband's or in-laws property or home, the dowry menace, discrimination under law etc.

Two significant conclusions emerge from the above classifications: the first is biological. This reflects that violence against women occurs only because women are on average weaker. The implication of this statement is clear that the position of women has been historically structured as hierarchy in which men possessed and controlled women. This become the cause of physical violence against women and is one of the most brutal and explicit expressions of patriarchical domination. The second is to consider violence in its social-cultural context. A greater understanding of violence against women will be achieved through a consideration of the social environment in which it occurs.

Statistics on Crime against Women : With the constant rise in dowry deaths, bride burning, rape, molestation, kidnapping and other crimes against women in the country, it has become difficult to determine the extent and nature of crimes against women accurately on the basis of cases reported to the police.

Reasons for under Reporting of Cases : Firstly, due to the social stigma attached to the victim of sexual offences (i.e., rape, molestation, uttering word, making gesture etc.). Secondly, in dowry cases, parents do not want to stress the issue to the extreme for the future of the victim. Thirdly, to shun publicity being given by the media. Fourthly, in certain societies (Tribal) such crimes are not viewed with concern. Another reason may be the inadequate strength of the women police (Misra and Arora: 1982:7).

Crimes against women may not be reported due to the social stigma attached to the crime. A victim of sexual offences like rape, molestation, etc., may have to suffer the severity of social stigma, if it is made public. Besides, the social situations, there have been increasing reports regarding the rate of crime against women, which gives us an impression that such activities are on the rise. Although statistics regarding criminality against women are compiled officially in accordance with the provision of existing status of our country and collected, codified and classified at the national level in crime in India reports, yet there are no officially recognized figures available except their depiction under broad categories in the publication of significance. Taking IPC crime as an index of the situation of crime, the rise in the rate of crime against women has been reported in all types of crimes ranging from eve-teasing to abductions and killings for the period 1977-1979.

Data which reveal an average percentage of crime against women committed during 1977-79 which represent that a little more than 80 per cent crime against women has been reported: for molestation (28.94 per cent); offences under SITA Act (24.67 per cent); Kidnapping and abduction (20.96 per cent); and rape (10.70 per cent). Moreover, these four crimes have gone up further during the 1983 to 1985. Besides these crimes, there is also an increase in eve-teasing and dowry deaths as reflected by the percentage change in 1985 over 1983. It was pointed out that against 2487 cases of rape in 1971, 4300 cases were reported in 1979 averaging 12 rapes a day or about one every two hours. The All India figures of dowry deaths is about 4000 per year. Similarly, 619 cases of bride burning were registered by the police in Delhi in 1982 against a total of 421 cases in 1980. Registered cases have also been going up alarmingly in the past few years though the number of cases reported is much more than the recorded ones.

Reported figures in Delhi for crimes against women reveal that dowry deaths rose from 43 in 1985 to 64 in 1986 and 59 in 1987 to 71 in 1988. The number of such deaths had risen to 132 between January 1989 and February 1990 as disclosed by the then Union Home Minister in Parliament. This apart, Delhi led all union territories in 1987 with 103 registered cases of rape; worse still innocent minors were the victims in most of these cases.

The total incidence of such crimes are estimated to be in the country with a population of about 700 million are estimated to be 50 times higher because of the inherent hesitation on the part of victims to complain about such matters. These figures do not represent the whole picture except in the case of murder and suicide. This is particularly so in the case of the offences of eve-teasing where the victim, as a rule, tries not to report the matter as they feel that in the absence of any strong provision in the law to deal with this crime, the only consequences of reporting would be unnecessary harassment to the victim and her witness. The crime of wife-beating goes almost cent per cent unreported for the same reason of the law and also the fact that reporting of such incidents to the police would put an end to all hopes of future reconciliation (Atray: 1988).

Misra and Arora (1982) conducted a study of six districts, namely, Hissar, Sirsa, Jaunsar Bewar (Tehsil Chakrota in Dehradun), Kanpur, Delhi and Bombay representing respectively the agrarian/ smaller towns; tribal areas; and urban/metropolitan cities. Crime against women constitute only a small proportion of the total crime reported to the police. On an average for every 100 cases of crime reported to the police during 1977-79, there were only 0.43 cases of crime against women. In tribal area this ratio was

2.27, in agrarian area the same was 1.68 and in urban area it was 0.42. It also reveals that the ratio of crime against women to the total crime increased in the urban/metropolitan cities and the tribal belt while it declined in the agrarian sector.

The overall ratio of crime against women to total crime has increased from 0.40 in 1977 to 0.43 in 1978 and to 0.47 in 1979. In the urban areas it increased from 0.38 in 1977 to 0.41 in 1978 and further to 0.45 in 1979. In tribal belt, it increased erratically from 0.69 in 1977 to 4.59 in 1978 and declined to 2.04 in 1979. In agrarian area the ratio had declined in 1979 over the year 1977. The ratio in 1977 was 1.63, 1.91 in 1978 and 1.54 in 1979 (*Ibid:* 79-80). The volume of crime against women rose from 12.64 per lakh population in 1977 to 14.18 per lakh population in 1979. In the agrarian areas during the same period, the increase was 10 per cent in 1978 and 11.1 per cent in 1979 over the year 1977. In the tribal area, the percentage increase in 1978 was 400.0 and 100.0 in 1979 over the year 1977. The urban area registered an increase of 0.8 per cent in 1978 and in 1979 by 20.2 per cent over the year 1977. Thus, we see that the crime against women had increased at a much higher rate than the other crimes. Moreover, the ratio of crime against women to the total crime increased in the urban/metropolitan cities and the tribal belt while it declined in the agricultural sector. Out of the total of 6483 cases of crime against women reported, the maximum (37.2 per cent) cases were of Suppression of Immoral Traffic Act, followed by kidnapping/adduction (21.7 per cent), molestation (14.2 per cent), rape (8.6 per cent), chain-snatching (7.2 per cent), murder (5.1 per cent) and enticing or taking away or detaining with criminal intent a married women (3.9 per cent). These offences together constitute above 98 per cent of the total cases of crime against women.

The other offences committed against women were very less in number. These offences in order of reporting were: Eve-teasing (0.8 per cent), dacoity (0.4 per cent), abetment to suicide (0.3 per cent), Dowry Prohibition Act, unnatural offences, importation and selling of minor for prostitution 0.1 per cent each, procuration of minor (0.04 per cent). In the agricultural sector the highest number of cases were of molestation being 46.8 per cent followed by kidnapping/abduction (23.2 per cent), rape (14.9 per cent), abetment to suicide (3.1 per cent). A solitary case of eve-teasing was also reported. In the urban areas the order of reporting was SITA Act (38.9 per cent), followed by kidnapping/ abduction (21.7 per cent), molestation (12.7 per cent), rape (8.2 per cent), chain-snatching (7.5 per cent), enticing or taking away with criminal intent a married women (4.1 per cent). The other offences committed against women are very less in number and the trend of these offences were similar to the total cases of crime against women as mentioned above. In the tribal areas, the highest cases (75.0 per cent) were of rape/kidnapping/abduction followed by molestation (25.0 per cent). Thus, the nature and extent of crime against women differ from area to area.

Offences of Many Types

The victimization of the fair sex has been showing an upward inclination and incidence of these crimes is on the rise. Eventhough the available statistics are very high, they don't represent even 25 per cent of the total because it is well-known that in actual practice hardly one fourth of the cases are reported. The reasons for non-reporting are obvious. A critical perusal of statistical data on crimes against women reveals that rape is increasing throughout India. According to Crime in India Report 1986, a total of 7,952 cases in rape were registered in 1986 against 7,289 cases in 1985 thereby registering an increase of 9.1 per cent in 1986 over 1985. The highest number of cases among the States was registered by Madhya Pradesh (1,506) followed by Uttar Pradesh (1,292), Maharashtra (804), Bihar (794), West Bengal (612), Rajasthan (598), etc. Thus, about 50 per cent of the total cases in the country are reported in four States of Madhya Pradesh, Uttar Pradesh, Maharashtra, and Bihar together. However, the highest volume of rape cases was reported from the State of Jammu and Kashmir being 2.8, followed by Madhya Pradesh (2.6), and lowest from the State of Punjab (0.3) and Karnataka (0.3) respectively. The volume of rape cases for each population was 1.0 in all the States taken together, in all the union territories taken together as well as in the country as a whole.

Overall the volume of rape cases to per lakh of population had increased critically during the period 1974-86. It increased from 0.5 in 1974 to 1.0 in 1986 exceptionally in 1979, it had declined to 0.66 as compared to the year 1078, which was 0.71. However, in the last one decade, rape cases have just doubled and it would be seen that the percentage victims of rape was the highest in the age-group between 16 to 30 years in all the seven years between 1971 to 1977, the average being 62.5 per cent followed by the age group below 30 years accounted for 14.6 per cent.

The incidence of kidnapping and abduction has also been increasing in our country. The total number of cases recorded in 1971 was 9,647. In 1973, the incidence under this head increased by 8.7 per cent over 1972; in 1976 the incidence increased by 10.0 per cent over 1977; and in 1978 the incidence increased by 11.2 per cent over 1977. The rate of this crime, per one lakh of population is 2.0 in our country. Manipur topped the list among the States with the average per annum volume per lakh of population being 13.33, followed by Jammu and Kashmir (6.85), Rajasthan (4.09), Uttar Pradesh (3.07) and so on. Delhi topped the list among Union territories with the average per annum volume of 5.0. No case was reported from Dadra and Nagar Haveli and Lakshadweep during the period 1977-79.

The average annual volume per lakh of population of reported cases of molestation of women and girls were the highest in the State of Madhya Pradesh being 5.56 followed by Jammu and Kashmir (5.36), Manipur (4.72), Tripura (3.48) and so on. The average per annum volume in these States was higher than the average volume (1.82) of all States taken together. No cases of molestation of women and girls were reported from the State of Sikkim and the Union Territory of Lakshadweep Islands.

Among the union territories the average per year volume of this crime was the highest in Andaman and Nicobar Islands, bring 12.27 per lakh of population, followed by Mizoram (6.04), Pondicherry (2.33). The average volume per annum in these Union territories was higher than the all Union territories average 7.87. Statistics reveal that the volume of molestation of women and girls per lakh of population on all-India basis had increased from 1.77 in 1977 to 1.92 in 1978.

Of the major crimes against women, the volume per lakh of population of cases of SITA taken together were the highest after cases of molestation of women and girls. The highest volume of SITA cases were reported from the State of Tamil Nadu being 10.57 per lakh of population, followed by Karnataka (6.55), Andhra Pradesh (2.37), Maharashtra (1.37) and Uttar Pradesh (0.50). In other States insignificant or negligible cases of SITA were reported. No case was reported during the year 1977-79 in the States of Gujarat, Meghalaya, Nagaland, Sikkim, West Bengal.

Amongst the Union territories, the maximum number of cases of SITA were reported from Delhi with the average volume of (0.77) followed by Pondicherry (0.36). No case of this offence was reported from the other Union territories during 1977-79. In the Union Territory of Delhi, the volume per lakh of population had shown a continuously rising trend.

The number of dowry deaths is on the rise despite the various legislative and other measures taken from time to time to tackle the problem. This has threatened our way of life (Mir, 1982). There were 162 cases of burning of women reported in the capital only between April 1, 1983 and June 30, 1983. Figures reveal that in many States, the reported cases of dowry deaths or deaths by burning or suicide more than doubled within two years. Andhra Pradesh reported 14 cases of dowry deaths in 1983, 27 cases in 1984 and 38 cases in 1985. In Uttar Pradesh the death figures of bride burning or suicide, were 323 in 1985 and 110 in the first four months of 1986. Madhya Pradesh reported 42 cases of dowry deaths in just five months June-October in 1985. In Maharashtra, there were 129 cases of dowry deaths in 1984, the number of such deaths recorded in 1985 was at 211 and it had reached to 247 in the first ten months of 1986. Maharashtra recorded 411 cases of suicide by young married women in 1983, 652 in 1985 and 662 for the first ten months of 1986 (Indian Express, 24.5.1987).

Statistics provided by the Home Ministry regarding dowry deaths also helps us to some extent in assessing the prevalence of this phenomenon in our country. The figures show a sharp increase in the incidence, year after year, which could partly be due to the increased awareness about the problem.

Official figures between January 1980-March 1981 show that there were 139 dowry death cases registered with police in various parts of the country. Of these Punjab and Haryana accounted for 231 cases each and 17 cases were from Uttar Pradesh. Whereas by latest figures, the number of dowry deaths for the year 1987 stands at 1649, and Uttar Pradesh on the whole is found to be the leading State in dowry deaths.

According to statistics, the figures of dowry deaths by burning or suicide are only a part of the actual number of deaths caused in this respect, therefore, the reported figures are usually misleading. Sources of information include the special cell in the Delhi Police Headquarters and numerous non-governmental organization which clearly prove the point of gross variability in information in this regard, the figures supplied in the Rajya Sabha could probably be treated as the third source of information. The number of cases of married women in the age-group 16-30 years with third degree burns admitted in the various hospitals of Delhi is yet another source of information. In the capital 736 cases of death due to burns, suicide and poisoning were reported in the year 1985. The number of such deaths increased to 775 in 1986 and 426 in the first six months of 1987 (Bhatia, 1988). There is no doubt about the fact that crimes against women are increasing in every country, but in India, like other developing countries the proportion of such trend is on higher level.

To sum up, on an all-India basis taking the 3 years (1977-79) average of all the selected offences against women, the highest number of cases were reported under the head 'Molestation' being 11642 (28.94) per cent of the total cases reported. This was followed by the cases under SITA and Girls 9926 (24.67 per cent) cases; kidnapping/abduction 8432 (20.96 per cent), rape 4305 (10.70 per cent); Enticing or taking away with criminal intent a married women 2736 (6.80 per cent), chain snatching 1298 (3.23 per cent) procuring minor girl 908 (2.26 per cent). Interestingly some of the offences like abetment to suicide and penalty for demanding dowry which are reported in the mass media were comparatively less. The average per year cases reported under abetment to suicide were only 169 (0.42 per cent), demanding dowry-Section 4 were 103 (0.26 per cent).

The vulnerability of women to various forms of oppression, exploitation and abuse should be given its due share while framing of policies and laws so that they can be given their share of respect and status long due to them.

7

Death in Womb

Slaughtering the Unborn

Infanticide is motivated by the necessity of getting rid of an illegitimate child as well as unwelcome offsprings whom the parents cannot afford. Infanticide means murder of an infant or a newly born baby. Infanticide as such has not been defined in the I.P.C. but since it amounts to the killing of a living person, the sections dealing with murder under the penal code is applicable to the offence of infanticide. Those who kill infants or newly born babies cannot claim the benefit of the right of private defence.

Infanticide of the female children in India is usually done out of the undermentioned necessity: (i) Family vanity among the groups of warrior class. (ii) Inflated dowy demand. (iii) Heavy expenses required to be incurred by the bride's party during marriages. (iv) Craze for a male child drives a family to sacrifice a daughter's life on account of superstitions at times under the influence of the miracleman of the community.

The infanticide of girl babies is widely prevalent in Thar desert area of Rajasthan, particularly among the Bhil Rajput family. The infant is subjected to asphyxial deaths through manual strangulation or through administration of opium. The male-female ratio in this area is 750 females per one thousand males, against All India figure of 929 and Rajasthan figure of 913 females per one thousand males. The figure of Jaisalmer district is 800 female per thousand males and among the Bhatti Rajput family, it is 550 females per one thousand males being the lowest among the Rajputs.

In October 1986, the Central Government ordered an inquiry into the alleged killing of a baby girl in the family of an MLA. A CID enquiry was conducted by two officers, an Additional Superintendent of Police and an Assistant Superintendent of Police. The common thing in both the enquires was that there is truth in the matter but since the Gujjar family in Rajasthan are well-off and carry on money-lending business and, therefore, no one was coming forward to give evidence. In the meantime a Public Interest Litigation (P.I.L.) case was filed before the Rajasthan High Court by Ms Summita Satyarthi, a Human Rights Activist, who pleaded for a direction to be issued for holding a C.B.I. enquiry. Great interest having been shown by the people, a case of murder was registered against the Legislator.

The Kellar community of landless farmers having a strength of about two lakh, the economic condition of the people are so deplorable that it is difficult for any family to foot the bill of marriages of their daughters. However, the people somehow manage the marriage of one daughter but the marriage of two daughters is an impossible task. Therefore, a second daughter on being born, becomes an unwelcome child and is quickly done to death by administering a paste made from poisonous oleander berries. The menfolk dig a pit outside the house, watch the cries of baby and when it is stopped, the dead body is slipped into the pit and buried. There are hardly any families where some or other child is not buried.

According to a *Times of India* news report, from Madurai, a 26 years old woman of Chokknathpuram, who had vowed to carry "Agni Chatti" (firepot) to a nearby temple during the "Panguni Uthiram" festival could not fulfil her vow as her husband declined to give her money for that and in frustration, she doused her three daughters with kerosene and set them on fire. Thereafter she herself attempted to commit suicide. On hearing the cries, the neighbours rushed and retrieved the children and hospitalised them. Only one could survive. It is pertinent to mention that she had a male child as well who was spared.

Killing Infants

In contrast to infanticide, foeticide is the unlawful expulsion of foetus. It is also called "criminal abortion" or "causing miscarriage". When used in the legal sense, it includes both abortion and premature labour. As per medical sense, premature labour means expulsion of a child that has attained viability. The term "abortion" or "miscarriage" signify the expulsion of foetus or ovum at an earlier period. Modern methods of detecting the sex of the foetus through amniocentesis are used nowadays.

Merciless Slaughter

Abortion may be classified into: (a) natural and (b) artificial.

Natural Abortion : Natural abortions occur due to such reasons as mother's ill-health, local disease, or diseases of the generative organs, shocks, fear, excessive joy, accidental falls, etc. Hence, appropriate care is required in respect of the health of the pregnant woman.

Artificial Abortion : Premature evacuation of foetus, whether medically, surgically or through indigenous method is known as artificial abortion. Artificial abortion is a criminal offence punishable under Sections 312-316 of the Indian Penal Code. The Sections run as under:

Sections 312-316 IPC

Sec. 312 Causing Miscarriage : Whoever voluntarily

causes a woman with a child to miscarry, shall, if such miscarriage be not caused in good faith for the purpose of saving the life of the woman, be punished with imprisonment of either description for a term which may extend to three years, or with fine, or with both; and, if the woman be quick with child, shall be punished with imprisonment of either description for a term which may extend to seven years, and shall also be liable to fine.

Explanation: A woman who causes herself to miscarry, is within the meaning of this section.

Sec. 313. Causing Miscarriage without Woman's Consent : Whoever, commits the offence defined in the last preceding section without the consent of the woman, whether the woman is quick with child or not, shall be punished with imprisonment for life, or with imprisonment of either description for a term which may extend to ten years, and shall be liable to fine.

Sec. 314. Death Caused by act done with Intent to Cause Miscarriage : Whoever with intent to cause the miscarriage of a woman with child, does any act which caused the death of such woman, shall be punished with imprisonment of either description for a term which may extend to ten years, and shall also be liable to fine.

If Act done without woman's consent, the offender shall be punished either with imprisonment for life, or with punishment mentioned above.

Explanation: It is not essential to this offence that the offender should know that the act is likely to cause death.

Sec. 315. Act done with Intent to Prevent Child being Born Alive or to Cause it to Die after Birth : Whoever, before the birth of any child does any act with the intention of thereby preventing that child from being born alive or causing it to die after its birth, shall, if such act not caused in good faith for the purpose of saving the life of the mother be punished with imprisonment of either description for a term which may extend to ten years, or with fine, or with both.

Sec. 316. Causing Death of Quick Unborn Child by act Amounting to Culpable Homicide : Whoever, does any act under such circumstances, that if he thereby causes death he would be guilty of culpable homicide, and does by such act cause the death of a quick unborn child, shall be punished with imprisonment of either description for a term which may extend to ten years, and shall also be liable to fine.

Illustration : A, knowing that he is likely to cause the death of a pregnant woman, does an act which, may cause the death of the woman, this would result in culpable homicide if the woman is, injured but does not die; but the death of an unborn quick child with which she is pregnant is thereby caused, A is guilty of the offence defined in this Section.

NOT ALLOWED TO BE BORN

Legislation : Except for saving the life of the pregnant woman, termination of pregnancy (Bhrun Hatya) was a penal offence in accordance with the provisions of the aforesaid sections of the I.P.C.

After India's independence and with the passage of time, population started growing rapidly with such an alarming speed that it began to be seen that available resources would not be adequate to meet the necessities of the people in the country. Thus, several family planning programmes were evolved and propagated among the people of the country through mass media. It was further thought that a legislation to legalise termination of pregnancy was another means by which the growing population could be checkmated. Thus, Medical Termination of Pregnancy Act (1971) was enacted as a means of population control. According to it (Sec. 3), the objectives of termination of pregnancy are two fold:

Objectives

(a) *Therapeutic :* When the continuance of pregnancy is likely to endanger the life of the pregnant woman and could cause grave injuries to her physical and mental health.

(b) *Eugenic:* When there is the risk of the child being born with serious physical or mental handicap. This may occur, if the pregnant woman in the first three months of her pregnancy suffers from: (i) German measles; chicken pox or small pox, viral infection including viral heptitis, toxoplasmonia or any other disease which would have affected the health of the woman. (ii) The pregnant woman takes certain medicines, whether under medical advice or otherwise which affect the foetus; (iii) The pregnant woman receives radio or any invisible ray therapy; and (iv) Insanity of the either of the two or both spouse.

(c) *Humanitarian:* When the pregnancy is in consequence of sexual assault.

(d) *Social:* When the pregnancy has occurred on account of failure of contraceptive device.

Abortion having become legalized, this act is a blessing for large number of nursing homes who are thriving through such operations.

Contraceptive means to ensure sex without reproduction. Surrogate motherhood, in vitro fertilisation and artificial insemination are advancements in genetic technology in which reproduction is possible without sex. New techniques have enabled the determination of the abnormalities as well as the sex of the child in advance much before the birth of the child. The prenatal sex-determination is done through amniocentesis, wherein amniotic fluid is drawn through the uterus of a pregnant woman to determine any defect or physical deformity in the child. Amniocentesis is risky as it constitutes the drawing of amniotic fluid from the uterus. This is the fluid on which the foetus lives until birth. This test is conducted after sixteen weeks pregnancy and if conducted earlier may prove harmful or fatal for the child in which case there can be legal proceedings against the wrong doers.

The determination of sex is also possible through Chorionic Villi Sampling (CVS) by vaginal extraction from eight to sixteen weeks of pregnancy. This method is also dangerous as it causes the pregnant woman to infect and in effect, spontaneous abortions can take place. It may as well result in fatality of the pregnant woman. The other method of sex determination is through ultrasound scanning which though non-invasive, is unreliable, even at the advanced stage of pregnancy.

Misuse of Science

Scientists have developed the genetic technology in order to ascertain in advance if the child in the mother's womb has any deformity. Unscrupulous people in the society are using the know-how to reduce the female population in an organised and systematic manner.

The dangerous form of genetic engineering by selectively aborting the newborn child has been flourishing in the capital city of India as well as in several big and small cities of the state on account of no value being attached to a female child in comparison to the male counterpart. Sex clinics have multiplied and mushroomed throughout the cities and towns. According to a rough estimate around 78,000 female foeticides were aborted after prenatal sex determination test through amniocentesis. In 1983, Bombay had only three sex clinics and over a period of next five years, it had multiplied to 258 private clinics in addition to the sixteen recognised Government clinics. No permit or licence is required to set up a clinic of this type. On account of the coming up of a large number of clinics, there is a competition in the market and the fees charged (which had become between Rs. 150 to Rs. 500) is within the reach of a common man. The popularity of the method has spread to small places in far-flung areas. The samples now can be carried to Mumbai or Delhi or Kolkata or any big city of the country from the nearby places. A survey made by Women's Centre has revealed that out of 8000 abortions checked, 7999 were in respect of females.

One clinic in Mumbai is reported to have advertised that the cost of abortion is cheaper than the amount required for the marriage and payment of dowry. Such statement provoking abortion openly advocate murder of the foetus. What more can be said of such a system. There is a battle being fought between doctors and feminist groups on the availability of medical technology which could assist pre-selection of sex. These organisations have demanded a total ban while the lobby of doctors who perform these tests, on the other hand, oppose the demand on the ground that if the ban is enforced, abortions would be performed by quaks. There is some force in the demand of the doctors also. The whole issue is dependent upon the attitude of the people towards the female child. The rate, the pre-natal sex determination tests are gaining popularity and being used in aborting female foetus, the day is not far when the woman may become an endangered species.

Legal Aspect of the Offence

The Medical Termination of Pregnancy Act, 1971 only ensures a legal sanction to a Medical Practitioner to abort a female foetus. Thus, the two together, that is MTPA and Sex-determination Technology have put India on its way to technological and legal femicide. Unregulated technology and the legal Act have created a new problem in bringing a decline in female population.

According to the Provision of Section 3 of the Act, a Registered Medical Practitioner is entitled to abort a foetus within twelve weeks of pregnancy and two of them can abort a pregnancy having a length of 12 to 20 weeks. In either case they will have to take a stand that abortion was necessary in the interest of the health of the woman.

The anguish of a pregnancy by sexual assault is presumed to constitute a grave injury to a woman's mental health. However, the failure of a contraceptive device cannot cause any such damage to the mental health. Assessment of the anticipated risk is rather vague and gives a licence to abort female child with the aid of pre-natal sex determination test. Directly or indirectly the MTP is a licence to kill the foetus as some of its statements lack logic.

Business in abortion became possible and flourishing on account of provisions of Section 5 of the MTP Act, 1971, which is an enabling provision for an emergent situation and permits non-application of provisions of Section 3 and Section 4 of the Act. The Section enables a doctor without any experience in gynaecology and obstetrics to operate after having formed an opinion with due care and attention that termination of pregnancy is immediately necessary to save the life of the pregnant woman. It may be pertinent to mention that while making a provision of the Section, care to provide any safeguard has not been introduced to prevent its misuse. A doctor can now be prosecuted under the I.P.C. only. The Act suffers from the following flaws:

Flaws in MTP Act

(i) The Act does not provide any guidelines for calculating the commencement of pregnancy and to assess the period of twelve weeks or twenty weeks. The matter has been left entirely to the wisdom of the doctor.

(ii) The Act does not require that the pregnant woman countersigns or affixes her signature/thumb impression on the key column of the register containing details regarding the duration of pregnancy. Thus, any evidence, which, otherwise could have been provided, is always missing.

(iii) .The evidence is further weakened by the type of consent Form C prescribed under the Central Rules. There is no column that the doctor makes a declaration that he has explained to the pregnant woman the reasons for the termination of her pregnancy.

(iv) As usual, the Act further ensures a cover for the doctor as per Section 8 of the Act which lays down that no suit or proceedings shall lie against the doctor if he has acted in good faith. It is very difficult to prove that the doctor did not exercise reasonable care and lacked good faith.

Initially nearly one dozen doctors in seven states of the country offered to perform these tests which, for the first time was introduced in All India Institute of Medical Sciences, Delhi, primarily to discover genetic disorders in foetus in those cases where the parents had the history of abnormality. Since in course of the determination of the genetic disorder, it was found that the method reveals the sex of the unborn child, it became popular as a method for determination of pre-natal sex of the child. The Medical Termination of Pregnancy Act, 1971, made it a convenient tool for selective abortion.

Consequent upon a widespread resentment against this test, the Maharashtra has taken a lead and the Legislature of Maharashtra Assembly passed the Regulation; "Use of Pre-natal Diagnostic Techniques Act, 1988".

Features

(a) Section 3 of the Act prohibits carrying of the pre-natal diagnostic tests by an unregistered genetic centre laboratory or clinic.

(b) Section 4 of the Act lays down the fulfilment of five conditions for the performance of diagnostic tests. The important conditions are that woman should be near about the age of 35 years and she has a history of at least a couple of abortions, family history of mental retardation and/or physical abnormalities.

8

Crimes within Family

Living in a society which is largely patriarchal though centered around the wife, the family has its share of marital violence in which the woman bears the brunt in spite of being the pillar of the home.

To maintain their dominant position in the home, men inflict some or the other kind of violence on women and harass her throughout her life. A common name given to wife battering is silent crime. Others are considered as domestic violence like spouse abuse and similar ones. If we examine the variety of names it is known by, besides wife battering, two points emerge at once: that the violence is located at home and the attacker is the husband. The site of violence being the home and the attacker being the 'husband' has distorted, confused and is responsible for the gross trivailisation of the crime.

Wife battering is a crime that is 'victim precipitated'. This has been largely proven by three aspects—social, legal and psychological—with large help from recent cases, at home or abroad and through the numerous myths or sayings. It is a widely prevalent crime that is under cover for being 'too private' to be spoken of. Being an old problem; it is assumed by some to have begun with the first monogamous pairing. What is new, however, is that the fact that the public admission of violence against women occurs in a civilised society and the insistance by the government and responsible citizens that such violence is no longer acceptable, that we are therefore compelled to discuss the problem of such a form of violence and search for solutions to alleviate it.

In the context of marriage, violence towards women becomes more significant when a husband who is supposed to love and protect his wife, batters her. It becomes a big setback for a woman, being battered by a man whom she trusted most.

Vicious Games

Wife battering has been largely supported by various cultures down the ages. It was part of the Napoleanic code until a decade back. The very code says: "Women like walnut trees must be beaten every day". In North Africa, the expression "women and camels need to be beaten" is still common. In Europe, they used to say that a man had the right to beat his wife with a stick not thicker than his thumb. In Indian culture we have the quotation of Tulsidas such as "Drums, donkeys and women need to be beaten".

So religion has played more or less a crucial role in reinforcing brutal attitudes to women which include "mortification of the flesh" deemed religious and more appropriate to the female. In fact over the ages, religions have constantly admonished woman to stay with her husband, no matter how cruelly he treated her".

Needs of Common Nature

Wife battering is the most prevalent form of violence against women which is commonly caused due to maladjustments between husband and wife. Also prevalent among working women as most mothers-in-law, who are non-working and under complete dominance of their husbands feel jealous of and frustrated at the sudden independence and freedom of their daughter-in-law. She counters by poisoning the ears of her son antagonising him against his wife.

The batterer rationalises his battering saying that it happened as he was not satisfied by the conduct of his wife. So she is made to feel guilty of her performance at home—be it cooking or general upkeep of the home. A housewife of Rajouli was beaten to death by her husband as she was not cooking good food and the house being untidy, for which she alone, often at times, is not responsible. Implicit in this viewpoint is that the husband has a right to beat his wife if she does not behave according to what he desires.

A young woman of village Taaddih under Amarpur police station of Banka was battered to death by her husband and in-laws as she refused to go out in rain to bring *ganja* for her husband. While attempting to amend her husband a pregnant woman of Samastipur was mercilessly beaten and sent to her parents' house by her husband. The battering resulted in abortion.

Her husband along with his two brothers used to commit dacoity. When the wife protested against this, the dacoit started battering her mercilessly. Consequently, an abortion took place and she objected to the illicit relation of her husband. A young housewife of Dalsingsarai was mercilessly beaten to death by her husband when she objected to his having illicit relations with his elder brother's wife.

Affordable Circumstances

To tame a woman who does not accept the traditional role of submissiveness and subordination, any means including violence is justified. Ironically counsellers and social workers also contribute towards this ideology when they question a woman who gets beaten: 'what did you do to provoke him? Due to this she often begins to have serious doubts about herself, to the extent that she starts questioning her identity as one who is responsible, intelligent or knowledgeable.

The women continue to live in a state of fear and uncertainty as it is unpredictable when, where and under what circumstances the violence may suddently erupt. The consequence of this is that she develops an inferiority complex, so much that she begins to look down upon herself and underestimates her value and potentialities loosing confidence in all her moves.

It is undeniable that some women are so arrogant, haughty, uncompromising and intolerant and make the husband's life so miserable through calculated and well planned acts of social misconduct that even the most reasonable man would lose control of himself beyond a certain limitation and beat up the erring woman.

Cases of women suspected of adultery come under this category. A man of village Janui under Nargar Police Station of Garhwa hacked to death his 28-year-old wife as she had illict relations with a man of the same village, in spite of being told to mend her ways, she paid no heed. In a fit of rage he hacked her to death.

Until the mid-1970s and the re-emergent women's movement wife battering was almost completely ignored. In USA many researchers in this field agree with Justice Stewart Oneglias' estimate that 50 per cent of all marriages involve some degree of physical abuse of women. Such statistics are not available in India, but there is no doubt that they would far exceed the American statistics. Being the most frequently referred to "crime in India" reports do not provide information on wife battering. So widely and pervasively is wife battering accepted and tolerated that very rarely it is publicly talked about and still much less written about in the media.

Might of the Humanbeings

Wife battering is seriously under-reported crime and the data hard to obtain because of its location, the home... "Gelles Straus and Steinmetz reported that physical assault occurs in one-third of all homes. "In Mumbai, HELP, a voluntary group received over 300 calls in less than a year in which more than 80 per cent were calls for marital violence.

No one dares to interfere or question the man even if he is seen battering his wife because it is considered purely something their family affair. The society also implicitly supports this attitude by leaving the husband and wife to themselves to settle their affairs. On the other hand, if two neighbours get into a fight, the people around immediately intervene to see justice prevails. But in the case of a husband battering his wife, the neighbours tend to be mute spectators. Wife battering is commonly accepted by society and not many people take much notice to it. If the wife happens to retaliate, she is considered a woman of low morals. It is ingrained in the mind of people that no decent woman would beat her husband. Whereas battering one's husband is considered shameful for the husband as well as for the wife, there is no shame attached to wife battering, society being what it is.

Wife battering falls under the general category of assault, under sections 319-326 of Indian Penal Code. Sections 319 and 321 are non-cognizable offences, i.e., the cases in which the police can take no action against the assaulter. Thus, there is no legislation against wife battering.

Grievous Offences : Under Section 320 of the I.P.C. the following kind of offences have been described as grievous:

(a) Emasculation;

(b) Permanent deprivation of the sight of either eye;

(c) Permanent deprivation of hearing of either ear;

(d) Deprivation of any organ or joint;

(e) Destruction or permanent impairing of the power of any organ or any joint;

(f) Permanent disfiguring of the head or face;

(g) Fracture or dislocation of a bone or both;

(h) Any hurt which endangers life or which causes the sufferer to remain for twenty days in severe bodily pain or unable to follow his ordinary pursuits. Section 324/326 of I.P.C. cover those cases where the assaulter uses dangerous weapons or means.

Thus, unless the wife is grievously beaten up resulting in one or more of the above injuries, the offence is non-cognizable, i.e., not punishable by law.

Measures to be Taken

Wife battering is the most under-reported crime in India. No woman wants to bring her agony and personal life to courtroom and throw herself open to having her *bonafides* questioned and her character maligned. She would rather prefer to cling on to a broken marriage that break up her family reputation.

The first point to be noted is that these laws are ineffective for protection of a woman under the general law of assault. Very often, because a woman's lack of interest in a separation with her husband, people say that she enjoys the batterings. But there are currently very few alternatives to help women to live an independent life.

The alternative for her is to go to her parents, only if they are in a position to maintain her with children which is often a rarity. Another option for her is to go to a women's rescue home run by the government which in the Indian context are very few and ill-maintained. Moreover, if she has children over the age of eight, then the children would be sent to a children's remand home.

Both these centres are largely, centres of exploitation. A

woman can leave her husband for cruelty but it is a ground only for a judicial separation and not for a divorce. It is essential that laws be changed to make wife battering a ground for immediate divorce. Custody of children of such women who are compelled to take divorce is another problem. A woman can get custody of children only after undergoing a lot of legal problems involving time, knowledge, money and of course judicial patronage. These hardships come in the way of making a decision of divorce for the woman and often she is forced to look back and face her destiny and torture.

Women belonging to the poorer groups are more easily swayed by emotions, can leave their husbands and start living alone. Being used to the hardships of life, they can rough it out even living alone. Their society gives them shelter and helps them start a new. Women belonging to the middle class, however, are more guided by social taboos and bindings. Right from the time of maturity, they are taught to be loyal to their husbands, to mould themselves to the whims and caprices of their husbands, bearing stoically the brunt of all hardships and all the abuses their husbands put them to. Under such conditions; they prefer not to leave their husbands in spite of extreme hardships and torture.

Causes of wife battering are high level family conflict, stress and violence in society, family socialisation in an environment marked by violence, cultural norms and sexual inequalities. (Straus, 1983). Wife abuse is seen as a reaffirmation of male self image as an aggressor which has been internalised and encouraged during childhood (Cotlin, 1974). According to (George, 1977) child abuse in own families or parental violence, alcoholism and the husband's experience of childhood battering are some of the factors leading to wife battering.

Moore (1979) looks into the social, legal, psychological and personal factors to explain the causes of wife battering. Newman hypothesised that the intake of alcohol, hostile dependency, extensive brooding on the part of the husband, husband's frustration in his work and other activities, and the husband having been battered by his parents in childhood, contribute to wife battering.

FACTORS BEHIND CRIME

There are two levels of frustration in a man's life, individual and societal.

Individual : Man's expectations of himself and his inability to face problem and failures which lead to a sense of insecurity lead to individual frustration. If frustrations in a man's life lead to violence, why is it that the wife is always an inevitable target of his violence? Frustrations build up in a woman's life as well, but why is it that this does not lead to spouse abuse? Some cases have been put forward to answer these questions:

1. The unquestioned authority of man in his home/marriage.
2. The consequent subservient role of the wife.
3. The wife's total dependency on her husband.
4. The social status which the husband provides to his wife.
5. Male confidence that he can make a woman forget and forgive the worst with a show of love and gifts.
6. The fact that a wife is least likely to show resistance to her husband's batterings.
7. If a man has witnessed wife battering during childhood or has been physically abused as a child, he is likely to adopt it as an acceptable way of resolving problems in his marital life.

Societal : The most fundamental factor which leads to wife battering is linked with the sex structure of the society as well as the family. The fundamental rights grant a man and woman equality but as long as the authority of man remains rooted in our culture and in the eyes of the law, wife battering will be perpetuated in society.

It has been seen that while economically dependent and

independent women are equally likely to be battered, an economically dependent woman is more likely to stay on in a violent home. Lack of education and poor job opportunities force the middle class women to remain married to men who constantly batter them. This, along with the burden of child care and parental responsibility forces women to remain in violent homes. Knowing this, men continue abusing their wives with relative impunity. They can be relatively confident that she will not leave him because: (i) She is not economically independent; (ii) She has no place to go and; (iii) She has the burden of bringing up the children because society feels that child care is exclusively a mother's job and women who leave children behind became social outcastes.

Immediate Causes : However immediate causes of wife battering may be noted as:

1. Monetary causes
2. Jealousy and suspicion
3. Instigation by in-laws
4. House work
5. Impact of alcohol
6. Economic independence of wife or wife's high self-esteem (she thinks too much of herself)
7. Dispute over children
8. Extra-marital affairs of husband.

VICTIM'S DEVALUATION

There are some myths common to all culture about the "kind of women" who get beaten.

1. The first myth is that middle class women do not undergo wife battering. In reality women come from all sections of the society, belonging to different religions, educational levels and from all socio-economic classes. If we hear

more about wife battering in slums or in chawls, it is because these women have less privacy. The middle and upper class women are battered behind closed doors. They live in total isolation and keep up the pretence of a successful marriage. Working class women talk, quite openly about the violence that they experience in their homes, and generally it seems to affect them less psychologically as they do not see it as being something unrelated to them as individuals whereas middle class women begin to question and doubt themselves.

2. The second myth is that the victim of violence is a small, fragile, helpless woman belonging to the working class. In reality, women holding responsible jobs as doctors, lecturers, journalists and models get beaten by their husbands. Many of them are quite capable of managing their lives. So there is no stereotype of a battered woman.
3. The third myth is that of provocation. This myth conveys the message that women who get beaten are masochistic and they want to get beaten. It further victimizes the women. The burden of guilt falls on her, increasing her shame and degradation.
4. The fourth myth is that the women who don't leave their husbands do not mind the batterings or that they actually like it. It is often asked: why women continue to live in a situation where they are eventually murdered or are driven to suicide. Why don't they seek a way out? The theory of learned helplessness gives an insight into the mental stage of passive resignation experienced by women. According to this approach, some events occur in the battered women's life during childhood and onwards with sufficient regularity due to which they acquire feelings of helplessness and poor self-image and resigning themselves to fate or accepting blame. Some important events in women's early lives which suggest a susceptibility factor include a high level of violence by members of their

families in childhood (e.g. being battered by the mother, battered by the father, the father battering the mother, the father-mother battering other children) perception of critical or uncontrollable events in childhood, and experiencing such conditions which place them at high risk for depression in future. The fear of losing the husband's affection and the fear of disruption of their home life status quo also prompts them to tolerate the husband's battering. The battered wives are thus afraid to stay and at the same time terrified to leave for fear of inescapable reprisals. They prefer to choose the devil than foray into the deep sea.

Recognising the Criminals

As there are myths about the type of women who get beaten, there are myths about the type of husbands, who beat their wives.

1. We generally tend to take it for granted that if a man beats his wife, he must be from the lower strata of society, being frustrated in his job, an alcoholic, or a paranoid person, aggressive in his relationship with the world at large and his wife being one of the victims. The act of wife battering is found elsewhere too, where the males are either professionals like lawyers, teachers, doctors, etc. or the well off economically like businessmen, politicians, etc. In some cases, the males are not alcoholic but they too are not free from this very act towards their wives.
2. The myth that loving husband does not indulge in wife battering is also false. Sometimes some males are quite sober, gentle and lovable to their wives but they too involve in wife battering in case of some frustration.

Hence, more or less from what is found, the wife battering is a general phenomena among all sections of male community of the society throughout the world.

1. A preventive rather than a curative approach to the problem should be taken by the institution which tries to deal with

the problem of wife battering. Unless the structure of the family changes, the help given to battered wife will prove to be only superficial. This does not mean that we should ignore the desperate and immediate situation in which millions of women find themselves, and live their lives in constant fear of violence and death. Despite occasional successes to expect lone women to fight individually against institutionalised family violence is both cruel and unrealistic. There is not only a desperate need for more homes for battered women, where such women can take refuge when their lives are threatened, we also need homes which will look at the problem of wife battering from a pro-women point of view, and which will help the women rebuild their shattered lives and induce faith and confidence in themselves. These can serve as important educational institutions and consciousness raising places. The time spent here can be utilized in teaching the women useful skills which can eventually make them self-sufficient. In case a woman chooses to go back to the husband, the home should lay down rules that the husband allows her to continue her job training and should not send the women back on their husband's terms. In most cases the husband is more anxious to get the wife back once she leaves, and this is the only time, terms and conditions can be laid for the man. This can be very useful in maintaining contact with the woman, so that when the batterings recur, prompt action can be taken against the husband.

2. There is a need to create an awareness in society so that the attitude of society— doctors, counsellors, institutions, social workers and the police is more sympathetic towards victims of marital violence.
3. Community action like having a *morcha* or a *dharna* outside a wife-battered house goes a long way in acting as a deterrent to marital violence. Men and society at large

should recognize once and for all that women are no longer going to take batterings lying down.

4. Support structures for women who decide to break away like legal aid, a place to stay and a job go a long way in bringing a feeling of security to the tortured and oppressed woman. The homes for battered women should be linked up with organisations which help women take up self-employment ventures. We need more committed lawyers who are sympathetic and understanding and would help to provide legal protection and relief to the women who are battered.
5. In cases where the marriages are resolved and reconciled, full precautions should be exercised so that any future attack on her is frustrated. This can be done by getting help from her neighbours, locking herself in a room, running away from the house, throwing objects or chilli powder at the husband can at times, deter a husband from being violent. There may be several hurdles to a religious mind which is conditioned to accept the husband as lord and master, but unless women can stand upto the batterings and fight back, the power relationship within the family will not change.
6. The situation of assaults by a husband on a wife being quite specific where the wife is economically dependent on the husband, and that the assault occurs in the house of common residence, it is essential that the police operate under different laws than those which cover general assault. A law such as Domestic Violence Act should be passed.

The point that women are often their worst enemies should not be forgotten. Mother-in-laws and sisters-in-law often instigate men to violence. Do they not poison the ears of their sons and brothers respectively and antagonise them against their wives? Voluntary social workers uphold women's dignity through glittering sessions and often have double standards as they subject their own maidservants to cruel humiliations.

Unless women are able to organise themselves, they cannot fight male domination. There is a need, therefore, to set up women's organizations in every area to fight this aspect of women's oppression. Forming into groups will help them raise their voices louder against the men and get them the desired results one day.

Crime of Homicide

In law, culpable homicide is differentiated from justifiable and excusable homicide (see Gibbons, *Society, Crime and Criminal Careers*, 3rd ed., 1978: 350).

Justifiable homicide is intentional killing sanctioned by law. It is committed on some legal demands, or discharging one's legal responsibility, such as the execution of a legal sentence of death, or the killing of a person in legitimate self-defence, or a police officer's shooting a fleeing dacoit, or a prison officer's killing a prisoner attempting to escape from the jail.

Excusable homicide is one which results accidentally from lawful acts performed by lawful means. It is unintentional killing where no blame is attached; for example, the death of a patient that results accidentally from a surgery by a doctor. *Culpable homicide* is one for which a person is held criminally responsible and is subjected to prosecution and punishment.

Culpable homicide is further divided into three sub-categories: (a) first-degree murder, (b) second-degree murder, and (c) manslaughter. These distinctions rest on the degrees of premeditation and malice aforethought. Premeditation designates 'intent' (to violate the law) formulated prior to the activity, i.e., a decision to commit crime and planning its execution, etc. Malice aforethought does not involve planning, though it involves 'intent to kill' at the time of the act. Thus, for a person to be convicted of murder in the first-degree, both premeditation and malice aforethought have to be established. In second degree murder, only malice aforethought has to be proved. In manslaughter, neither premeditation nor malice aforethought are present. It (manslaughter) is, thus, unintended homicide.

All types of homicides in this chapter are used as a generic term as 'murders'. Although not all homicides are murders, yet if an act is a homicide it states a reason for regarding it as murder and hence as wrong. Calling an act 'murder' presupposes that the act is homicide; that is the reason why the act is wrong. We could thus say that homicide is morally neutral but not murder.

Official statistics reveal that murder has been on the rise in India during recent years. The figures had gone up from 25,786 in 1984 to 38,577 in 1994, i.e., by 50 per cent (*Crime in India*, 1994:8). Rates also vary by region and by the size of a city, though we cannot say that murder is primarily a city phenomenon. The rates for the rural areas have been higher than the rates for the urban areas. It is rare that murders go unreported and it is also rare that a suspect is not apprehended and charged with murder.

All-India figures of murders in which female victims may be classified on gender basis are not available. No official records are maintained on the incidence of spouse murder. But it is estimated that spousal murders in intra-familial homicides may account for 20 per cent to 30 per cent of all murders and wives killed by their husbands (in comparison to husbands being killed by their wives) make up 68 per cent to 70 per cent of all spousal murders.

Any meaningful study of spousal murder requires to concentrate on four major aspects: the kinds of persons who commit murders, the situations in which murders are committed, the categories of murder, and motivations in murder. We also focused our attention on these and a few other issues. The main concerns of the study of the murder of females were:

* to gain insight into motivations in murder;
* to examine patterns in murders;

* to assess the kinds of men who commit murders;
* to find out the types of women who are usually murdered;
* to study homogeneity-heterogeneity in the offender-victim relationship in murder; and
* to analyze the role of victim in murder.

The data for the present study was collected from prisoners in a jail (all 'lifers' having served one to eight years in jail) and court and police records. In all, 52 cases were studied.

Familial Relations in Common

The offender and the victim were closely related to each other as members of the same family in 92 per cent cases and knew each other as acquaintance in 8 per cent cases. Of the 48 cases in the first category (members of the same family), the victim was related to the murderer as wife in 90 per cent cases, as illegal wife in 4 per cent cases, as daughter-in-law in 4% cases, and as sister-in-law in 2 per cent cases. Thus, a large number of murders by men were murders of their wives. Of the four cases in which the victim was not a member of the murderer's family, one was the landlady (the killer being her servant), one was the offender's old co-tenant (a girl of 19 years of age) and two were colleagues (a teacher in school and a clerk in office).

It could, be said that familial maladjustment in general and marital relations in particular are very crucial in female homicides. Or, what needs to be understood in female murders is adjustment and role performance in family relations. Von Hentig's (*The Criminal and his Victim*, 1948: 392) investigation of murders in Germany in 1930 also brought into light a startling fact that 62 per cent of the women murdered were killed by their husbands. A similar finding was earlier given by McDonald ("Death Penalty and Homicide" in *American Journal of Sociology*, 1911:16) in his perusal of criminal statistics covering the late 19th and early 20th centuries in several countries. Similar conclusion was made by a study in England and Wales for the years 1885-1905. Out of 487 murders committed by men, 124 were women murdered by their husbands and 115 were mistresses or sweethearts of their assailants. Wolfgang's (*Patterns in Criminal Homicide,* 1958:11) Philadelphia (United States) study during the 1950s also revealed the relationship between gender and murder. He emphasized that homicide is directly related to "relatively close, intimate, personal and direct relationships or primary contacts". His research indicated that primary group relationships, accounted for 65 per cent, of all victim-offender relationships, and that the number of wives, homicidally assaulted by their husbands constituted 41 per cent of all women who were killed. Gibson and Klein's study of homicides occurring between 1957 and 1968 in England (Statistical Report on Murder in England and Wales, 1969) also revealed that wives were usually the most frequent victims.

As regards age, out of 52 victims, 14 per cent were 20 years of age or below at the time of murder, 44 per cent were between 21 and 30 years of age, 27 per cent between 31 and 40 years, and 15 per cent between 41 and 50 years of age. The mean age of the victims was 29.4. Against this, 7 per cent of the murderers were 20 years or below, 52 per cent were between 21 and 30 years, 25 per cent between 31 and 40 years, 10 per cent between 41 and 50 years, 4 per cent between 51 and 60 years and 2 per cent above 60 years of age. The mean age of the murderers was 30.5 years. This indicates that:

(i) three-fifths of the victims (58%) and three-fifths of the murderers (59%) were young, i.e., below 30 years of age, and

(ii) the ratio of middle-aged offenders to middle-aged victims was 1:1.2.

It may be hypothesized that most victims of murders as well as their murderers are young persons (of 18 to 30 years of age) or that young husbands are more likely to kill their wives than older husbands. This does not support Wolfgang's finding that murderers are generally younger than the victims; though it supports Bensing and Schroeder's contention that relatively young persons carrying out most homicides.

The age difference between the murderer and his victim was less than one year in 11 per cent cases, between 1-3 years in 33 per cent cases, between 4-6 years in 31 per cent cases, between 7-9 years in 17 per cent cases and 10 and above years in 8 per cent cases. Thus, the age difference between offenders and victims was very less. On an average, the killers were about 4.5 years older than the victims. A significant fact to remember here is that the murderer in our study was the victim's husband and in Indian society the age difference between husband and wife varies from 2-5 years. The above figures also support Richard Block's (*Homicide in Chicago,* 1973) finding that the homicide offender is young.

Marital Life : As regards the marital life, of the 48 victims who were married and members of the offender's family, 9 per cent had enjoyed a married life for less than 1 year, 44 per cent between 1-5 years, 26 per cent between 5-10 years, 14 per cent between 10-15 years, and 7 per cent for more than 15 years. The mean period which the victims had spent with their husbands/in-laws was 6.2 years. About 33 per cent of the victims were married before the age of 18 years, 46 per cent in the age group of 19-22 years and 21 per cent after the age of 23 or more years.

Children : Further, 65 per cent of the victims had children and 35 per cent had no children. Of those 31 victims who had children, 31 per cent had one child, 35 per cent had 2 children, 23 per cent had 3 children, and 16 per cent had 4 or more children. The mean number of children was 2.4. The age of the children varied from 1 year to 38 years. Of the total (71) children, the age of 31 per cent of the children was 5 years or less, while 24 per cent of the children belonged to the 6-10 years age-group, 17 per cent to the 11-15 years age-group, 14 per cent to the 16-20 years age-group, 10 per cent to the 21-25 years age-group, and 4 per cent were more than 25 years of age. The mean age of the children was 11 years. Thus, since a little more than half of the victims (53%) had spent one to five years with their husbands/ in-laws and a little less than two-fifths (38%) had one to two children, it may be concluded that:

(i) the rates of murder among women with a marital span of less than 5 years are greater than the rates among women with a marital span of 5-10 years or more than 10 years.

(ii) as the marital span increases, the rate of murder decreases, and

(iii) problems of adjustment of a girl arise not soon after her marriage but after spending several years in the family of procreation.

Education : Regarding education, 29 per cent of the murderers were illiterate or had no formal education, 35 per cent were educated up to the primary/middle level, 19 per cent up to the secondary level, 8 per cent up to the higher secondary level, and 9 per cent were graduates/post-graduates or had a technical degree/diploma. Amongst the victims, 40 per cent were illiterate or had no formal education, 31 per cent were educated up to the primary/middle level, 21 per cent up to the high school level and 8 per cent were graduates and/or postgraduates. Thus 7 out of every 10 victims and 6 out of every 10 murderers were either illiterate or less educated. This indicates that educational achievement or level of education is significantly related to murder.

Caste : In terms of caste, of the 47 Hindus (five were non-Hindus) 55 per cent belonged to the upper castes, 30 per cent to the intermediate castes, and 15 per cent to the lower castes. The ratio of upper caste to lower caste victims was 3.6:1. It may thus be averred that among lower castes there is no high rates of murder as against the common belief. Further, 60 per cent victims hailed from rural areas and 40 per cent from urban areas, showing thereby that female murder largely tends to be a rural phenomenon.

Occupation : In terms of occupation, 39 per cent offenders were cultivators, 17 per cent businessmen (including shopkeepers) 21 per cent service-men (including teachers), and 13 per cent were self-employed (tailor/sari-printer/nagina-maker/rickshaw-puller/mason/advocate/black-smith). Of the remaining 10 per cent offenders, two were unemployed and one each was a student, a beggar, and a salesman. Thus, 62 per cent offenders were engaged in occupations of low status. Or, it may be said that homicides of females are more common among low status occupational groups.

Economic Status : Finally, analyzing the economic status, it was found that 88 per cent of the murderers were working and earning while 12 per cent were non-earners. Of the 46 earners, 26 per cent were earning up to Rs. 1,000 per month, 48 per cent between Rs. 1,000 and Rs. 2,000, 20 per cent between Rs. 2,000 and Rs. 5,000, and 6 per cent above Rs. 5,000 per month.

Nearly 27 per cent of the murderers were the sole bread winners of their families while 73 per cent had co-earners also in their families. Thus, taking the income of all the earning members in the family, 25 per cent were found belonging to lower class (with an income of less than Rs. 1,000 per month), 29 per cent to lower middle class (with an income of Rs. 1,000-2,000), and 46 per cent to middle and upper-middle classes (with an income of Rs. 2,000 and Rs. 6,000 per month). Amongst the victims, only seven women were earning.

These figures reveal that the rates of homicides of women from the lower and lower-middle classes exceed those from women of middle and upper middle economic status. In other words, economic factor is inextricably related to female murder. Our study, thus confirms Bensing and Schroeder's (*Homicide in an Urban Community*, 1972) thesis that low-income families have high rates of murder. It also supports Wolfgang's contention that murderers are largely located in the low stratum of society. Further, it supports our own earlier study on female murderers in India

(*Female offenders in India,* 1969) that female murderers generally come from the lower income groups. This makes it necessary to critically examine the link between homicide and lower and lower-middle class adjustment. Scholars like Miller and Bullock (*Urban Homicide in Theory and Fact,* 1952) Wolfgang and Cohen (*Delinquent Boys: The Culture of the Gang,* 1956) have attempted to trace the root of the violence behaviour pattern in what they call 'lower-class sub-culture'. We will examine this theory later on.

Taking all variables together, it may be concluded that:

(1) murderers of females by and large are members of their own families;

(2) they are not-so-young, but are generally illiterate or less educated and moderately poor persons; and

(3) a positive correlation exists between the incidence of homicide and the level of familial adjustment.

Since the last feature makes an analysis of offenders' families essential, we will now attempt to examine the family structure and family relations vis-a-vis murders.

STRUCTURE OF FAMILY

The family structure pointed out that 37 per cent of the murderers were living in nuclear families, and 63 per cent in joint families. The high incidence of murderers from joint families is probably attributable to the predominance of joint families in the social structure of our society, particularly in rural areas.

It was further found that out of the 48 cases in which victims were members of the killers' families, in 65 per cent cases the murderers were heads of families and in 35 per cent cases they were ordinary members (non-heads). Since the number of murders by heads of families was about two times more than that of non-heads, one must ask if this indicates any relation between murder and the role which the head of the family has to play as leader of the family group.

On the other hand, as far as the status of 48 victims is concerned, 33 per cent of the victims had no young children to bring up in the families, but 67 per cent had small children to look after. Does this not indicate a difficult problem of adjustment in families?

How were relations among members in the families studied? The persistent belief is that if a family is normal, members must love one another and violence must be totally absent. Were then the families of murderers studied abnormal? The respondents did not agree to this contention. Conflicts while common in many families were certainly not abnormally frequent in the homes analyzed. By and large, the families functioned nonviolently. The threat of murder or even physical violence never hung heavy in the air.

The murderers interviewed revealed that the victims of their murder had broadly speaking strong feelings for them. That love and threat of murder can coexist in a family is perhaps the most insidious aspect of murderers' family life. Men do hit the people they love. Then what went wrong in the family that led the respondents to commit murders. This is discussed in the following paragraphs on murder motives.

Objectives behind Killing

The most common homicide situation starts when the parties to the fatal interaction are involved in arguments and altercations, often over matters that might appear relatively trivial to many people. In our study too, quarrels over behaviour with the in-laws, money, children and sundry situational disputes were found to be the precipitating circumstances in many homicides. Petty quarrels resulting from illicit relations, a dislike for the wife, the wife's chronic illness or property conflicts were also found to be the motivating factors in murders.

An in-depth study showed that the main causes of murders were as follows: petty quarrels — 27 per cent, victim's chronic illness 15 per cent, irritating behaviour of wife — 11 per cent, offender's illicit relations — 10 per cent, victim's illicit relations— 5 per cent, fear of victim's revealing offender's secrets — 6 per cent, property conflict — 6 per cent, feeling of revenge — 6 per cent, wife's insistence on visiting parents — 4 per cent and wife's constant demand for money — 10 per cent. Thus, marital maladjustment (58%) because of domestic altercations or wife's chronic illness and sexual infidelity (15%) were the two most important factors in the murder of females.

It was further found that there was no significant relationship between motivation and planning. The planning was associated only with murders committed for revenge. Murders because of petty quarrels or wife's chronic illness or wife's irritating behaviour or irrational demands or illicit relations, etc., were not always planned.

On the basis of this analysis, we can identify the following four types of murders:

(i) Non-malicious emotional murders.

(ii) Non-malicious accidental murders.

(iii) Malicious murders without explicit intention to kill (say, beating with a view to teaching a lesson).

(iv) Malicious murders with premeditated intention to kill.

Of the 52 murders in our study, 27 per cent fall in the first category, 19 per cent in the second category, 31 per cent in the third category, and 23 per cent in the fourth category. This indicates that a large number of murders are committed in the heat of passion or in a state of high emotionalism or in a situation of negligence.

Only a small number of offenders kill females in a cool and calculated manner with malice aforethought. Thus, since the real intent to kill is absent in a large number of the cases, it may be pointed out that homicide is the product of a situation characterized by lack of social control.

Numerous Paths

Murders vary not only in terms of causes and relationships between the murderer and the victim but also in terms of operational dimensions like the place and the time of murder, modes of murder, planning in murder, weapon used, help sought, and alcoholic state of mind. We will examine these important dimensions separately.

Place of Murder : In 88 per cent of the cases, murders were committed in the homes and in 12 per cent cases outside the homes. The data further showed that there was a direct relationship between the locale and the type of person killed. Primary (43) and secondary (3) kin were mostly killed in their own homes and acquaintances (4) were killed outside their homes. Thus, our finding that a very large number of murders of females are usually committed in home supports Gibson and Klein's thesis (*Murder: 1957-1968*) in their study of homicides occurred between 1957 and 1968 in England that most murders of women occur in their homes. However, our finding is different from that of Wolfgang, Bullock and Pokorny.

Mode of Killing : In analyzing the modes of killing, it was found that women were killed by stabbing in 23 per cent cases, by strangulation in 19 per cent cases, by hacking (cutting body in pieces) in 25 per cent cases, by poisoning in 15 per cent cases, by slashing (making cuts with sweeping strokes) in 12 per cent cases, and by shooting, electric shock and burning in 6 per cent cases. Of the 21 cases in which weapons were used in killing, a knife was used in 26 per cent cases, an iron-rod in 23 per cent cases, an axe in 35 per cent cases, and a pistol, gun or sword in 5 per cent cases. Thus, the availability of a licensed weapon has no bearing on murder. It was further found that there was some relationship between the mode of killing and the planned and unplanned nature of murder.

Planned Murders : Of the 28 planned murders, 18 per cent were committed by stabbing, 29 per cent by poisoning, 14 per cent by strangulation, 21 per cent by hacking, 7 per cent by shooting and 11 per cent by slashing.

Unplanned Murders : Against this, of the 24 per cent unplanned murders, 29 per cent were committed by stabbing, 25 per cent by strangulation, 29 per cent by hacking, and 17 per cent by strangulation and then burning, by electric wire, and by slashing. Thus, there was no great difference in the methods of both planned and unplanned killing.

Influence of Alcohol : Only five murders were committed in a state of intoxication and 47 in a sober state of mind. This does not mean that all murderers in the second category were non-alcoholics or all murderers in the first category were necessarily alcoholics. If alcoholism is defined as 'habitual drinking' and is operationalized in terms of physical and psychological dependence of individual on alcohol, it was found that murderers by and large were not alcoholics, although 37 per cent did take alcohol occasionally or once in a while. Thus, we cannot demonstrate any positive correlationship between murder and alcoholism.

Presence of Accomplices : Three-fourths of the murders (73%) were committed by the murderers alone while in one-fourth of the cases (27%) someone's help was sought. Of the 14 cases in the latter category (in which the offenders had accomplices), in 12 cases they had only one accomplice and only in two cases did the murderer have two accomplices. Amongst the accomplices, in two cases the accomplice was a member of the murderer's family, in four cases a friend and in one case a brother and his friend. Further, the accomplices were found only in planned murders. The help sought was in terms of killing the victim (9 cases) and in disposing of the body of the victim after the murder (5 cases).

Element of Planning : Nearly 54 per cent of the murders were planned and 46 per cent were situational. That is, the latter type of murders were committed in a state of momentary outrage, in a situation of tense interaction with the victims, while the former type of murders were committed in a cool and calculated manner.

Several researchers have held the view that many victims of murder precipitate their own deaths. This mostly occurs when offenders and victims know each other and their tensions and mutual aggravations reach a point where both indulge in violence. Our study, however, indicated that the number of cases in which victims induced their death through their own menacing actions, was not very high. Only in 15 per cent of the cases, was the first initiative for violence taken by the victim, i.e., a large number of homicides involving women were not victim-precipitated. While more husbands have been found to have provoked their wives, the number of wives provoking their husbands is not large. When our earlier study of female murderers (*Female Offenders in India*, 1969) had shown that in quite a large number of cases, husbands had provoked their wives, our present study of women being murdered by males showed that only 15 per cent wives provoked their husbands. Boudouris's work in Detroit (*Homicide and the Family*, 1971) has also revealed a similar pattern.

A few victim-precipitated cases show the pattern of victim-precipitated murders, are described below. The use of scurrilous language by the victim, supplemented by outrageous behaviour, characterizes the most common victim-precipitated homicides. Though these cases exist they are not very large.

Cases : In one case, the husband accused his wife of having illicit relations. Once when he was beating her for this, she taunted him that he should kill her if he did not want her in the house. Thus challenged, the husband stabbed her. In the second case, a man (the accused) had married for the second time after paying Rs. 5,000 to have a woman to look after his young children from the first wife. Soon he found that his wife was neglecting the children as well as him (the accused) as well. He tried to argue with her but she always abused him. On one occasion when she started abusing him, he struck with an iron rod and killed her.

In the third case, the victim wanted to visit her parents, but the husband (the accused) refused to let her go. On her insistance, he attacked her with an axe.

The blow was so fatal that the victim died within a few hours. In the fourth case, the second wife of a husband (the accused) took away ornaments and a lot of cash and gave these to her brother. When the accused went to her house and asked for the money, his brother-in-law started beating him. His wife also started abusing him with a fit of rage, he gave his wife several blows and then struck her with an iron rod. In the fifth case, a husband used to beat his wife regularly; generally the beating was preceded as well as followed by a violent quarrel. One day the wife attacked her husband with a knife. The husband snatched the knife from her hands and stabbed her. In another case, the daughter-in-law and her mother-in-law very frequently quarrelled on petty issues. Both sought the husband's/son's sympathy. The husband tried to pacify both but the quarrels persisted. One night when both started quarrelling in his presence, he physically attacked his wife to calm her down, but the injury was so severe that the wife died in hospital.

Any Logic?

A number of theories have been advanced to explain violence in general and homicide in particular. Four important theories which have absorbed the attention of scholars in this connection are:

1. the Instinctive Aggression Theory (bio-psychological view),
2. the Frustration-Aggression Theory (psychological view),
3. the Learing Theory (sociological view) and
4. the Theory of Sub-culture of Violence (sociological view).

We do not consider these theoretical explanations (including the Theory of Sub-culture) adequate explanations for explaining the murders of females in one's own family, particularly of wives.

IDENTIFYING THE CULPRITS

Abrahamsen (*The Murdering Mind,* 1973), a psychoanalyst psychologist, has given the following characteristics of a murderer:

1. hateful impulses,
2. feelings of distrust, helplessness, fear, insignificance, and loss of self-esteem,
3. emotional disturbances,
4. inability to withstand frustration and find sufficient gratification by expressing hostile aggressive feelings,
5. suggestibility,
6. a tendency toward transforming identification,
7. an inability to change persistent egocentricity or self-centredness into a healthy conscience resulting in contempt for authority,
8. suicidal tendencies with depression, and
9. a history of a previous antisocial or criminal acts.

An umpteen number of the respondents confessed having the first four attributes, but they denied having the last five characteristics. It is, therefore, difficult to accept the 'personality-type' explanation of Abrahamsen and other psychiatrists of the dynamics of murder. A murderer, in most cases, is a normal individual who acts in an extreme way due to anxiety, fear, anger, or confusion caused by a specific situation.

Having said this, it cannot be maintained that we accept the 'emotional-type personality' explanation of a murderer. People who cry at the slightest provocation or who smash things when annoyed are often characterized as 'emotional' people (Newman, G., *Understanding Violence,* 1979). Some studies have referred to the relationship between emotions and aggression, which includes murder. Emotions like fear or rage, etc., erupt as a result of external stimuli though environmental conditions which can lead to a woman's murder cannot be ruled out. However, we do concede that these fear or anxiety or aggression complexes might have developed due to extreme deprivation (of love, sustenance, etc.) at an early age (Kuo, Z.Y., *The Dynamics of Behaviour Development,* 1967).

Reasons behind the Crime

A theoretical perspective is needed to explain why a man murders a woman belonging to his own family, particularly his wife. For this, we have to understand the following:

(i) What are the broad expectations from a woman in a specific family setting?

(ii) Why does a woman fail to adjust herself or fail to perform roles according to familial expectations?

(iii) Why does a man (i.e., husband or father-in-law or brother-in-law etc.) react to this failure in a specific way?

(iv) When does the (reacting) man use "murder" as a reaction to woman's failure to familial or individual expectations?

Context-specific Approach : To answer these questions, we have to use a 'Context-specific Approach' as proposed by Wegner (*Pacific Sociological Review,* 1975) and used by Dobash and Dobash (*Violence Against Wives,* 1972) in their researches. In this approach, instead of viewing situations, personalities, feelings, etc., in general terms, we view them in specific contexts and specific domains.

With this approach in the background and drawing on contributions from psychology and sociology, our answers to the questions raised above are:

1. The roles and behaviour expectations from a woman vary according to sub-cultural patterns existing in a specific community and a specific family.
2. The failure of a woman to adopt herself to these expectations is circumstancial and partly her personality

traits. Thus failure affects her inter-personal relations in the family.

3. A man's reaction to woman's failure and her specific behaviour is the result of his learning, through the process of socialization, a set of beliefs regarding relationship between man and woman and man's authority over woman, and the demonstration of this authority in certain situations.
4. A man's own personality type determines his aggressive ways in enforcing his authority and domination.
5. A passive man with a submissive personality will tolerate woman's failure, but an aggressive man with a domineering personality will react and use violent techniques in enforcing control.
6. The nature of the precipitation in the specific situation determines a man's violent reaction leading to murder.

Thus, in our theoretical explanation, we do not give importance to unfulfilled childhood experiences, or to pathological personalities, or a sub-culture of violence. Our focus is on the social situation (including family structure, family norms, and intra-family relations, man's status in the family), personality characteristics (like impulsiveness, depression, immaturity, etc.) and socio-cultural interpretations given by man to woman's roles, that is, response learned in the process of inter-personal relations.

Cultural attitudes about women and about violence as a means of self-expression and solving problems are at the root of private violence. There is urgent need to bring about a change on this account. Various social factors may be related to different patterns of murder but we need to consider that people have choices as to how they will respond to immediate crisis and stress. Cultural legacy of violence may, in many ways, influence what choices people consider appropriate.

Since our finding is that most of the murders of women are within the family, particularly of wives by husbands, and these murders are not planned and premeditated but are crimes of violence and passion which occur in the heat of inter-personal conflicts and tensions, it may be said that if women adjust in certain situations while dealing with domineering, aggressive and authoritarian males, and if in certain other situations instead of acting as submissive and passive females, they act as efficient and active females, most of the murders would not occur. The level of violence in family (including murder) is the greatest when wife is either too submissive or too dominant in decisions.

Patriarchal Violence

India a democratic country with more than a half century of independent existence which gives the world the message of non-violence has a history of systematic violence and aggression among large cross sections of population. Violence with its latent and manifest forms always reveals negative consequences on the part of the victim. From the very beginning of our existence it is being used as an instrument to exert power over others.

History is the testimony to the fact that discrimination of sex always remained effective in particularizing one's treatment. While men and women these two are the wonderful creatures of nature whose mutual understanding and cooperation are essentially needed to guide the activities of the world, it is most unfortunate that throughout the history Indian women remained victims of various forms of violent actions induced by men's society. Increasing rate of dowry deaths, rape, wife battering, eve-teasing, prostitution and many latent and manifest forms of tortures have disturbed the equilibrium of our living. It is, however, a matter of satisfaction that there is a growing awareness of this problem in our society. So now it has become an agitating issue.

The question is often asked as to why should a man abuse a woman, inflicting all sorts of physical injuries and occasionally kill her? This seemingly simple question is not easy to answer.

Several factors account for this state of affairs with regard to women in this society. Factors which are deep-rooted are numerous, but most of them are basically of socio-psychological nature. Some factors may operate at personal level such as maladjustment, emotional instability, lack of mutual understanding, dissimilarity in beliefs, but these are not so important because they are the precipitating factors which may lead to their manifestations only. Now the question is what are the predisposing factors? What prepares the ground for the occurrence of such violent acts?

Cultural conditioning, rapid social changes and resultant frustration leading to aggression, perceptual discrepancy regarding the status of women, institutional structure of the society and to some extent women themselves are responsible for the increasing trend of violence against women in India.

Moulding Culturally

Violence is an acquired phenomenon. It is learnt in the society during the course of socialization through the technique of imitation and identification. Virtually our society is male-dominant. It does not provide equal treatment to both the sexes. When a child takes birth he remains completely raw. He learns whatever he observes in the society and that constitute his personality. A boy finds that he is getting preferential treatment by the society so he learns only the immediate gratification of his needs. He fails to get the opportunities to learn the use of such defensive-mechanisms as repression and suppression in controlling his desires more frequently so they remain weak.

A boy also identifies himself with his father. He imitates his reactions, aggression and hostility shown towards his wife. He also observes that his father is leading an independent life, being the master of the family. So he develops an anticipation of individual existence or separate entity which ultimately generates self-confidence, assertiveness, encouragements and initiation in him. All these characteristics are associated with dominance. In fact boy learns to develop authoritarian attitude towards his surroundings.

On the contrary a girl learns to control and suppress her desire. She observes that her father and brothers are enjoying all the privileges and whenever she tries to revolt, her parents teach her to develop tolerance, sacrifices, cooperation and submission. In this way she is forced to accept the dominance of males. How does this conditioning occur? The reasons may be the following:

(a) Discrimination exists from the childhood itself. Brownmiller, a well known sociologist has written that from the childhood a male is encouraged to build his muscles and toughen his fists and a female is encouraged to value, soft skin, and slender waist. His clothing gives him maximum mobility and her clothing hampers from movement by design and fragile materials add to her vulnerability.

(b) Our sick rituals and customs are also responsible for this faulty conditioning. We are prejudiced by religious attitude to secure spiritual benefit by son for the purpose of offering funeral cakes and libations of water to manes. A son is expected to become an heir and perpetuate father's name. Daughter is expected to leave her home after marriage. So no more expectations are associated with her.

(c) Our socio-religious norms have affected the women's status which has become another causative factor. Right from the post-vedic era down to the modern times, the religious practices, rituals, scriptures, precepts historical force which have created for women their existing secondary status in Indian society. Barring the vedic age, the women appear to have enjoyed a low status in society. In the major period of history womanhood has been treated as varna like Brahmin or Shudra, with a variety of functions and practices, even it was prescribed which foods to eat and when, with whom, which rituals and festivals to celebrate. Women under mensuration are treated as untouchables. They are considered as a property of man, to be disposed of as the master pleases. The chief apologists for lowering the status of woman was Manu, the father of Hindu caste system, who lived around 200 BC. He wrote " women is as foul as falsehood itself, when creating them the lord of creatures allotted to women a low of their beds of their seats and ornaments, impure thoughts, wreath, dishonesty, malice and bad conduct. From the cradle to the grave she is dependent on a male, during childhood on her father, during youth on her husband and in the old age on her son. Manu was also responsible for the defication of the husband. He wrote whether a drunkard, laper, sadist, or wife beater, a husband is to be worshipped as god".

(d) As psychologists suggest our belief and values condition our behaviour. Further these behaviours get reinforced by their success. In terms of reinforcement, it can be said that, if violence succeeds, there will be temptation to make use of it. Mostly, we see that women tolerate all these because they find no alternative. They perceive themselves inferior to men. Dependency on males makes them to feel lack of self-confidence and ability to recognize self-potentialities. They lack consensual validation of their revolt and all these lead to their withdrawal into themselves.

Many raped girls or women remain silent and they try to conceal facts predicting that otherwise they will be outcasted and perceived as disgrace to family. A woman who is beaten is often told that it is probably her fault as if her husband has a right to beat his wife. In case of dowry deaths which are usually burnt cases, we lack adequate punitive measures to prove them. All these make the revolt silent which strengthens the authoritarian mentality of males. In this way violence became a way of life, an accepted mode of behaviour, sanctioned by folkways and conventional morality, a subculture. Males are unaware of the fact that they are doing something wrong, so they do not have any guilt feeling.

Speedy Social Transformation

Increasing trend of social change and resultant frustrations leading to aggression is another contributing factor. Today many developmental changes are taking place and people are trying to catch them and to get them but the means are limited. The aspirations and goals are increasing improportionate to these available means and so people are facing strong competition where often they have to face failures.

Frequent failures generate frustration, a painful and discomfortable state, acuteness of which may threat ego boundaries. In order to overcome it one may unconsciously or consciously develop aggression which strives to be projected against some weaker object, outside himself and a female a weaker sex, always available before him becomes the scapegoat or target of his aggressive impulses.

Most social psychologists would agree that frustration does increase the likelihood of violence, but that a number of other factors help to determine whether violent behaviour will really occur. Berkowitz makes an important distinction between deprivation and frustration. I would like to say a person is deprived if he or she is unable to get an object which is desired but is frustrated only when he had been anticipating the pleasure to be gotton from the object and he cannot fulfil this expectation.

The statement that violence is related to rapidity of social change may mean that such changes bring with it new expectations, and as a consequence new frustrations leading to violence. A greater rate of change is associated with greater instability, Gurr summarizes "violent conflict is greatest in developing nations, least in modern nations, intermediate in the least-developed, most traditional nations".

Usually Indian males are more egoist, and self-centred. They develop feeling of superiority over females and so they perceive themselves as more powerful. They cannot tolerate their failure before women so they try to overcome their lackings by reacting more and by showing more hostility and aggression toward themselves. Rape can be considered as an important manifestation of aggression projected against the victim or an attempt to exercise power with means of deviant mode of behaviour.

Mackellar aptly verbalizes this tendency as follows; A man who rapes does so because he lacks a better means for making the point: I am a man. Similarly Bart observes rape as a power trip and not as a passion trip. Rape is considered as a male tendency to become genetically programmed in the fight for the survival of the fittest.

Dowry deaths may result from the frustration deprived by unfulfillment of expectations, which most of the in-laws used to have regarding their sons who have spent sizeable part of their earnings in educating them.

Organisational Set-up

The Institutional Structure of the Society also victimizes women. The organized institutional and structural patterning of the family and the economic, cultural and political systems that determine that some individuals shall be victimized through the withholding of social benefits, and be reduced more vulnerable to suffering and death than others.

The structural patterning also determines, the socialization practices that induce individual to inflict or to endure according to their roles. Women experience violence more sharply than men because social definitions of their biological equipment assign them to a special secondary descriptor as a limitation of their social status at every level in a given social hierarchy. The effects of the unequal distribution of resources, which is hierarchically determined becomes "extra unequal" for women when food tools and supplies are short, woman do without, man do.

Pregnant and lacting women and adolescent girls are culturally assigned less food than their bodies need. They face risks of death in child birth. Usually women carry a heavier work load than men responsible for the triple production loads of breeder, feeder and producer for the family unit, where men have only a single production role. In addition they must be ready at any time to render sexual service to men often involuntarily concomitantly, they are excluded from decision-making roles, both domestically and in public affairs.

Thus women are being kept deprived of many things for which patriarchal family structure itself is responsible. Our patriarchal household is such in which the male hand of the household as the power of life and death over the women and children of his family.

The patriarch family husband will protect his women from other men, but there is little or no protection from the patriarch. Court intervention to protect abused women has always been very limited, the practice of such intervention being even more limited than the concept. Therefore the vulnerability of women to the vicissitudes of the male temperament within the household is one aspect of the structural violence inherent in the institution of the patriarchal family. Another face of this violence shows itself in the situation of unmarried, widowed, unpartnered, deserted or divorced women, who maintain single-parent households unaided, and are totally vulnerable to rape and economic exploitation, they have neither patriarch nor court to protect them.

By the inverted logic of the rules of the patriarchy prostitution and rape and the anxiliary institution of pornography are seen as safeguards to the institution of the family. By providing men with sexual satisfaction outside the family, they protect wives from unreasonable demands. The underlying perception of women on the part of men that makes pornography, rape and prostitution possible is that of objects varyingly available for erotic stimulation.

Broadly speaking, the patriarchal imprint keeps women from sharing in economic, cultural and political roles according to their abilities, because of stereotype notions about what is appropriate for women.

Prejudiced Impression

An stereotyped image of women in our society is another causative factor. In fact, the image of women is very contradictory. They are kept on two ends of a continuum indicating extremely good or bad images. Thus on the one hand, position is exalted to the Goddess and on the other hand, lowered to the slave. Rig veda (composed sometimes between 1500 and 900 B.C.) and some other Hindu Shastras tell us that women enjoyed great respect in the society. They were even evaluated to the position of Goddesses and given different celestial names like Prithvi, a vague personification of the earth, Aadit; the great mother of Gods.

Ushai the Goddess of the dawn, Ratri; the spirit of the night, Aranyani; spirit of the forest and so on. Society thus makes an idealized or glorified image of a women. But this is injustice on her part because her elevation to the status of Goddess made men to expect unquestionable amount of loyalty and sacrifices from her.

At the same time woman is considered as a low creature. It is told that women have fickle and uncontrollable mind. Bhisma and Yudhishtara, two highly respectable figures of Mahabharata, regard woman as the vilest creature on earth and root of all evil. That's why people believe to treat woman as a slave. As if woman is a sub-species. These two stereotyped images of women have made them to suffer a lot. Woman is also a human-being with a mind to think and heart to feel. The craving in her mind to develop her ego, to think independently, to take important decisions about social order side by side with men, is not dead in her. When these aspirations in her are suppressed, it often gives and has given rise to spiritual discontent. But man has taken care to avoid the affront to his vanity by not giving her a chance to think and fearlessly express her against him.

Nietzsche has told - "Every one carries in himself an image of woman derived from the mother, by this he is determined to reverse women generally, or to hold them in low esteem, or to be generally indifferent to them".

Women's Self-image

The women themselves possess negative self-image which also helps to maintain the very structure that victimize them. The deep rooted factor is their wrong socialization. Our social norms and values are such that women learn to misperceive themselves. Usually women are being evaluated on a scale having three dimensions - sexuality, fertility and labour their ideal image and role expectations are-judged on these dimensions. This becomes the sad point on their part. Conformity with these social norms and values distort their perceptions and so they themselves become their worst enemies.

In a cross-section interview eve-teasing was viewed as reaction and not as action. According to some of the interviews "Eve-teasing occurs only when girls provoke. They incite others by their actions, dresses and mannerism. It's a form of admiration. Girls dress not for themselves, but for boys. Then why not let them be aware that they are looking great. But this is a partial statement. Girls interviewes showed another views. They said they dress themselves in modern way only to show that they have equal status and not to attract boys. So it can be said that eve-teasing may result due to misperception of girl's image by the boys."

What is wrong with Indian women is that there is basic difference between how men view themselves and how women view themselves. Usually women understand who they are, in terms of their relationship with their husband, while men understand themselves in terms of work they do. It shows that the feeling of insecurity and incompleteness misguide them. Many educated girls do not seem to bother about their career the reason is simple, marriage will decide their future. Some do study in view that educational qualification enhance their chances of better bridegroom. Women in their roles as wives and mothers give vital reinforcement to military structure of socializing battle-readysons and docile daughters. Since boys spend much of their prepubertal life with their mothers, it is impossible to minimize the role of mothers in creating the aggressive, fight-happy, male. By forcing male children to repress tears and expressions of emotion of pain, mothers directly contribute to the emotional infantalism of the adult male, who has grown up without adequate techniques for working through his feelings. Techniques for hardening boy children exist in every society. The pressures put on women by their own position as objects have historically been translated by women into practices of treating children as objects. Infanticide is a crime usually committed by women.

Thus, there are several socio-cultural, historical, and psychological reasons to the violence being committed against women in this society. Each one is deeply embedded to our way of life, to our mode of thinking, and the socialization process. Any plan to improve the condition of women, therefore, must take into consideration. These deep-rooted causes 'of violence and degradation of women.

9

Marriage Related Crimes

Victims of Dowry

Violence against women is a global phenomenon. Since times immemorial, women have been subjected to violence, atrocities and supression in almost all the countries around the world, whether developed or developing. However, it is only recently, since the mid seventies, that a growing concern has become visible on the issue of violence against women. Due to the sincere efforts of the different women organizations, media and developmental programmes, now, it has become an acrimonious topic for public and parliamentary debate. In fact no Govt. can be a silent spectator on the issue of the majority group "Women", constituting half of the total population. In fact Reddy's (1987) remark seems to be pertinent in this matter stating that, "In her (women) is symbolised the suffering and the indignity inflicted on the Indian masses".

The Indian constitution provides equality of status and opportunity to all its citizens irrespective of sex. Our state has enacted several laws to safeguard the interests of women and to bring socio-economic change in their status. Inspite of all the legal provisions, the rate of violence and crime against women is constantly increasing. The leading newspapers of India and Bihar almost daily find a place as banner news for violence against women in various manifestations i.e. dowry -death, bride burning, rape, abduction etc. After more than half a century of Independence women are still being raped, tortured, insulted, burnt and battered. Why have the changes brought into the economic, social political and legal sphere of the life in the 21st. century not brought any change in the status of women? The question is not one of mere enactment of laws or policies, rather their social implementation and rightful awareness. Minattur rightly opined that "from a study of the ameliorative legal provisions relating to women and the actual situation in which they find themselves, it is clear that something more than legislation is required. Perhaps the first attempt is to make women aware of their rights".

In this perspective the present paper aims to analyse the recent trend of violence against women in Bihar with special reference to cruelty to married women related to dowry, and some of the new legislative measures to curb violence. But before proceeding to the focal point it is relevant to discuss the social causation of violence manifested in different types of criminal behaviour like murder, physical torture, rape, burning etc.

Violence against women can be viewed in a multi-dimensional perspective. Psychologists like Brenner (1958) Kohn (1959) and Andry (1962) have ascertained psychological attributes like frustration, aggression and relative deprivation in the socialization process for violence. But the psychological attributes alone cannot explain the phenomenon as it also depicts a form of social behaviour. In this perspective it appears that violence generates from the basic milieu of social structure and cultural values of society. It is only the culturally determined gender role and socialization process which ascribe a second grade status to women in every walk of life though thinkers like Tiger & Fox (1972) and Parsons have applauded biological determinants for gender discrimination. Here reference may be made to Oakley's (1974)

Scathing remark on Parson's 'expressive female' in saying that explanation of gender role is simply a validating myth for the "domestic oppression of women" because researches have shown that in many societies biological basis appear to have little influence on women's role. Oakley rightly noted that women form an important part in the armed forces, administration, industries and agriculture in many countries like China, Russia, Cuba, Israel and India. Therefore it appears true that the universal degradation of women is mainly due to the social structure, cultural norms and the values rather than biology as Ortner and Friedle have accepted. Even in the Soviet Union where Engels predicted that sexual inequality would end with the emergence of Communism, inequality between male and female persists in many sphere of life as Lane has pointed out.

In India too, it is mainly the cultural milieu that accounts for the gender discrimination and dominance of patriarchy. The major reason behind the subordination of women is the institutionalization of the mother-housewife role as the primary role for all women. Papanek also supported the contention that"It is generally true that in India, Women's sense of personal worth is related to her fertility performance and the social standing she achieves as a mother of sons." Hence marriage is considered to be the primary career for every women and home is supposed to be a women's citadel. But ironically within the wall of her home and family she is often a victim of violence. She has been battered, or burnt within her prison-like home or molested, assaulted or raped outside it. Dowry death has been the most discussed and glaring form of marital violence inflicted upon women. At this juncture it is high time to probe and research in the realm of violence against women related to the practice of dowry.

Dowry, a common phenomenon prevalent in all over India was initially a kind of premortem inheritance of daughters in parental property which was given at the time of marriage ceremony for better status at the in-laws house. This social evil has plagued the society since ancient times as Chatterjee has mentioned.

Hindu religious scriptures provide evidences that Lord Shiva and Rama received valuable items such as Jewels, gold, horses, elephants, vehicles, cows etc. as Dowry. During the Mughal period too the *Ain-e-Akbari* has traced the evil of dowry. Now the custom of giving and taking of dowry has increased in all groups - Hindus, Muslims, Christians all alike through a process of sheer osmosis. The Hindu dowry tradition is firmly entrenched among the Roman Catholics of Goa and the Syrian Christians of Kerala as Verghese found during her studies. Now dowry has become a menace to society often compelling girls to commit suicide. It is nothing but an extraction of money or valuable items from bride's father. On the one hand it has lowered down the status of women in society and on the other hand it has given as impetus for earning black money and several malpractices at social level.

MAIN DIFFICULTIES

Hence the practice of dowry has become an important problem in marriage resulting in cruelty to married women. Education and developmental programme, instead of eradicating the evil have worsened it to a scandalous proportion. The society has adopted the system for a variety of reason like religious recognition, better, status for girls and growing belief that a good dowry hooks a good 'catch'. The evils of dowry have become so pernicious that a large number of women are being murdered, burnt or assaulted every year on the alter of dowry.

To curb the evil practice of dowry the Dowry Prohibition Act 1961 was passed, but it has not been much effective. In fact, women, are legally protected against violence but it is shocking to note that the rate of violence against women has been on constant increase as manifested through the police records and the media. Hardly a day passes, when the news of suicide, murder or bride burning for dowry are not flashed in the dailies in some or the other parts of the country. Surprisingly enough, the *Hindustan Times* published a banner news, "Dowry torture on increase in U.K.", stating that bride-burning and other dowry related brutalities among the Asian families are on increase and have become now a major problem in London, Leicester, and Birmingham. In Delhi too, in the first ten months of 2001, 56 women were killed for dowry and about 3,108 dowry complaints were filed inspite of stringent laws. In Bihar also, the evil has been like an epidemic. A large number of women are being forced to commit suicide or are burnt to death for dowry. *The Hindustan Times* daily reported 125 dowry deaths in Begusarai area only every year.

In this context reference may be made to the staggering statement given by the Parliamentary Affairs Minister, Bihar on violence against women as 113 dowry deaths, 459 rape cases, 442 kidnapping cases and 448 cases of eve-teasing in the State during 2000. Hence it seems relevant to present the records data in police station just to show the trend of violence against women in Bihar.

It is a fact that the nature of violence does not permit the victim women or her family to go to police-station and report the incident as its nature is so sensitive that it brings prestige of family immediately at stake and in most of the cases the incident is hushed up in the name of the family privacy or by the reluctant attitude of the victims themselves or by the negligence of investigating officers concerned. The incidence is much higher as the majority of the cases are not reported.

Practice of Evil Nature

To curb the evil practice of dowry, the Dowry Prohibition Act was passed in 1961, but has not been very effective. In view of the increased dowry deaths and cruelty to married women it is being discussed widely by Govt., welfare agencies and women organizations, Consequently the Act was amended in 1984, 1986. Dowry Prohibition Act amended as in 1984, 1986 incorporated suitable amendments with a view to take straight measures against the evils of dowry and tortures on brides. The word "Dowry" has been clearly defined as any covert or overt means of offering dowry thereby making a person liable to be held up under non-bailable offences. In the Dowry Prohibition Act 1961 dowry means any property or valuable security given or agreed to be given either directly or indirectly before marriage or at the time of marriage or after marriage by the parties" as consideration for the marriage".

In the amended act the words "as consideration for the marriage have been replaced by the words" in connection with marriage". Persons found guilty of dowry offences are liable to be imprisoned for a period of five years in addition to a fine of Rs. 5000 to Rs. 10,000. Under the revised Act, some restrictions on matrimonial advertisements have also been imposed. A person found to be advertising alluring terms such as share in wealth, money or business through media can be sent to jail for a minimum of six months to a maximum of five years or be fined a sum of rupees 15,000.

To sharpen the teeth of the Dowry Prohibition Act reference may be made to the criminal law (Amendment Act 1983) and the criminal law/(Second Amendment Act 1983) which are important steps, the enactments have amended the Indian Penal Code (I.P.C), the criminal procedure code (Cr.P.C.) and the Indian Evidence Act (I.E Act) and have inserted new sections, which provide remedial measures against cruelty to women, bride-burning etc.

Cruelty to married women has been made a substantive offence by inserting a new section 498 A in the Indian Penal Code by criminal law (Second Amendment Act 1983) section 498A of I.P.C. defines cruelty as:

(a) Any wilful conduct which is of such a nature as is likely to drive the women to commit suicide or to cause grave injury, danger to life, limb or health.

(b) Harassment of the women with a view to coercing her or any person related to her to meet any unlawful demand for any property or valuable or on account of failure by her to meet such demands is an offence as cruelty on married women.

A new section 113A has been inserted in the I.E act (Indian Evidence Act) which provides that when suicide is committed by a married woman there is presumption of abetment by husband or any one of the relatives;

(a) If a woman commits suicide within seven years of her marriage; and

(b) her husband and relatives have subjected her to cruelty. Section 174 (3) of Cr.P.C provides for the postmortem by a civil-surgeon or by a qualified doctor in case of suspicious death or if the police officers considers it desirable. Under this section, it is mandatory to go for the examination of the body when a woman dies in the following circumstances:

(i) Suicide by a woman within seven years of her marriage.

(ii) Any circumstances raising a reasonable suspicion that some other person committed an offence in relation to such women.

(iii) The case relates to the death of a women within seven years of her marriage and any relative of the women has made a request on this behalf.

Hence it appears that there are legal provisions no doubt, but how far these provisions safeguard women's interest ? Mere enactments and legislations do not always bring the desired change and impact. In reality implementation of law accounts much importance.

Because these legislations and enactments are still a matter in the books of law alone and the rate of bride burning, murder and cruelty to women is on the increase. Here it is relevant to cite an example as a case study to focus how does law work in actual practice.

It so happened that on 9.8.86 Mrs. X., a graduate of Patna University and State Govt employee working at Muzaffarpur, S.D.O. Office was strangulated and burnt to death by her husband the accused, but not confirmed by the court of law as yet. The accused admitted before the police that he committed this heinus crime for the Group Insurance claim of Rs. 96,000/- payable to the legal heir of the deceased. All formalities by the police were completed as on 13.10.86 and charge-sheet was submitted under section 302/ 201. The session trial case No.51/ 87 was in process for more than a year in the session court Muzaffarpur. Viewing the delay, the deceased's mother, a widow lady requested the Chief Justice of India in May 1987 and she got a reply much later with the contents that the case was beyond the jurisdiction of Chief Justice and the applicant should request the court concerned, where the trial proceedings are in process for quick decision.

Exposing Callousness

Another case, revealing the cruelty to the married women, is that of Mrs. Y who was killed on July 25, 1987 by her in-laws in Hilsa, Nalanda district, Bihar State. The deceased's father lodged F.I.R. with the Hilsa Police Station on July 29, 87. It was more shocking and suspicious that the father of the deceased was not even informed in time and the body was disposed off in a bid to hush up the case. It was revealed that Mrs. Y was killed by her husband and inlaw's as her father failed to pay the agreed dowry in terms of gold due to financial constraints. Thus this case also tells the inhuman story of woman's suffering and torture. These events transpire the following facts:

(1) Crime like strangulation, murder and burning to death could not be finalised by the court of law till-today i.e. after more than fifteen year. Thus the time lag between the incidence and judgment adversely affects the demand of justice in such cases.

(2) 'Justice delayed is justice denied' appears true as the law authority even has not made any effort for quick disposal

or expeditious decision. This situation will certainly stimulate the antisocial elements of the society, psychologically to proceed for such crime as justice is much delayed.

(3) The delayed justice will automatically spoil the situation of witness as most of the witnesses will lose sympathy towards the victims as time-lag is the greatest healer. The witnesses may also move from previous place to other place for their convenience. In such cases the court seldom cares to locate such witnesses after lapse of time.

(4) The time-lag and delayed justice do not impose confidence in people in the effectiveness of the justice, and therefore in most of the cases police is not reported.

(5) Such cases are dealt with by the Govt. pleader and generally victims are not required to appoint their own lawyers. If people want to appoint the competent lawyers to defend the case, it is not always possible to bear the financial burden by the poor. Our social-moral values have become so much questionable that to get proper justice appears to be doubtful for the poor masses. In this context statement made by Justice Iyer is quite significant, "Indian law system is administered and shaped by the British pattern not wholly indigenous or agreeable to Indian conditions, scaring away or victimising the weak through slow motion justice, high priced legal service, long distance delivery centres, mystiques legaless and lacunaes".

Thus it is evident that though there are legal provisions against violence to women with the recent amendments filling the gaps of legal lacunae, still the gap is vast between theory and practice. As far as the enforcement of law is concerned gaps still remain to be plugged. There are administrative, socio-economic and cultural constraints which come in the way of effective enforcement of laws.

As far as the administrative constraints are concerned the investigation process and the trial is so lethargic and time taking that people lose faith in it. In fact in many cases crime against women is not reported immediately . If reported, it is not recorded properly by the police officers due to unsympathic attitude towards women involvement of elite groups, the politicisation of the civil and police-service or on any other pretexts. Under such circumstances the witnesses are usually won over by accused persons or can become hostile. In most of the cases of bride-burning junior police officers investigate the case who may be more susceptible to be influenced by the local elite class.

Section 174 (3) of Cr.P.C. provides for the postmortem by a civil surgeon or qualified doctor no doubt. But the situation of postmortem is well known to every body as to how it is done and the circumstances under which it is done in ill-equipped hospitals of Bihar.

At this juncture, it appears desirable to have some concrete suggestions. Women should be more aware of their legal rights as Sachidananda & Sinha have observed that even after several decades of the introduction of social legislation, very few women know the legal rights and are unable to enumerate provisions incorporated in these rights. Hence there is more need for the voluntary organizations from grass-root level to upper most strata of society. They can play the role of "pressure group" and information agencies to mobilise Government, administrators and society to raise voice against violence to women. There should be more efforts and coordination between the different departments related to violence and crime from reporting to investigation, prosecution and punishment. Legal proceeding should be speedy and easily accessible to the masses. For this the free and mobile legal cells should be opened up at grass-root level. These cells can be attached to community centres, social workers, mahila mandal etc. In this regard a little effort has been made by the Govt. agencies, but their working is not upto the mark as Kishwar reported about the Anti Dowry cell set up by Delhi Police. She rightly opined that the creation of this cell is a leizarra mockery. Now one has to knock at four more doors instead of two or three. It is just the cretain of bureaucracy".

Legal literacy should be provided at school and college level. School and college curriculum can have a short course on legal literacy. For it para legal workers like social workers, community teachers and local leaders should be trained. To spread legal literacy the Family court should be set up in slum areas and centres of poverty. The roles of the main mass media is also very significant, they can play a vital role in mobilising public-opinion against social evils.

Reasons of Violence

Last but not the least, the cause of violence against women steming from the socio-economic and cultural set up of Indian society should be changed. Although the Hindu Succession Act (1955) provides equal share of property to daughters in parental property, but tradition hardly dies and the net result is subjugation of women. The entire socialization process of Indian psyche is so much deeply rooted to male chauvinism that this Act has remained a page of law books only. In many cases neither the parent care for rightful heirship to their daughters, nor the daughters claim for it and consequently girls become the victim of dowry and cruelty at their in-laws hands. Due to economic dependency on the husband and the in-laws women are at the mercy of their in-laws and are forced to tolerate suffering and torture.

Marx is quite right in his saying that, "the emancipation of women and the equality with men are impossible and must remain so as long as women are excluded from socially productive works and are restricted to house hold work which is private". Women too should change their attitude. They should not consider themselves as burden. This can only be done by a creative, rather than a conservative approach in the planning of a new type of society and economy which will contribute immensely to the cause of women's emancipation. The first step in this direction by the State can be the reservation of economic opportunities for females according to their population.

Dowry, a Menace

Dowry is generally believed to be given by the girls parents to the groom to ensure her a happy married life by fulfilling the basic necessities to give a comfortable living. But the greed of the groom's family is growing day by day. Starting from basic needs, the custom has become rigid enough to become an evil associated with social status and family prestige. Monetary considerations receive priority over the merits of the bride. Never before have the demands for dowry been so exorbitant and so widespread as today. It has taken the form of bridegroom price and has developed into a great social evil.

There is hardly a day when the cries of dowry victims are not echoed by the media. One day we read that the bride was burnt to death, as she could not bring the expected dowry. The next day, we come across a case where the bride was taken out on the pretext of sightseeing, and pushed from the hill top or into the swelling river. And these are just those cases which are reported in the media. There still remain countless other cases which do not come to the notice of the media or the police or the women's organisation.

Meaning : Dowry normally means gifts given during the marriage to the son-in-law or his parents in cash or kind. From the point of view of women's status, however, dowry has to be looked at as constituting:

(a) what is given to the bride, and often settled before and announced openly or directly; the gift though given to the bride may not be regarded as exclusively her property;

(b) what is given to the bridegroom before and at marriage; and

(c) what is presented to the in-laws of the girl.

The settlement often includes the enormous expenses incurred on travel and entertainment of the bridegroom's party. The gift-giving ritual continues throughout early married life, during festivals and celebrations.

The Justification : Indirectly it is assumed that it is a way of providing a girl with a share of the family property. The Hindu laws on property and ownership do not, in their present form, grant women their due share of family income and property. The Hindu Succession Act gives women the right to a share of the family property. But tradition dies hard, and in most cases the property of the family is given to sons. Daughters usually do not contend this, and hence inadvertently strengthen the argument that the dowry system alone ensures them fair share of her father's property, which will help them tide over any crisis. The latter also explains the importance attached to gold and jewellery and other constituents of dowry. For, unlike land and other immoveable property, they are both easily transportable and readily converted to cash. Demand for dowry is justified on many grounds. Firstly, since they have to pay dowry for their daughters, why not take it for their sons? Secondly, fathers of educated boys want to get back the money spent for their sons' education.

Non-fulfilment of Demand : Dowry today is being demanded and paid without any relation to the bride's father's income and wealth: One Ganaur Mahto of Keshopur village under Sakra police station of Muzaffarpur self-immolated as he failed to meet the dowry demand of his son-in-law even after five years of his marriage. With the increased desire for quick money and the luxuries of life, these demands are not confined to the middle class alone. Dowry is being demanded by all levels of people, be they high, middle or low, items of dowry may differ ranging from flats, cars, electricals, furniture, clothes, cash and jewellery. Failure to meet these demands results in ill-treatment to young wives, often driving them to commit suicide. A 22-year-old bride of Banka committed suicide by throwing herself into a well after constant nagging by her in-laws over inadequate dowry. In many instances they have been murdered. These deaths are generally represented as accidents to save the future of the children and the parents from social stigma.

Growing Keenness among Girls : Surprisingly now-a-days girls themselves are keen to collect their own dowry without any consideration of the plight of parents and the future of younger brothers and sisters. It is surely their socialization and the influence of the social milieu which have shaped their attitudes and expectations. If they have no rights of membership in the natal family, they also have no obligation to contribute towards its maintenance. Their main concern is to establish themselves in the new family and acquire status there. They look upon dowry as a necessary contribution towards this process and a compensation for their share in the family property.

The Concept : Social scientists differ widely in their interpretations of the concept of dowry reflecting the particularistic features of the societies which they have studied. It is very difficult to arrive at a universal definition from these varied explanations. The sociologists who have analysed the dowry system in South Indian societies define dowry as "female inheritance" because dowry is often termed as 'streedhanam' in South India. On the other hand, those who have studied dowry system in north India emphasise the *daan* or the gift aspect of dowry as it is variously called *daan dahej* (in Bihar) and *Dayaj* (in the Awadh region). They also view it as a compensation related to the institution of hypergamy.

The problem of protecting young married women against harassment on account of dowry has been engaging the attention of social workers and women's organisations for quite sometimes. Unnatural deaths of newly married young women beat headlines in the newspapers. Hardly a day passes without a news item on a tragic event like this. Some social organisations have been urging the government to make suitable provisions both, legal and administrative, to give protection to young married women against cruelty at the hands of their husbands and in-laws.

Women as Perpetrators : Women being the enemy of a woman in cases of bride burning is an interesting feature of this crime. It has been usually found that attitude of a woman as a mother is different from that as a mother-in-law. As a mother she gives all what she has to the daughter but as the in-law she attempts to extract the maximum possible dowry and can go to the extent of causing death of the bride, if the demands are not met to her satisfaction. In other words, in bride burning cases, crime is normally abetted and even committed by the women themselves. It is ironical that in many cases where one woman is killed for dowry another woman with a more handsome dowry is prepared to "console" the bereaved husband.

The government of Bihar set up "anti-dowry cell" in 1976 headed by a Superintendent of Police to give protection to women and Harijans against atrocities against them and the name of this cell was subsequently changed to "Offences against Women Cell". What is interesting is the fact that during the wedding season in 1983, IAS and IPS officers, engineers and doctors fetched more dowry; as IAS officer was paid Rs. 10 lakh as dowry and his marriage ceremony was attended by high officials (*The Statesman*, 18 August, 1983). Thus, if government servants are the perpetrators what more can be said and done is a matter to ponder.

Prohibition by Law

The first attempt by the Government of India to recognise dowry as a social evil and to curb its practice is the Dowry Prohibition Act of 1961. The Act was modified with the Dowry Prohibition (Amendment) Act of 1984 and 1986. Women's organisations have played a key role in this process of change.

The 1961 Act defines dowry and makes the practice of both giving and taking dowry, a punishable offence. Any agreement on dowry is void. If it is given at all, it will be the women's property. With increased awareness of dowry deaths and consequent public condemnation, women's organization made a thorough analysis of the implication of 1961 Dowry Act and criticised it for being theoretical and lacking in clarity.

Amendment 1984 : The Dowry Prohibition (Amendment) Act, 1984 makes the offence cognizable by enlarging the meaning of the term "Dowry".

The main features of the Amendment Act are as follows:

> Any property given or agreed to be given in connection with a marriage to the bride or bridegroom or any other person is considered as dowry. It is not necessary to show that the same has been given as consideration for the marriage. It also provides for the preparation of list of presents which are given at the time of marriage to the bride or bridegroom in accordance with the rules made under this Act.

Any person giving or taking dowry or abetting the giving or taking of dowry is also punishable with imprisonment which is not less than six months, but which may extend to two years and with a fine which can extend to Rs. 10,000 or the amount of the value of the dowry whichever is higher. Neither the bride nor the persons giving presents to her at the time of marriage is liable for punishment if the presents have been given to her without any demand on that behalf and the presents are entered in the list maintained in accordance with the rules. Demands of dowry continue in spite of this significant new amendment of the Dowry Prohibition Act 1961, failing which the bridegroom or his parents take to violence against the bride and sometimes such violence results in her death. Further there is a need for legal registration of gifts to be made compulsory, so that women may not be cheated of her dowry. The 1984 Amendment however makes it a cognizable offence and empowers recognised welfare institutions or organisations to take cognizance of the offence.

Amendment 1986 : The Dowry Prohibition (Amendment) Bill 1986 was introduced in the Rajya Sabha. It attempts to tighten the provisions of the Act and includes dowry deaths in the list of offence in the Indian Penal Code. The Bill provides that if a woman dies within seven years of her marriage due to causes other than natural, her property would be transferred to her children and if she has no children to her parents. The burden of proving that no dowry demand was made will be on those who took or abetted in the taking of the dowry, the aggrieved person will be subjected to prosecution. This amendment bill has made the offence non-bailable and raised the minimum punishment to five years and fine upto Rs. 15,000. Provisions for appointment of dowry prohibition officers and their advisory board with two women members had been made. According to this new amendment in the Indian Penal Code whoever, being husband or related to the husband of a woman, subjects such woman to cruelty shall be punishable with imprisonment which may extend to three years and shall also be liable to fine. The cruelty for the purpose of this provision means any wilful conduct which is of such a nature as is likely to drive the woman to commit suicide or cause grave injury and danger to life, or health (whether mental or physical) of the woman. The cruelty also includes harassment of the woman where such harassment is with a view to coercing her or any person related to her to meet unlawful demands for any property or valuable security or on account of failure by her or any person related to her to meet such demand. Under this amendment the police have been empowered to investigate and report cases of unnatural or suspicious deaths of women.

Factors Initiating Investigation : Further, they have been empowered to investigate in the following cases: when

(i) The case involves suicide by a woman within seven years of her marriage, or

(ii) The case relates to the death of women within seven years of her marriage in any circumstances raising a reasonable suspicion that some other person committed an offence in relation to such woman; or

(iii) There is any doubt regarding the cause of death.

A new Section 198A has been inserted in the Cr. P.C. 1973, providing that "No court shall take cognizance of an offence punishable under Section 498-A of the I.P.C. except upon a police report of facts which constitute such offence or upon a complaint made by the person aggrieved by the offence or by her father, mother, brother, sister or by her father's or mother's brother or sister or with the leave of the court, by any other person related to her blood, marriage or adoption".

The Section takes into account the various circumstances under which a court can take cognizance of an offence registered under Section 498-A of the IPC.

A new Section 113-A has been added in the Indian Evidence Act, 1972, to the following effect, in relation to the burden of proof:

> "When the question is whether the Commission of suicide by a woman had been abetted by her husband or any relative of her husband and it is shown that she had committed suicide within a period of seven years from the date of her marriage and that her husband or such relatives of her husband had subjected her to cruelty, the court may presume, having regard to all the other circumstances of the case, that such suicide has been abetted by her husband or by such relatives of her husband".

This Section empowers the court to assume that the suicide has been abetted by the husband or a relative of the husband, unless otherwise established. Under this provision, the burden of proof is shifted from the prosecution to the accused. Thus, there is a total departure from the fundamental rules of evidence. The guilt of the accused is assumed if the death of the woman is caused within seven years of marriage and if cruelty against such woman at the hands of the accused is established. However, the accused is at liberty to prove his innocence. He will not be entitled to any benefit of doubt, provided under the law of Evidence.

In spite of this amendment, dowry deaths in the country have not undergone any decline.

THE TRANSITIONS

The names vary. The circumstances differ. The amounts in question are vastly dissimilar. But the victims of dowry death all share one thing in common—an untimely, unnatural, grisly end. Shorn of superficial differences, each story reads the same: the demand for goods and/or money by the boys' side, the inability or the unwillingness, of the girls' parents to pay up: the lack of support structures available to the girl and, therefore, her incapability to walk out of the marriage; the mental, and often physical torture that follows. The barbaric bestial act turned on by the flick of a match stick on kerosene drenched victims marks the end to a helpless being. The demand for dowry and the victimization is carefully planned and plotted by the culprits so as to leave minimum evidence of the crime which they term as accident. The culprits allow some time to pass to give the impression that the couple had good relations. Demands for dowry are conveyed to the bride's father and others in a variety of direct and indirect ways. When demands were made after marriage, it is perceived either as an exercise of the rightful prerogative of the groom and his family, or to express discontent at what was given at the time of marriage or in social comparison with neighbours, at a later date, the dowry was perceived as inadequate.

The list of dowry demands are numerous and diverse and stretch beyond imagination ranging from cash for starting business to TV, tape recorder, motor cycle, refrigerator, car, even wrist watch, cycle or few *tolas* of gold. There are even demands for buffalo or a fan or a job for the groom or transfer of name of husband in fixed deposit. Demands of a grand wedding, share in property of bride's father are also few other demands which may precipitate into serious consequences.

No correlation exists between the level of the education of the bride and her murder on dowry issue is a matter of great surprise. Parent's belief that proper education of their daughter will diminish the margin of dowry is proving wrong . The more a girl an educated, the greater is the demand of dowry. A sixth year Chemistry student of Bihar University was burnt to death by her in-laws and husband for a car. Her parents are said to have given Rs. 4 lakh a few days before she was married. Her father said that a week back his son-in-law had sent a letter threatening him with dire consequences if he was not given a car. In the meanwhile due to constant pressure her father sent two ceiling fans, one cooking range, one table fan and four electric irons. Even working women are not spared for dowry.

Victimization starts immediately after the marriage in most of the cases. But sometimes victimization starts even after several years of marriage. In Gaya town even after eight years of marriage, a mother of two children narrated a woeful tale before the police after regaining consciousness that her husband and mother-in-law with the help of other members of the family inflicted hot iron injuries from her waist to chest till she became unconscious as father of the victim had expressed his inability to comply with the demand of her husband and this led to inhuman treatment with her.

A total of 1635 cases of bride burning have been reported during the period 1981-88. This was analysed to examine the rural-urban differences and then regional variation across four regions, namely, Magahi, Maithili, Bhojpuri and Adivasi.

The per cent of distribution of dowry deaths shows increasing trend in Magahi region. When the figure is compared with other regions it is found that all other regions showed a decreasing trend. This result showed that dowry system is more rampant in Magahi areas than in Maithili and Bhojpuri areas, while Adivasi people did not have concept of dowry. Statistics reveal that incidence of dowry death was always double in urban areas compared to the rural areas during the same years in the four regions. The gap between rural-urban cases was the biggest in

Magahi region (39.71) followed by Maithili (35.42), Bhojpuri (29.60) and Adivasi regions (26.21) in that order.

Harassing brides in the name of dowry is not caste or community specific. The dowry deaths are not confined to the Hindu community alone, they are now noticeable among the Muslims. A Muslim girl of Siwan was murdered by her husband. First of all, the boy refused to take his wife to his house. Soon he took her to a place and after a month he sent a message of burning in an accident of her parents. A young Sikh housewife was allegedly murdered by her husband and in-laws for dowry in Punjabi Colony, Chitkohra in Patna.

Impact on Muslims

Though dowry has been widely prevalent among Muslims in Bihar "dowry deaths were relatively unknown. It is only in recent times that such incidents have been coming to light. A glance at media reports over the years make it amply evident that no longer are Hindu women alone victim of dowry-related violence, it is taking place among Muslims as well although data available on the topic is inadequate. It is beyond doubt that the incidents of dowry deaths among Muslim is much lower in absolute number, yet their occurrence can no longer be described as a "stray incident" or "an isolated case". Wife battering and torture have always been indulged in by men in a male dominated society. Even Muslims come from the same kind of society and so the problem exists among them too and they are no exceptions to the nature of men all over. But burning of women has been rare occurrence in comparison to Hindus reason being that Muslims have recourse to divorce, a provision in Islam much misused by Indian Muslim men.

There are also cases of Muslim brides who are constantly harassed physically or mentally for failure to bring sufficient dowry. Approximately thousand applications of women are pending before the Imarat Sharia, Phulwari Sharif, seeking to get their marriage dissolved as Muslim women have as such right as men to get out of an unhappy marriage through *Khula*. Many of these applicants have complained to the religious heads of the constant torture by their husbands for dowry and gifts. Maulana Mujahidul Islam, Head Qazi, of the Imarat Sharia told that increasing number of applications seeking divorce in the last two years, have forced the religious leaders and Muslim intellectuals of Bihar to sound a warning to Muslims to distant themselves from such practices in future and not to fall prey to the evils that have gripped the Hindu community of late. If this is not done, the dowry death and burning of brides among Muslims would become common. (Muslims asked not to take dowry, *Times of India*, Patna, April 2, 1992).

All the Casualties

Domestic violence related to dowry takes a particular form of reporting. A dowry victim would be one who is harassed, beaten up, mentally tortured by her in-laws or her husband for failure to bring in the demanded dowry or more dowry; or would be one who has been harassed or deserted; or one who has been burnt to death; or who has committed suicide due to excessive harassment. Though the dowry death is generally perceived to be the murder of a woman on the dowry issue but before the act of killing, several forms of harassment and humiliation take place against the victim. An innocent bride of Hazaribagh was kept confined in a room without food for days together before being murdered.

Death Penalty for Dowry

Dubious Acts : It has been gathered from the newspapers that five different methods were alleged to have been adopted in killing the victims.

Sometimes the victims are first strangulated and then hanged from the roof to make it look like suicide. We shall not attempt to define what exactly is meant by harassment and cruelty, since they are largely subjective terms. At best, some of their physical manifestations on death or injury to body are cognisable. What is more important is that it must be recognised.

Malpractices in Prevalence

The most common form of harassment of a woman in her in-laws family unfolds in the forms of taunts, abuses, threats, which generally escalate to battering, even abettement to suicide or murder in some cases. However, what remains hidden from us are experiences of woman battered by their husband — for various reasons including inadequacy of dowry. This is viewed by the police as a simple case of domestic assault and by the society as "normal interaction among intimate couples". Women will be women, always striving to keep the family fabric intact. Blinded by the patriarchal notions about the privacy of family matters and because of their assumed weakness, woman seldom choose to get out of these relationships or even complain about it. Putting up with violence becomes the order of the day for an indefinite period until it becomes unbearable when they have to take hard decisions and escape torture by suicide or walking out. Keeping relationships together, despite violence, is also important for practical reasons such as financial support and shelter. Setting out is almost as bad as staying in the relationship. The threat of male violence outside the home is an acutely intimidating reality of women who endure violence within their own homes. Living among constant threats of killing and desertion become a daily ordeal for them, they have to take it or leave it, in most cases they keep taking it.

The mother-in-law, sister-in-law nexus along with an unsympathetic husband make life a living hell for them. Indian conjugal relationships are typically much less closer than those between mother and son: frequently the mother-in-law instigates the harassment against the young bride using her son as her agent. The actual or supposed inadequacy of dowry becomes an excuse for the mother-in-law.

On the slightest pretext the bride is sent back to her parental home—usually to refurbish her "inadequate dowry". To make matters worse and continued harassment, the quality and quantity or whatever she gets from her parents are made the excuse.

On the other extreme the girl is discouraged from frequently visiting her parents. Her isolation from her earlier natal source of support being complete, her natal family is kept in the dark under the impression that all is going well not having an inkling of idea what their daughter is going through.

That torture and harassment could reach such limits can be seen in cases where clothes for daily wear were given to the woman by mother-in-law each day; where for a pair of slippers and handkerchiefs she was not given money but was asked to get these from her parents; where every time, she went to her parents, she was not given the rickshaw fare, but was asked to make her parents pay it where the battering has permanently disfigured her finger, where a newly married bride tried to commit suicide because of the hopeless situation she was in and had a miscarriage; where she was not allowed to sleep with her husband or communicate with him for one whole year after marriage; where a woman was tied with a rope, beaten, after which she was burnt, where a woman was burnt within a week after her marriage, and where a girl had been accused of being insane and cast out. These are few of the many instances of harassment the women may have to undergo each day of their lives.

Difficult Chances

Reasons : The question that confronts us now is why do so many girls come back even after they have undergone such torture beyond endurance? The first reason being the wish of the girl herself who really sees no respectable position outside her husband's house. Women often feel inadequate to cope with self-sufficiency and consequently the lack of self-confidence often acts as a trap to keep a woman within a violent home. Putting up with physical abuse is the very reason that there is no decline in domestic violence against women.

A daughter's change of status and her transfer from one family to another have a strong cultural sanction. It is said that at marriage the girl dies and is reborn as a new person. The formal advice given to her is that as long as she is alive she is not to leave the house she is entering. The parents themselves ignore the case of the daughter who is being harassed and wishes to come back. They advise her, pressurise her or even force her to stick to the "real" home and try to adjust. They are afraid of the stigma of a married daughter leaving her home and returning to her parents. Their constant advice to her is to "adjust" to maltreatment, the common saying being. "It is nothing unusual or so unbearable—so many women are coping with it" In most cases of wife murder, suicide, maltreatment, the women feels so burdened by the expenditure undertaken by her parents, that she feels duty bound to present a brave picture of "silent courage".

Parents justify their succumbing to these demands, saying that it was done for the daughter's well-being ... the well-being of continued torture, within the four walls rather than independent survival for their daughter. Most women would also undoubtedly opt for the former precisely because they have been conditioned to think along similar lines. Both society and religion sanctify the patient and suffering women.

Women see their recognition in society through matrimony and for this she has to sometimes pay a heavy price. A home for a woman is synonymous with the home her husband would provide her. This is the general understanding of the man, of the parents, of the women, and indeed of Indian society in general. In our culture divorce or widowhood for a woman is worse than death. However, this is in many cases not true for the women of lower castes, as there is greater autonomy to women among them.

Reason of Death

It is not always dowry which can lead to woman's burning there are other problems related to adjustment which confront her after her marriage and precipitate into serious consequences. After marriage an young bride joins a new family and she is expected to "adjust" her needs, her behaviour, her personality and her entire self - according to her husbands and his family needs as soon as possible. This adjustment problem creates conflicts between husband and wife and daughter-in-law, and father/mother-in-law and brother/sister-in-law. In this situation of conflict the husband does not always know when and where to side with his wife. Over small conflicts, therefore the girls go to their parents home to get their (parents) sympathy.

The parents generally advise them to go back and adjust. The girls, therefore remain frustrated; unable to cope with the harsh realities of married life and getting no emotional support from their husband or their own parents, they seek the easy way "ending it all" by committing suicide. Some of the cases thus reported as dowry-deaths are in fact cases of impulsive suicides. Earlier, it was held that women in the autumn of their life had suicidal tendencies. But nowadays psychologists are of this view that teenagers form the highest risk group, because in this age, rapid hormonal changes in her body which make them more excitable, depressive and vulnerable. When they experience tensions after marriage instead of love and affection from the husband and the family, they take their own lives, often on filmsy pretexts. The young girls with dreams in their eyes fall victim to tension on experiencing small disappointments making them big issues. This makes them excitable and prone to suicide.

A lady Commissioner of Police in charge of the Anti Dowry Cell of Delhi corroborates the view that 90 per cent of the cases that have been registered with Anti Dowry Cell have no link with dowry and many of them are directly related with the problem of non-adjustment between husband and wife due to variety of factors like physical or mental incompatibility, the wife resenting her mother-in-laws domination and wanting to live separately etc.

Earlier also there were suicides and murders due to conflicts, but now they are reported in the newspapers, due to the awakening of womens rights and the pro-bridal wave. Many women's organisations take up the issue of the so-called "silent sufferers". Thus, it is not that all of a sudden in-laws and husbands have been savages, but that the mass media gives these cases prominence, at the same time not declaring mother-in-law as completely innocent in case of dowry death.

Circumstances Leading to Killings of Wife : It is gathered from newspapers that there are many circumstances in which, ill treatment of young wives, often driving them to commit suicide and many times they have been murdered, take place which are not linked with the dowry death in any way.

It is, however, desirable to be remembered that all broken and problematic marriages do not have dowry as the roots. There are cases where a girl who had been married by the parents against her will, may be because she did not like the proposal or intended to marry some one else with whom she was in love before, cannot adjust with her husband or in-laws and concocts a story of cruelty against her, returns to parents and sends a legal notice levelling dowry and torture charges and uses blackmail to demand a handsome life time maintenance. If this is not met, she might involve the husband and his parents in a criminal case under the Dowry Prohibition Act. Such cases are coming to light in which ultra-modern working women are involved. They do not re-marry but live in adultery with men of their choice.

The laws and bouts of propaganda have created panic, trauma and suspicion all round, without helping to do with the dowry menace. To a great extent, the matrimonial relations in general and the rapport between the parents and in-laws, in particular have deteriorated under the stress of suspicion. It would, however, not be forgotten that the dowry deaths and ill treatment of married women are not as common as they are made out to be, by the recent publicity. In comparison with number of happily married couples and contented families, they are a microscopic minority. So, the generalisation of plights of some particular brides and rampant in-laws baiting will cause immense harm to the social fabric. Every case has to be dealt with individually as all aberration and not as a part of the general state of affairs. After all, marriage is still the cementing factor of the social edifice and nothing should be done to weaken it.

THE DESTITUTES

In some rare cases parents are also equally responsible for the plight of their daughters. Why do they select such boys for their girls for whom they even have to borrow money or spend all their life savings? Why do they marry their daughters in dowry—greedy families? Why do they not bring back their daughters from their in-law's home when they come to know of their harassment? Why are they so concerned about the social stigma and send back their daughters to their in-laws when they are tortured by their husbands and parents-in-laws? Why do they acquisce in the demands of their daughter's in-law? Why do they sacrifice their daughters for the sake of the legality of a tag marriage? Why do they spend thousands of rupees on dowry as demanded rather than spending a little less amount on their daughters to make them economically independent? We may therefore come to a conclusion that the parents of the girls and the girls themselves cannot be absolved of the responsibility. In several instances, the girl has been known to have written to her parents or visited them, just before she died and told them about the cruelty.

The girls as victims to oppression are equally questionable as to — why do they submit to oppression? Why do they not realize that a divorce is better than a marriage where money is the all and end-all of all relations? Why do they not walk out of their marriages and try to stand on their own legs? Why do they not realize that by committing suicide, they are creating problems for their children and an emotional trauma for their younger sisters and parents. Marriage is not the ultimate end in life but happiness certainly is.

Ideally the parents of the girls should take a firm decision to report the matter to the police and to the court, as well. At the same time the girl must also take a decision as to her future course of action. She must decide whether she would continue to live in a state of growing tension, or whether she would prefer to secure release from that tension once and for all.

There have been suggestions for establishment of special or separate courts may to deal with cases of dowry and bride burning. These courts would contribute to the speedy and efficient disposal of dowry death cases.

Moreover, court proceedings should be made time bound, laws amended to make it more effective, particularly by giving recognition not only to written but oral dying declarations made in the presence of a doctor, or a police officer or a magistrate or any respectable citizen. Neighbours who can really be vital witnesses should come forward more often and be involved in a dying declaration.

There is no let up in the rate of crime despite the law. What can be done to prevent dowry violence and crimes related to dowry? People should stop exhibiting dowry items. They must socially boycott dowry seekers. The young girls must fight dowry and take a pledge not to marry those who demand dowry.

Along with amendments and changes in the present law and providing more teeth to police force, the girls, their parents, their husbands and the people at large who matter, can only prevent the bride burning. There is also need for structural changes like assuming easy and less costly education, taking effective measure to reduce unemployment among educated youth, devising a system to eliminate bribery in the process of getting employment, providing housing facilities to the employed and simplifying the procedure for lodging complaint to the police, may definitely go a long way in minimizing the rate of bride burning.

Moreover, mutual respect for each other and a degree of tolerance of opposing viewpoints will, in a great measure, contribute to harmonious solution. Men have to be taught to respect women and not treat her as an object of exploitation. Further on, only if women respect themselves can command respect from others.

Dowry Propelled Torture

Women's oppression today, then has to be seen in a wholistic perspective, according to which "What links sati with dowry deaths, female foeticide, sexual harassment, sexual crimes is the fact of woman being regarded as a nonentity, a non-person, with no identity except that bestowed on her as some man's daughter, sister, wife, mother etc. These very forms of oppression of women are rotten fruits delivered by the vicious and decadent tree of Indian patriarchy". Even Britishers found dowry as a factor which could exculpate their colonial rule for impoverishing India and rationalise their brigandry. In 1913 Sydney Brooks wrote, "The poverty of India is, it is true, abject and pitiable enough, but to charge it to British rule is grotesque. The social habits of the people, their improvidence, their reckless expenditure on dowries and wedding festivities [emphasis mine] have infinitely more to do with it than any external agency has or can have. You might remit the whole of the land revenue, and abolish the salt tax and the custom duties, and India would still be abjectly poor, and famines would still occur."

"The same socialization strategies that prepare boys to be soldiers and policemen also co-opt women as mothers, wives and sisters into that preparation process. The concept of structural violence, that which frames behavioural violence refers to the organized institutional and structural patterning of the family and the economic, cultural and political systems that determine that some individuals shall be victimized through a withholding of society's benefits, and be rendered more vulnerable to suffering and death than others. That structural patterning also determines the socialization practices that induce individuals to inflict or to endure according to their roles. This latter aspect of structural violence is conceptually related to the fact that structural violence establishes the culturally accepted threshold for physical violence in a society". This is an apt analysis, which could be stretched to our understanding of violence related to dowry. But we would still go beyond such an observation arguing that violence is not merely physical but psychical as well. The trauma, anguish which the unfortunate women would have been facing before committing suicide, definitely caused serious damage to their being. Violence is not merely an end product, it is a process. Thus the whole process radiates violence.

The question which appears, then is who are the persons we are going to punish in the present case of suicide? Could the people who were demanding dowry be prosecuted now'? If not, why not? Is there no redressal? Wouldn't it be having a viciously debilitating impact on the other two sisters and millions of other girls? Have not the recent Gwalior ostentatious wedding of children of Madhav Rao Scindia and Karan Singh contributed to dowry violence? The links are made nebulous, in reality they are not. We have to use not merely sociological imagination but sociological intuition - phenomenological in nature. Once we debunk this dowry phenomenon the culprits stand exposed. Unfortunately they are de facto above law as they happen to be Members of Parliament or members belonging to the elite sections.

The Classification

We would categorise the oppression of Indian women into three manolateralistic forms. All these three take the form of victimisation namely, (i) Patriarchal victimisation (inter-gender: man v. woman): in this men are responsible for crimes like sexual harassment, wife battering, rape, dowry murders, and setting in processes like patriarchisation, genderisation ("a process of ossifying social differentiation based on gender"), commoditisation etc;

(ii) Patriarchally propelled self-victimisation (extra-intra person); here the present suicide committed by four girls of Kanpur (three sisters and the other drawing cue from the former) and the suicides committed by brides figure.

In the former case it is the patriarchal forces which compelled the three sisters to commit suicide notwithstanding their being educated. They felt "helpless" because woman even today remains a slave, a vassal in short an entity-with-no-entity. Having no patriarchally endorsed worth in herself, a woman is made to look for material consumerables to enhance her value. Thanks to capitalism and our commercial media (commercial films, advertisements (in T.V.) have bolstered the process of commoditisation of women) a woman today finds a lot of new commodities to decommoditise herself. But woman who has been made into a commodity, fit to be exchanged for patriarchy to prevail, fails to decommoditise herself with the help of other inanimate commodities, which in the ultimate analysis is nothing but commoditisation of the very process of existence - manolateralistic to the core.

Whereas in the case of suicides committed by the brides, it is abetted proximately by the harassment and torture of the bride at the hands of her in-laws and remotely by the patriarchal compulsion of 'izzat' for which the bride's parents are not willing to accept their daughter back, for only their daughter's corpse—as the customary saying goes—can come from her in-laws house; and (iii) Victim propelled victimisation (intra-gender; woman v woman): here the publicly celebrated rift between mother-in-law! sister-in-law versus daughter-in-law to discredit woman as oppressor of her own sex figures. For instance, Ashis Nandy notes that "...even man's cruelty toward women is no match for the cruelty of women toward women". "Indeed", observes A.R. Wadia that "the greatest enemy - and the only one that ultimately counts - of woman's 'Emancipation' is woman herself". To Renuka Singh "The worst deprivation of the 'deprived class' takes place when the woman vs woman battle begins resulting in the loss of support of women for the cause of their own liberation". K.L. Sharma observes, "it has been observed that it is women who obstruct the path of other women even more than men do; as is the case with mothers-in-law and colleagues at work". "What a pity", says S.C. Taneja, "that man has reached the moon and has made tremendous progress in every field but has not been able to end the social evil of dowry. And a more shocking aspect is that women are murdered by women themselves". Refuting the aforementioned superficial views we would argue that the intra gender nature of women's oppression is a manifestation of the "scapegoat sydndrome". For instance, the mother-in-law who has herself been made a scapegoat earlier (exceptions notwithstanding), searches for another on whom she can project the frustrations of her life-situation. And she finds in her daughter-in-law the object, who can be the target of her pent-up feelings.

We further maintain that it is unjust to say that in every crime or injustice against a woman there is a fellow women. This is the most decaying argument for intra-gender (woman vs woman) oppression, which tries to exonerate the male. This is so because we are merely perceiving the surface structure of reality. Only when we reach the deep structures of reality, we find not woman but man - his ethos, ambience, mores and norms-culpable. The mother-in-law and sister-in-law versus daughter-in-law phenomenon has roots not in a woman's mentality and her essentialistic characteristics they are illusory—but in the existing reality in which we have fixed her, where all the meanings of her life emanate not from herself but from man and his milieu. Thus we see that intra-gender oppression has roots in inter-gender oppression. "Through our sociological insight which pierces the facade, the picture which forms in front of us enjoins on us to perceive the problem of dowry in the broad framework of the male -dominated society and thereby seeing women as nothing more than a cog in the machine and thus being detrimental to their own genre" . Agreeing with such a view Ruth Vanita argues "every oppressed group perpetrates its own oppression. It was

Indians who, at British orders fired on Indians. But in doing so, they strengthened British imperialism. Women who oppress women increase the power of men as group. Mother-in-law and daughter-in-law are forced to compete for the favour of a man on whom they are both dependent. If the dependence disappeared, so would the competition".

Statistics of Dowry-related Incidents

The data on dowry in Delhi shows an increase in dowry deaths between 1985 to 1987. There is a decrease for the same period, in dowry murders and cases registered under the Dowry Prohibition Act (DPA), 1961 (amended 1984 and 1986).

The question which emerges from the data is as to whether the cases registered under Dowry Prohibition Act has reduced because of increase in dowry deaths? Can't we correlate it with the increase in dowry deaths, that's why less of cases registered under DPA? What definitely is clear is that DPA still has not been able to make much dent on the dowry problem - the magnitude of the problem has rather enlarged. Dowry deaths are on the rise (however under reported the data may be) while DPA remains a mute spectator. Physical violence related to dowry continues, while psychical violence transcends the hold of law as it remains unrecognised veiled under the private domain of a woman's life.

Moreover, the data on dowry deaths in Delhi provided by the Police given above is at variance with those of the women's organisations.

The preceding data shows failure on the part of police in not investigating these cases, which is why as few as 43,64 and 79 dowry death cases have been registered in year 1985, 1986, 1987 respectively. Even after having registered these cases there has been not even one conviction.' The official data which then tries to conceal the magnitude of the problem of dowry beleaguering women is just an ostrich like attempt to come to grips with reality. While women continue to be sacrificed on the altar of patriarchy, the Policemen grumble of not making good money in Crime Women Cell at Police Headquarters and the district Crime Women Cells, though they extort money from the offender and his family as a price to exonerate them of their heinous deeds. So also Policewomen (constables, who actually investigate the cases) curse the government for opening up Crime Women Cells - an outcome of androcentric training (concomitants of patriarchal value system) imparted to them without sensitising and conscientising them on women's issues. What more, then, can we expect from such a machinery except harming women and their interests.

Further, notwithstanding DPA being amended its scope still remains limited in terms of "gifts". "No doubt dowry is given at the time of marriage (in many cases) by the bride's parent but that is not the end, it is rather a rehearsal for the gifts to be given to the bride throughout her life on different occasions like festivals, marriage anniversaries, birthdays etc. Thus we see that though we may have done away with Zamindari (feudalism) (though notionally) at the macro-level, analogously speaking we are reviving it at the micro-level by turning the in-laws into lords and the bride's parents and family into serfs - who have always got to be on their toes at every beck and call of the in-laws or else be prepared to tolerate their daughter being tortured both mentally and physically -which comes to an end only with the death (either being burnt or suicide) of the bride". Violence (psychical or physical) is encountered not only then by the daughter-in-law but her parents as well.

What further undermines DPA are questions rationalising in the ultimate analysis the practice of dowry giving and accepting. It is asked, "when a husband is jailed at the behest of his wife, can the marriage survive in such an estranged relationship between the couple?"' It is further queried, "Is it possible for a husband, who has been subjected to police action by his wife, to enjoy and realise the conjugal bliss with her, which is the ultimate aim of a marriage?" Such questions are meaningless, as the husband by demanding dowry and torturing her directly or indirectly by being a mute spectator would have already ruined the marriage. There are multifarious ways in which dowry seekers and givers rationalise their demands and compulsions for giving dowry, respectively. Some of these are:

(a) prestige of both sides are involved and if dowry is not given the izzat of both the sides (mainly groom's side) would plummet;

(b) to make one's daughter's life comfortable, to ward off psychical and physical injury;

(c) "it is not uncommon to hear the daughters themselves asking for dowry from their parents on one pretext or the other";

(d) demanding dowry for one's son's marriage in order to finance daughter's marriage;

(e) if elder daughter gets married without dowry the younger one would have to bear the fear (along with her parents) of not getting any forthcoming proposals because the would-be groom's family will think that she too would not be given any dowry;

(f) what would samaj say if the only daughter among brothers or with no brothers was not given anything?

(g) who else except bride's side is going to give sarees and dresses to the intimates on the groom's side; etc.

If one has to quit dowry and thus curb its spread, one has to challenge these rationalisations.

Remedies in Possibility

Some of the solutions to the problem of dowry which occurs to us are:

(a) more and more of young people (women and men) coming together on an equal footing to shape their lives (ours was a dowryless and giftless wedding);

(b) enlightened older generation, who not only believe in dowryless marriages but also actively encourage them;

(c) men rejecting the patriarchal (feudal) prerogatives entrusted to them, thus becoming humans;

(d) depatriarchising education;

(e) women becoming economically independent by taking jobs;

(f) women refusing to marrying men who demand or accept dowry directly or indirectly, as Ratna'8 of Nagpur did on May 22, 1985;

(g) giving equal property rights to daughters which does not stand void in case the father Will's it to his sons (making such Wills ultra vires). Also making daughters coparceners (in the Mitakshara system) as has been done in Andhra Pradesh;

(h) ensconcing a depatriarchised socialist society, etc.

While outling the solutions we still remain aware of the fact that:

(a) Mr. Sharma is worried about his two daughters marriage, arranging their dowry even though he has given them best of education in an expensive school;

(b) Mrs. Vina, mother of two daughters (eldest being around nine years young) has started saving right now for their dowry;

(c) Worry seems writ large on Mr. Bhushan's face, father of three daughters (and a son), eldest of them being 18 years young. What else is his worry than making provision for their dowry?

We end this chapter with the question we began, while not overshadowing our optimism. Beating of the wife or wife battering is perhaps the most pervasive and age-old method of subjugating women to the males in marital life. It is the commonest form of violence towards women in marital life. It is however, amazing that until the latter part of the past century, women were bound by law to stay with their husbands, however brutally they were treated by them even in a country like U.K. If they ran away, their husbands had every right to drag them back again, and if need be to lock them up to prevent their future escape. It was in 1870 that Francis Power Cobbe, a Victorian feminist and philanthropic worker wrote a phamphalet called 'Wife-Torture' which crystallized a growing unhappiness with the law among many thinking men and women and in 1878 a Matrimonial Clauses Act was passed, enabling magistrates to grant judicial separation with maintenance and custody of any children to wives whose husbands had seriously assaulted them, in U.K.

This issue lay buried for nearly a century until Erin Puzzey almost single handed brought marital violence into news again. Through her efforts mainly wife-battering became a highly publicized subject and in July 1975 the House of Commons published their "report from the select committee on violence in marriage".The report remarked on the paucity of information about domestic violence and made urgent recommendations to the British Government and other bodies that future research on this matter should increase.

Despite the paucity of research and data we can, through our day to day observation, easily acknowledge the fact that a very high percentage of women are battered by men in every country of the world. India, with its rigid patriarchal structure of a family and society and the hold of feudal values is no exception, but a glaring example of such violence. Sociologists and lawyers Freeman & Maidment both agree that the problem of violence against women is a deep societal one, arising out of a family system in which the husbands authority over their wives creates a particular "marriage power relationship" and a subordinate status to wives and mothers (Dobash and Dobash).

Patriarchy can be held as a strong reason, and in communities where male-dominance is strong, wife battering is likely to be more frequent (Jean Renvoire 1979) for centuries the laws of Lord

Manu as regards the role and behaviour of women have been rigidly adhered to in the Indian society (Hindu society). Manu propounded a theory of perpetual slavery for women. She is to be under her father's guardianship in childhood, husband in youth and son in old age. She is to remain in the home and would or should have no part in the wider affairs of the society. Obedience and subservience to the male was prescribed as her supreme virtue along with chastity or "pavitrata". Her only utility was producing male children and whatever respect she commanded was as a mother of children. In such a set-up beating of the wife can easily be understood as a way of life. She can be beaten if she disagrees with her lord and master, if she does not produce male-children; if she does not readily submit to sexual intercourse, if she spends more on the household, then she is entitled to by her husband. The list is endless. And yet, she deserves beating on charges of assumed or proved infertility, while it is normal for the male to be sexually bigamous.

It is amazing that hardly there has been any research on this most common form of marital violence. It is almost always shrouded and concealed by the 'myth' of 'family privacy' while wife beating is clearly observable among the low-caste and low-income group, in the so called high-caste and middle income group communities it is almost always concealed. Even the 'victims' of such violence hesitate to speak about it and seek redress because it is so humiliating and disrespectable. The women's organisations, (Action group) have put up many forms of violence on their agenda such as dowry-deaths, sati, desertion, rape etc. but this form of violence has not been taken as on exclusive issue for action. Neither has the media, given it much importance. But the fact remains that it acts like a slow-poison ultimately producing women in hollow shells, or in some cases in suicide.

Torturing Wife

Wife-battering has been often taken as physical assault on the wife and it undoubtedly includes such assaults, but an important part of this violence is mental battering which is so subtle and slow, and yet devastating in its after effects. In U.K. mental battering accounts for a high percentage of women in the "refuge or shelter homes" (Joy Melville). Very often, it is the constant humiliation by the husband who is set in ridiculing his wife in public or proving her wrong to reinforce his own authority. Insults and constant criticism can reach intolerable heights whether sexual taunts, or accusations about being a bad wife and mother. When it goes on for hour after hour, the women is as bemused by it as after physical battering. She loses her confidence in herself, and her ability to cope (Joy Melville). The conterbury refuge in U.K. reported that quite a lot of the women who came there were mentally battered by incredibly petty restrictions on their basic women's liberties, which made life unbearable (Joy Melville).

This paper refers to cases of wife battering in Bihar. The sample is cross-caste, cross-religious and cross-economic status confirming the fact that this sort of violence on women cuts across,education, caste,religion and economic barriers. It happens everywhere, not exclusively among low-income and illiterate people.

My information is based on two sources observation of wife-battering in high-caste high-income and educated families, and secondary data as regards such violence in low-caste and low-income groups.

The cases under observation have been eleven and comprise both of house-wives and working women.

A. is a doctor in Arrah and she is very well placed. She is a gynaecologist and earns much more than her husband a doctor. Thus bank accounts are joint and this is no hassle on their salary. The problem is one of 'ego' and the wife is beaten on any petty ground, her refusal at times to submit to the sexual demands of her husband, being proised as a doctor by a third person, a doing to disagree with her husband in any conversation. Yet, they are living together. The wife is unable to decide whether she should leave, her husband.

B. is a housewife and has been battered ever since she got married. The husband not only ridicules her in front of friends and relatives at times even hits her in front of other people. Inspite of all this, they have three children and the wife continues to live in this violent situation. She has no support from her parents.

C. is a muslim woman belonging to a very good family and working in one of the schools in Patna. Her husband has always been cruel to her and hits her whenever he feels like it, even while, she is eating. She lives in her parental home, but her husband does not deter from violence even in the presence of her mother.

D. is a working woman, an associate professor in Patna University, with a very vivacious personality. She was married very young and her husband almost shaped her,getting her educated and helping her to get this job. The husband has been a very ambitious person, and also wanted to take up politics, go into movies for acting and taking part in all social activities. She was able to accomplish all these things to a certain extent. But after 20 years of marriage, the husband started beating his wife, on pretext of infidelity. The battering went on for four years, and ultimately the wife decided to separate and finally she was able to take up hostel superintendentship in one of the girl's hostels. According to her version, she was forced by her husband to ask for loans from his male-friends, in Banks, for constructing their house which was not even in the name of the wife and has been ultimately sold by her husband. She is continuously being harassed by banks for repayment of the loans which were taken on her name by the husband.

E. is a working woman belonging to a low income background and backward-caste. Her husband is a clerk while she is teaching in the University. The clash is due to the 'low-self-esteem' of the husband in himself, and jealousy on his part of his wife's position. She is not allowed to wear even clothes befitting her position and is beaten quite often by the husband. Yet they are living together.

F. is a well established journalist in Patna, after her break with her husband. She belongs to high-income and bureaucratic background. For ten years she lived with her husband and faced mental and physical battering. She was forced for sex and it resulted in the birth of two children, while all the time she was abused, not provided the basic amenities of life, and even burnt by glowing cigarettes by her husband. She has ultimately separated and now has made a place for herself as a journalist.

G. is a Gujarati house-wife. She was selected for the boy among fifty girl-candidates for marriage, was good-looking, healthy, although not much educated. She had no relatives of her own in Patna. She was beaten almost everyday, not only by her husband but also by her in laws. This was the first observation of wife- beating in an educated and high-income family.

H. is a working woman. She was married while she was a student. Immediately after marriage she felt the abnormality of the situation and after a couple of months, she was confirmed that her husband was having incestual relations with his own younger sister. She dared to object, and thereafter she was subjected to intensive mental torture. She kept isolated from other members of the family, and never went out with her husband, because he would never take her out, with him. She had no right to manage the household affairs and was not even given proper meals. There was constant altercation between her husband and herself which culminated at times in physical assault not only by her husband but also by her brother-in-law. Her husband remained silent spectator of such scenes.

Ultimately she separated and was able to obtain the decree of divorce after a high court case. She is now placed in a senior teaching position in an University.

I. is a housewife in Jamshedpur. The husband is a Junior Engineer. She was not living in a joint family, still she was beaten by the husband, because she did not agree perverse sex acts. That was the main reason behind her being battered.

J. is a housewife belonging to business community. The wife faced mental battering during the day and at night she faced physical assault. The husband was a chronic alcoholic and was very conscious of his money and status. He abused his wife and thought himself to be superior than his wife. The pressure of family ties was also there, also the couple did not live in a joint family.

K. is a housewife turned working woman. She teaches in the school of the factory where the husband is working. The husband feels that his wife has ceased to be docile after getting this job. So she was beaten up by the husband inside the four walls and even in public places before friends and neighbours. This was done to keep her in her proper place.

An observation of these cases reveals the following factors:

Penalty for Differing

Wife-battering follows almost always when the wife dares to disagree. The issues of disagreement may be vital one's such as infidelity of the husbands, intellectual issues, sexual pervisity or on petty issues of house-hold management. Low self esteem on the part of the husband and jealousy are important reasons. The wives inability or refusal to act as an instrument of satisfaction of the husband's ambition also lead to violent situations. In certain cases, total economic dependency of the wife over the husband forms the root cause of violence against the wife.

The second part of the study is based upon secondary data from the unpublished Ph.D. Thesis "Depressed Communities in Transition: Case of Bhangis and Musshar's of Bihar" of Renu Ranjan (1985). In her sample some 60 musahar women and 60 Bhangi women were interviewed. In the Musahar sample around 45.75% have admitted to beating by their husbands. These wives are comparatively of young age. Through informal conversation the reasons that came up for wife beating were:

(1) To get money from the wife. Wives in such communities always earn money by working as agricultural labourer, collecting wood and coal from road side and railway tracks. Husband's earn more than their wives but they think that they have a right on the earnings of their wives.

(2) These communities are heavily alcoholic and this is one major reason behind beating of the wife.

(3) Adultery-while the husband might be having illicit relationship with another woman or openly living with her, he beats his wife on assumed or real charges of adultery.

(4) Sometimes it is just habitual. The husbands beats his wife just to project that he has full control over his wife.

In the Bhangi community, almost all the wives accepted that they are beaten either by their husband's, sons or father-in-laws. As regards the reasons, they are almost the same, excepting the one major difference that women openly admitted that their husband's force them to go to other men(rickshaw-pullers, police constables, etc.) to get money, and if they disagree, they are badly beaten up. They also claimed that all women do this, some accept while others deny.

The observations about middle class and upper class educated wives and working women, and of low-caste, low income group wives and working women reveal many facts in common and prove the findings that wife-battering is not confined only to illiterate and poor families, but also to high-income and educated families. Let us now get down to the roots of such violence on women.

Firstly, violence against women is very much gender specific because the forms of control and coercion exercised in the case of women are related to gender and arise out of a heirarchical gender relationship where men are dominant and women are subordinate. The forms of control exercised over women cover essentially three areas sexuality, fertility and labour. Secondly, women become instruments through which systematic inequality is maintained. This is achieved through rules of legitimacy of offspring, through controlling access to women(as, for example, in caste-endogamy rules) and in general through the establishment of possessional rights over women which men have as husbands or fathers or older males. Such possessional rights include promise of protection (whether actually fulfilled or not in reality) in return for submission or exclusive use.

This is further maintained and strengthened over time by the socialisation process that embeds women strongly within the familial structure and heirarchic gender relations such that they have little or no independent status and transgression outside the family and male authority expose them to swift retribution and confirm their vulnerability. The situation of wife-beating arises out of a patriarchal family system in which the husband's authority over their wives create a "particular marriage power relationship" and a subordinate status to wives and mothers.

Financial Aspects

The economic dependency of women continues to be a fundamental feature of any society, especially with regard to middle class and upper class families. Attempts by women to leave violent relationships, or to find viable alternatives to them, continues therefore to be constrained by this basic inequality. They are subject to primary poverty irrespective of the family income level(Majore, Homer, Anne Leonard and Pat Taylar 1985). Financial hardship, burden of responsibilities and the prospect of deeper poverty ahead preserve a violent relationship to a great extent. Majority of women in Homer's sample were either powerless to gain an equitable distribution of family resources in the first place or felt unable to withstand persistent demands made by husbands to give the money back. Hence the nominal pattern of income distribution turned out to be largely unrelevant; for the concept of husband's right in what Bell and Newly describe as the "differential relationship" appears to have been constantly reinforced by his might. Kalmus and Straus maintain that economic dependency on husband is the reason for violent beating of the wife. Evidences show that the husbands power of the purse is an important factor. Economic dependency along with the acceptance of responsibility for the care and welfare of the children is important factor in this regard.

However, the study of low-caste and low-income groups adds a new dimension to these facts, which is that despite economic independence, women are subject to beating. The husband demands more than a share of the wives earning. In well to do families also, the income of the wife is more than the husband, creates problems of ego and it leads to mental battering if not physical beating. Low income creates strong feelings of "inadequacy and low self-esteem" leading to violent behaviour of the spouses in the small sample studied by Jean Moore (described in the N.S.P.S.C. (1074) Booklet-yo-yo Children). The American researchers Snell, Rosenwald and Robey came to similar conclusions in their small middle-class research sample.

10

Widows, the Victims

Normally, the status of Women in Indian Society has been subordinate to men, right from very beginning. They have to undergo from various lands of discrimination, exploitation and torture, both mental and physical in the society and within the four walls of the family. In the family which is supposed to be the safest place for its member's protection and development the women are not only tortured, exploited, discriminated, but they are occasionally killed or burnt.

If this is the case of normal life of a woman, what can be expected of such women who have lost their husbands in a male dominated society?

The concept of violence against women here does not include only physical assault on her, but also physical and mental torture, harassment, exploitation, discrimination, which she has to undergo for being a woman. The creation of an atmosphere of terror, a situation of threat and reprisal also come under the concept of violence. The life styles of Hindu widows, represent the climax of violence against women in our society.

The state of widowhood in Hindu society is considered as the worst and the most dreaded period of a high caste women's life; among the lower castes atleast, the stigma of widowhood is removed, since remarriage is socially accepted and is popular among them. A widow in Hindu society has to undergo various kinds of socio-religious-cultural oppression as well as economic hardships. The present paper is based on an analysis of the data collected by interviewing 80 widows. Forty widows have been interviewed from urban Patna and forty from rural Patna i.e. the rural areas just on the periphery of urban Patna.

A Review

An agewise distribution of the widows under study reveals that maximum number of widows (50%) were in the age group of 35 to 44, 35% of them are of 45 years and above and 15% of them are of the age of upto 34 years.

A good number of the respondents i.e. 43.75% are educated more than graduate level. Obviously, they were urban in majority and formed working class also. 25% of them were educated upto matric level and rest (31.25%) were just literate i.e. could read and write only. A few respondents who were urban based and educated upto matric level were trying for further education, which would help them in earning their livelihood. Out of 35, who were found highly educated, only 20 were found working, out of 20, ten respondents got their service after their husband's death in respective offices on humanitarian grounds. Income-wise distribution reveals that about 31.25% respondents belonged to upper income level, 50% to middle income and only 18.75% to low income level.

Violent Expression

In the present paper one is seeking to find out whether these widows underwent any violence and if so the different ways of violence specific to the widowhood. A widow in high caste Hindu society, is considered to be an evil omen, a Kulakshini in family and society, who has 'eaten' her husband. Widowhood is regarded as the punishment for horrible crimes committed by the women during her present or earlier births. Disobedience and disloyality to the husband or murdering him in an earlier existence are some of the grave crimes, which results as punishment in the present birth by widowhood (Saraswati, 1984; 69). Thus in Hindu society a women's worth is nil without her husband and the widowhood is associated with the idea of inauspiciousness.

Just to know the existence of inauspiciousness in present day, the respondents were asked how the society and family treated them after widowhood. All the respondents under study reacted very sharply. Their status in the family and in the society changed overnight just after the death of their husband. They were being treated inauspicious by their in-laws and parents too. Following this the society too treated them as inauspicious. In rural area the feeling of inauspiciousness was even more intense. To see the face of a widow in the morning before seeing any object is thought as unlucky; a man will postpone his journey if a widow crosses his path at the time of departure. There is hardly any day when a widow is not cursed for the death of her husband. The mother of her husband gives vent to her grief by using all terrible abuses and language against the widow of her son (daughter-in-law).

It was found during study that a vast majority of the respondents i.e. 70 out of 80, suffer from guilty feeling thinking that it was their bad luck which brought them into such a condition. Only 10 out of 80 were of the view that by virtue of circumstances beyond their control, they had lost their husbands. These respondents were urban, educated and working. But the other 30 respondents, which included educated and working widows, (besides the rural widows) were found to be torturing themselves. They were also the victim of superstition and ignorance.

The Impoverishment

The moment a women lost her husband, she is deprived of average living conditions and benefits of worldly desires. A widow, irrespective of age, has religious and social sanctions to discard colourful clothes, jewellery, glass bangles, weaving of flowers, make up, good and delicious food etc. They are allowed only such bland food, which is enough for survival. Thus, their are numerous ways for restricting the life of widows and restraining them from enjoying the pleasure of life. Life long mourning is imposed on them, which emphasizes that her existence in the society is worthless with the death of her husband. A widow is expected to go the extreme of self-immolation with her husband's pyre and this gets the sanction of the widows, themselves, as they don't want to get tortured in remaining, life.

It is quite clear that even these days i.e. in twenty first century, which is called as computer-age, widows of high caste Hindu family suffers from the age old deprivation of average living condition. It was observed during study that all the rural respondents and except six urban out of 40, agreed that they do not wear bright coloured saris. None of them ever used coloured glass bangles and bindi after their husband's death. Only 6 urban widows were found using perfumes, occasionally, not regularly. While a good number of urban respondents (23 out of 40) and one fourth of rural respondents (10 out of 40) accepted that they feel attracted towards all these. The six urban widows, who were found using perfumes off and on, admitted that they rarely use the perfumes in social gathering or family functions.

Beauty parlour has become recently a very common phenomenon for Patanites, even for those who are living in its periphery. It was found during survey that 5 out of 40 of rural Patna and 13 out of 40 of urban Patna were visiting beauty parlours before the husband's death, but after their husband's death, except three urban widows, none of them had visited beauty parlours.

Regarding their food habit, it was found that except 5 urban widows, none of them were taking non-vegetarian. Though 25% rural and 62.5% urban respondents showed their liking for it. A widow even accepted that sometimes without knowledge of anybody,she was eating non-vegetarian food. Actually widows in Hindu society are not allowed to take non-vegetarian meal. It is believed that non-vegetarian meal is tamasi food which is not 'Satwik'. It will initiate the sexual urge of widow, which is immoral for them.

It was a traditional norm that widows should be allowed to eat only one meal in 24 hours of a general day and compelled to abstain from food totally on sacred days in disguise of various religious customs.

During the study, it was observed that some of them were compelled to eat only one meal in 24 hours. There is a normal phenomenon that women take their meals in the last in family. So, this was not specific only to widows. But there were some instances, when women were forced indirectly to observe fast for the welfare of the family or children, specially those women who were widows. During study it was found that rural widows specially aged widows were observing the fast at least twice in a month. But this was not found in case of urban educated; working widows under study.

A widow who had lost her husband in early age is deprived of normal sex life, as there is no provision of remarriage among Hindus except in lower castes. Remarriage of a widow was not favoured by Smritis. According to Manu, a widow must not mention the name of another man after her husband's death. With the efforts of social reformers, widow remarriage Act came into existence as early as 1856, but the attitude towards widow remarriage has not changed upto the mark yet and cannot be said to be encouraging.

Respondents under study favoured in good number (approx. 54%) widow remarriage but not in all cases. According to them when widow is of very young age, childless, they should be allowed to remarry. Those who have children, then in that condition, they should not be remarried, as children will have to suffer. But there are many difficulties in remarriage of widows. There are a few person who will come forward boldly for marrying the widows. It is easy to talk about something, which is unapproved custom, but it is not an easy task to practise in behaviour. The old values are very deep rooted in society and difficult to remove. Dowry system is also a great obstacle for the remarriage, as parents can't manage dowry again and again for the same daughter.

It was asked from the widows under study whether they felt the physical and emotional loss of the husband due to their death. All the respondents, responded in affirmation which was quite expected from them. But about their sexual urge, at first they were not ready to say any word. After continuous probing only 27 out of 80 opened their mouth in positive. Of course, all of them were comparatively of younger age urban widows and only seven rural widows.

Those respondents, who advocated for the remarriage also pleaded that the young widows, deprived of their normal sex life, were always looked upon with suspicion. The society and the family may bring disgrace for them any time by committing some improper act and are exploited on this account also. Many of the respondents under study, also admitted that there are many cases in which widows have been sexually exploited by their own family members and close relatives. They also added that in many cases, the young widows, who are deprived of their normal sexual life, cannot sustain the social pressure for long and hence are swayed by their emotions. In such cases they are often trapped by such persons who compel them to accept a life of infame and shame or to commit suicide.

Besides five aged urban widows all accepted that they have been invited in functions and they do attend. But regarding the participation in functions, they have been kept aside and most of them do it willingly. As it was quite clear from their response, respondents themselves were suffering from guilty feeling and thus torturing themselves. Though, on certain occasions, they felt humiliated also but not always, only sometimes when pricks are direct. But none of them reacted on such behaviour, rather kept mum.

It was observed during study that respondents even in their son's or daughters marriage did not participate in rituals and customs, rather they kept themselves far aside on such occasion.

Financial Difficulties

The economic status of most of the women in our society is determined by the economic status of their husband. After husband's death, as life-partner, economically they become helpless. During study it was found that majority of the respondent except few i.e.75% (60 out of 80) were economically dependent. Only 20 were employed, out of which ten widows had got the job in place of their dead husband according to the Government's scheme on humanitarian ground. All the widows who got the job were urban based and educated. Three widows got jobs in A.G. office, three in Banking services, two in private organisations and two in College library. The other ten widows who were employed, had got the job of their own.

Three fourth of the respondents under study were not earning. Their source of livelihood was either their property or dependence on their family members. The rural respondents, were living in villages, dependent on agriculture. Most of them had their property joint with sons or with husband's brother or living with parents-in-laws.

Most of the respondents under study had some property, but they could not claim it and thus they had to depend on their family members economically. Regarding their own property right, it was found that they were just aware that they had equal property and inheritance rights. Only ten out of 80, who were urban widows were knowing that there is Hindu Succession Act, but they were not aware of the details of the Act.

Respondents under study reported that they were rarely given their due shares in their property. According to the respondent whether illiterates or literate, it is very difficult for them to fight for their property, while living in the same family. Six rural widows told that with the connivance of patwari and Tehsildar their properties were grabbed by family members. Widows under study preferred to remain as they were, as there was no way out, neither they could dream to go out of their present home. Because they would have to face more crisis.

The Hindu Succession Act, 1956, has given absolute powers to the female owner no doubt. A widow is entitled to the share in property, the husband had. If the husband had self acquired property she inherits it or shares the same with the children. Thus discussing the Hindu Succession Act Sec. 8, it is quite clear that this act has brought about a radical change in the position of women, in the matter of succession to the estate of the father or the husband. As the preferential heirs, according to Sec.8, specified in class I of the schedule, includes daughter, widow, mother, daughter of a pre-deceased son, pre-deceased daughter, widow of a pre-deceased son.

The property of a Hindu male dying intestate shall devolve the above preferential heirs. But there is grave flaw in the Act, as the line of succession opens as a matter of right in the case of a property of a male Hindu dying intestate, the owners may circumvent the necessity of devoting the property to female members. Hindu Women's Right to Property Act (1973) conferred the right to enjoy her husband's share in coparcenary property for life time without a right to alienate property. Under the new Act, the daughters, the widow and the mother can inherit the property of the deceased simultaneously. As between them, each takes an equal share, except that when there are more widows than one, all the widows together take one share. This is the position with respect to the self acquired property of the deceased. With respect to coparcenary property, the son takes his own share in such property and in addition takes a share in the father's share of such property as well, unless he had separated himself from the coparcenary during the life time of his father. Nevertheless, the acceptance of the right of the daughter to inherit is itself a big step forward.

None of the respondents under study were found aware of these details and was found that majority of the widows under study were deprived of their property, but could not open the mouth. The moment they raised the voice against the close relatives, whatever help they were getting , would be withdrawn away from them.

Most of them were waiting for setting down their children, some for marrying the daughters etc. It was surprising to know that not only in-laws, but their own brothers, fathers also exploited them economically.

Thus from the above analysis it is quite clear that widows are not only debarred of average living conditions and normal sex life, but are deprived of property also and economic independence which leads to chain of miseries in their life.

The life styles of Hindu widows which came out from the study, shows how much women are exploited and tortured just being a widow. The state of widowhood, which has been imposed upon them, is not due to their own fault, but it is just a natural phenomenon. Birth can be checked, but death can't be. Any of the life partner can die any time, but it is the woman, who has to undergo through different types of harassment—mental, physical, economical etc. just being a women, as well as a part of patriarchal society. Because no male after his wife's death is called by bad names, declared inauspicious, deprived of average living condition, normal sex life and economic independence.

Widowhood for a woman is a permanent feature in Hindu Society. Among the lower castes, it is believed that the widows could and did enjoy the privilege of remarriage. But even among the lower castes, due to the process of Sanskritization, the well-to-do lower castes people began to follow this custom in order to have respect in society. In a study of scheduled castes of Bihar, (which included urban Patna) also, it was found that the two communities, Bhangi and Musahar were in majority of the view that remarriage of widow should not be permitted. They pleaded on the ground that in case of remarriage, children have to suffer. But those, who are young and childless or having one child should be permitted to remarry. Like upper caste Hindu boys, lower-castes boys also were not ready to marry with the widows or deserted women. Prevalence of dowry system was also one of the important factor, going against remarriage of widows.

The life of the Hindu widow is at its best one of incessant self sacrifice and at its worst a reward of unredeemed sorrows and sufferings, a long tale of troubles and tribulations, hopelessness and helplessness.

Thus the life styles of the Hindu widows is in itself expressions of violence against women. "Deprived of property right, excluded from productive work, debarred from any chance of remarriage, high caste Hindu widows were doomed to a parasitic existence....., malnourished, devoid of any security by their own right shut out from all luxury, they were condemned to a sort of living death. For a widow, the maxim is "once a widow, always a widow."

Thus the continuous, mental, physical and economic torture and harassment and systematic dehumanisation of widows, develop some sever mental problems for themselves.

Though, the Government has introduced some programmes for widows such as old age homes, pension schemes etc., but they are abysmal and erratic. The religious holy places like Haridwar, Rishikesh, Kashi, Vrindavan, have become the widow's last refuge. But these places are the den of their exploitations. Here, also the older women have to depend for their subsistence on beggary, while the young widows have to do perennial chores and are exploited by religious contractors of the society.

Divorced Unfortunates

Despite the fact that we are living in the Twenty first Century which is making great strides in the spheres of science, technology, socio-political rights of the individuals and economic development, atrocities on women have not ceased in any part of the globe or in different societies. It is as true in the developed countries of the west as it is in the traditional societies of the "Third World"

Violence against women cuts across religion, culture, race, class and geographical boundaries. So it is that, in the context of India. Violence against women exists equally in the Hindu society as well as in the minority communities of Muslims, Christians or Sikhs. In the Muslim community, which is the largest after Hindu community, it is increasing and spreading like a virus. It is so despite the fact that Islam gave women, considerable rights for the first time in the world. Among the important rights given to women by Islam is the right of divorce. It is within the tenets of Islam to annul a marriage which has gone wrong, as different from Hinduism. However, has this facility eased the pain and sufferings of women in the Muslim society? It is open to debate.

Before the advent of Islam, women were treated badly even in Arabia. Women were penalised for giving birth to female children. A female child could even be killed by the father. If ever the female child escaped death, and grew up to be a woman, she was treated as a slave, both in her parents' home and in his husband's family. Women lived on the mercy either of their father, brothers, husbands or sons. Their status was no better than that of a bonded labourer.

However Islam and the Holy Prophet of Islam through his teachings and actions gave women respectable position in the family and society at large. They were given a share and rights of inheritance in the family property. Husbands were directed to treat their wives with respect and provide them with comfort and all the necessities of life. Islam also permitted women to obtain divorce in the form of "Khola". Marriage in Islam is a "sanctified contract entered into by both parties with solemnity and sincerity". If the marriage goes wrong both the parties have equal rights to end the marriage by seeking and obtaining divorce.

'Khola' or Talak' or Divorce is obtained by the wife if the husband is found guilty of neglecting or torturing his wife and his guilt has been proved beyond doubt. It can be obtained if the husband is physically and mentally incapable of performing his marital duties or denied his wife the position of honour she is entitled to.

There is another provision called "Fiskh" in favour of the wife. This is obtained by the wife under the orders of the "Qadi" (authority in Shariat laws) (Abul Samad) when it is proved that the husband has been traceless since long and it is not possible to find him. After "Fiskh" the wife is at liberty to find and select a new husband if, she so desires.

The Holy Prophet himself set an example by marrying a widow and treating her with utmost respect, affection, honour and care. Not only this, although polygomy is permissible in Islam, he did not marry any other women during her life time. Even after her death, he remembered her with tearful eyes and respect. Relatives of his former wife Hazarat Khadija were treated with honour and respect in his house whenever they happened to come there even after her passing away. With this glorious background, one would hope that the position of a divorcee in the Muslim society would be free of the Stigma' so commonly applied to such women in other religious communities and that such women would be leading a life full of respect and facilities for a normal life.

However the picture does not appear to be that in practice. Early Islamic jurists like Jamaluddin Afghani held this view that the Quran enjoins to have only one living wife. Similarly the Holy Prophet has said that the most despicable thing in the eyes of God is divorce and there are restrictions with relevant verses of the Quran (V.2.2.28-289) on the right of divorcee. It is thus, obvious that both husband and wife should live in such a way that there may not be any occasion to such a drastic action as divorce. With the passage of time and influence of several other factors, divorce has become a weapon of torture and violence against Muslim women. They are considered worse than widows. Their fate is worst than widows because they have to suffer from not only humiliation but also character assassination.

SOCIAL CRITERIA

The social norms do not support the move of divorce by women. Any such move creates a flutter in the community. It is a matter of shock and humilitation for her family. Often such women are branded as women of easy virtues and are exposed to severe mental, emotional and physical torture. She is shunned by the society, at times even by her parents. If at all they get shelter in their parental homes, things do not become easy for them. Often they are treated harshly and with disrespect and are compelled to work like maids in their own parents home.

Despite the fact that a divorcee is not a widow she is treated as one. Even if she has courage to remarry, she is not looked with respect. Rather she becomes target of all sorts of taunting and sarcastic remarks. The women are forced to bear torture and atrocities also because of their economic dependance on their male relatives. Nearly 90% of Muslim women in India are illiterate and consequently ignorant of their rights. They are entirely dependent on their husbands for the bare necessities of life, such as food, clothing and shelter. Once they are divorced there is no one else to provide them with these basic facilities of life.

The Muslim women are entitled to get Mehr, a sum fixed during the marriage ceremony, which the wife is entitled to get. The husband is under moral binding to pay pain Mehr. According to the Islamic shariat this is the first charge of the wife on the property of the husband. However, it is very seldom that the divorced wife gets the Mehr from her husband. Also, the amount fixed as Mehr is never sufficient enough to maintain the wife after she is divorced. She is entitled for maintenance from her husband only for the period of Iddat. After which she may become the responsibility of the Wakf Board or her parents, brothers, nephew or any other relatives. The net result is that in majority of the cases such women become destitutes and end up as maid servants in their relatives homes.

Of course, the children from her former husband are entitled to maintenance up to a certain age by the father and inherit the property left by him. Although Islam permits marriage of a divorcee it is a well known fact that it is considered as stigma in the Muslim society, specially in higher circle called Ashraf. Thus the marriage of a divorcee is not an easy affair. The result is that most of the Muslim divorcee women remain unmarried with no body to look after them.

In the recent past the Shah Bano case caused a stir in the circle of fundamentalists. But those who raised issue of interference in religious matters forgot the cardinal principles of Islam which lay stress on the fundamental rights of Muslim Women. Is there any scope in Islamic laws to harass, torture and commit all sorts of violence to weaker section of the society, can anybody prove that in Islam divorced women has no place in society ? On the contrary it provides and allows all facilities to such helpless women.

The famous Urdu Poet and Islamic scholar Iqbal has observed, the teaching of the Quran that life is a progressive creation, necessities that each generation, guided by the works of its predecessors, should be permitted to solve its own problems. Yet today in India, inequalities in the status of Muslim women are not only tolerated but are encouraged due to ignorance of Islamic law.

Mr. J. J. Akbar has tried to explain the tenacity with which Indian Muslim men are trying to preserve Muslim Personal law in its out moded form. But the same men have manipulated the Islamic injunctions to suit male chauvinist interests regarding the practice of polygamy and maintenance etc. Another example would be regarding the freedom given to women to select their life partner and their consent as a necessary part of the marriage ritual (Levy 1957). But in how many cases this important provision of Shariat law is adhered to? It is clearly laid down that the marriage without the consent of the women is null and void. If it is found that the marriage has been performed without consent of the female, it may be cancelled. But in practice it is not so.

The Sword of insecurity always hangs over the heads of Muslim women contrary to the teachings of Islam. If they do not agree to their husband taking a co-wife, they can move for divorce and ultimately maintenance and 'Mehr'. Although the Quran clearly lays down that to divorced women a reasonable provision is due, this is the duty incumbent on those that fear God. (Khan-Khutbat-137-163 in Bashir Ahmad, Religions Thought of S.S.A. Khan), but maintenance after divorce is rarely given. And with the passage of the new act Muslim women has have no legal protection as regards maintenance.

Thus the women in Muslim society undergo perpetual mental agony and torture and are continuously exposed to situation of mental and physical violence. Despite the provisions of protection in Muslim personal law, they are hardly given any. The injunctions are so interpreted and manipulated to serve the male chauvinistic interests. Shariat lays down in detail the code of conduct for every Muslim, men and women in every detail, but how many Muslims in this country follow the Shariat except those provisions which suits them after misinterpreted meaning for suppression of women. In face of growing instance of violence it is necessary for me to suggest some preventive methods. But the real purpose of the law will be seldom served without changing social outlook and normative system.

Divine and Viable

To marry a divorced helpless women has been considered a sacred and desirable affair in the eyes of God. But unfortunately the mental set up is otherwise. The attitude of society towards divorcee has to be changed. It is a fact that a woman left her house out of distress, mental tension and adverse circumstances and life necessity, as such a divorced woman deserves all sympathy in help. Due to illiteracy women are slaves, old and out dated custom and traditions besides following the path of blind faith. It can't be denied that education is powerful medium to remove all these maladies, proper education will certainly change the mental set up and help the Muslim women to stand on their own legs. They can be freed from the fetters which are in their legs for centuries. Education will help them to recognise theirselves and wake up their will power. It will also improve their financial conditions and make them independent from all sorts of troubles. Proper education will teach them that no religion permits slavery.

The recourse to atrocities, violence and harassment is taken under the wrong interpretation of provisions of religious laws and sayings. This mental out look and selfish attitude of the man dominated Society should be changed. This can be done through logical study of the religion and proper education to illiterate. One who violate the cardinal principle of Shariat that a divorcee should be treated as a human being, should be condemned by all, Maulvi Abdusamad Rahmani Nayab Shariat in his book Islam Main Aurat ka Mokam (1986) has given a clear picture of the rights of women in Islam. In the light of several verses of Holy Quran and Sayings of the Holy Prophet. At one place he has mentioned with reference to suras Unvisan and Al elmtah that in many respects woman is better than man. He has further proved that man and pious woman are equal in the eyes of God. It is true that according to Islam the woman is required to respect the wishes of her husband, but it is equally incombent on the husband to treat his wife with dignity and honour. It does not permit violence, torture and harassment to any woman. The religious sanctions are respected but not strictly followed and most of the practices are tradition oriented and not Islamic. There should be nothing immutable sacrosanct or rigid about the Shariat.

11

Acts of Embarrassment

Eve-teasing has been a serious menace in our society. The commission of this crime is an indicator of extent to which the women folk are insecure in our society. Eve-teasing which involves the verbal and physical harassment of women is the scourge of the urban society. A woman cannot go out in the street without the fear of being harassed by strange men. In busy crowded areas the women get pawed and pressed, jostled, rubbed and squeezed, the miscreants taking advantage of the press of the crowd and indulging in whatever physical intimacy the situation permits. The miscreants hurl indecent remarks. There is no woman who has not suffered this menace of society. In daily life if not all men are potential eve-teasers, all women are potential victims. All women suffer from the fear of being teased, irrespective of her age, health, appearance, mental state etc.

Having largely affected the peace of mind of women as they are not able to move freely and participate in the social life of the community. This is a challenge to our constitution which ensures all citizens the right "to move freely throughout the territory of India". There is no safe territory left for women, not even in their "mohallas". In a cross-section interview, a girl of Patna women's college says "Eve-teasers are everywhere outside our campus, in the markets, in parks and in buses, you have to face their hooliganism". Do we not understand why girls avoided attending classes on the day Saraswati idols were to be immersed? The girl students avoid attending classes much before the closure of the colleges during Holi festival. The boy students of St. Columba's College, Hazaribagh have started celebrating Holi festivals before fifteen days, creating panic among the girl students. Even the girls' common room which was locked to avoid any ugly scene was also attacked. As a result the police which was already posted there owing to an earlier incident of damaging a car, escorted the girl students to their houses. Now the girl students are missing their classes and practicals because college authorities are unable to control the hooliganism in the college. Great resentments is prevailing among girls and their guardians. Eve-teasing hinders healthy academic atmosphere and damages the career of girl students. It is an irony that we talk of the 21st century and don't allow girls to enjoy freedom in society.

The culprits are not only those who belong to goonda class but they belong to the so-called educated and cultured and affluent families. Young men include sons of senior government officers have been named in an eve-teasing case off and on. In case of anti-social elements, eve-teasing is a group activity and often assumes violent proportions. On several occasions eve-teasing led to communal disturbances. Three persons including a woman of Bhabhua were injured when members of the two families clashed over the issue of eve-teasing. A man of village Chhata of Siwan district was killed by an angry mob for teasing a girl of the same village. In the case of boys belonging to educated, cultured and affluent families, eve-teasing is individual and a concealed phenomenon.

Being no longer confined to students, unemployed and un-married youth only, this evil has no boundaries. Some recent news report eve-teasing committed by professionals like lawyers, teachers, and civil servants. Of course, the elite class is a bit sophisticated in nature. They play with their subordinate working women in lighter form and watch the response of the opposite sex in this regard.

VARIOUS DIMENSIONS

Eve-teasers are in the age bracket of 15 to 40 and some of them are married too. In a cross section interview a girl student has given an interesting twist to the story more than the young boys, middle aged men with receding hairlines and broken teeth, indulge in eve-teasing.

Their despicable deeds cover the following:

1. Indulging in cat-calls, waving wolf whistling, winking and uttering indecent remarks about female anatomy or singing obscene songs in such a way so as to be heard by women. Songs are deliberately chosen from popular film so that these could appear innocuous if it came to an argument.
2. Brushing past hurriedly, pressing against women, trying to pinch the bottoms or the breasts and disappearing in the crowd is very common for such perverts. If caught they pretend that rubbing was all accidental. They get a free hand during the breakdown of power. In the process sometimes the aged women are not spared from this kind of menace.
3. Eve-teasers board crowded buses and trains, prefer to stand or sit next to ladies and depending on the situation, the teaser sometimes gets himself sandwiched with her in the crowd and leans on her.
4. In recent years, in some universities these forms of eve-teasing have replaced with brazen acts as *dupatta* snatching, back patting and in some cases even forced kissing.
5. Eve-teasing has also taken the form of telephone to a girl and uttering obscene and suggestive words.

6. Mailing anonymous love letters in the most filthy languages.
7. Exhibiting male genitals in front of women and thereby deriving strange perverted sexual pleasure out of it.

Such vulgar acts occur in educational institutions mostly around women's college and girls' schools. The very act gets intensified particularly during festivals when pre-festivals shopping is on or in the puja pandals, which remain crowded with women folk in the evening.

Multi-faceted Factors

Eve-teasing by itself is not an offence under any law at present. But a close reading of Sections 294 and 354 of the Indian Penal Code would clearly indicate that the substance of the act of eve-teasing would be covered by them. Section 294 states that "whoever to the annoyance of others (a) does any obscene act in any public place, or (b) sings, recites or utters any obscene song, ballads or words in or near any public place is liable to be punished with imprisonment or with fine."

The section is very wide in nature and a person can be hauled up even if the acts forming part of the substance of the offence are addressed to the public at large, provided these cause annoyance. Clearly, a girl or a woman who feels annoyed by any obscene song or words can take recourse to the provision of the section and put up a complaint before a police station. The offence is cognizable, i.e., a police officer can arrest the offender without a warrant but it is bailable. A graver form of eve-teasing is accompanied by the use of gesture indicating threat or use of force. In such a case also, action can be taken against the person using it. It would be covered by section 352 of the Indian Penal Code, which provides the punishment in such a case.

The substance of the offence is given in section 351 and is known as assault. The making of gesture should be accompanied with preparation so that the person against whom it is directed has the apprehension that criminal force will be used against her.

Apart from this, there is a special provision which recognises the gravity of the offence when it is directed against a woman, and has been given in section 354 of the Indian Penal Code.

The punishment in such cases is imprisonment for two years or fine or both. The offence is cognizable. The only condition is that the person should have the intention or knowledge that such an action would outrage her modesty. Small cases of eve-teasing, social disgrace and other inconveniences are rarely brought to the notice of courts, fewer still are challenged in the courts and negligible number end in minor convictions and that also after a long lapse when the offenders and his likes continue committing many more such acts.

The provocation coming from the opposite sex like the style of dressing, talking, walking etc. should not be overlooked while condemning eve-teasing. It is not that all women behave in identical provocative manner. Sometimes women consciously or unconsciously invite such hazards. In a cross-section interview eve-teasing was viewed as reaction and not an action. According to some of the male interviews "Eve-teasing took place only when girls provoke. They incite others by their action, dress and manner. It is a form of admiration. Girls dress not for girls but for boys".

Then why not let them be aware that they are looked great. But this is a partial statement. Interview at girls gave another point of view. They said they dress themselves in modern way only to show that they have equal status and not to attract boys. Thus it can be said that eve-teasing may result due to wrong impression of girls' image by the boys.

The social malaise of harassing the women is assuming such proportions that one shudders at the shape of things to come. The exercises of passing annoying and embarassing comments from a distance, if unchecked, are found to lead to more serious forms and proportions. Eve-teasing, if not properly checked will end up in entering a house and committing criminal assault or homicide. Every eve-teaser is a potential murderer.

MEASURES TO BE TAKEN

1. The need for creating an awareness in society has always been there and as a result the attitude of common people in general and the police may be more sympathetic towards the victims themselves in particular.
2. Girls should be bold and give back to the ruffians in the same coin. They should be taught a lesson. If he gets even a slap from an opponent, he takes to his heels. Training in 'Judo' and 'Karate' to girls is very helpful and for this the government must open training centres.
3. At times tact can be of great help until she is able to sight others who can come to her rescue or get hold of any lethal substance with which she can strike at.
4. It is a must for the case to be reported to police. There should be no leniency exercised on this account.
5. The Parliament should pass stringent laws for the police to enforcing them vigorously. This can be expedited through public pressure.
6. The public have also to help damsels in distress and not behave in an unconcerned and impersonal way. It must encourage the victims to report the incidents to police and help the police and the courts in punishing the offenders by deposing truthfully and by being not won over by the threats or lures of the culprits.
7. There should be a massive boycott by public of eve-teasers and they should make it a point that they do not prevail. The names of eve-teasers may be written on big hoarding to be kept at a public place for days together in every 'Mohalla'. Voluntary women welfare organisations that we have in the country like the All India Women's Conference, Nari Raksha Samiti, Mahila Dakshta Samiti, etc. could well bring awakening and alertness among eves in this regard.

8. The parents must ensure that their children dress properly without an effort to expose the anatomy unncessarily which invites the attention of the evil minded.
9. Parents should be initiated to talk about basic sexual matters with their children. Failing this they gather dangerous knowledge from footpath publications which are worse than anything else. Talk about sex is taboo in Indian society. Society need to change its attitude towards sex education. In fact, eve-teasing is only a superficial manifestation of the imbalance in the relationship between man and women.

What we need is public consciousness and a serious rethinking about our morals and values and public action can go a long way in acting as a deterrent to eve-teasing.

Basic Reasons of the Evil

Greater degeneration of the male vis-a-vis eve teasing is a symptom of social, economic and moral disorder. It is a symptomatic of a combination of varied and complicated disorder. First and the foremost is the abandonment of the traditional moral values, the lack of religious education and the absence of the sobering effect of the family and the teacher. Secondly no body is born an eve-teaser. If he is neglected at home, he grows rowdy. Thirdly, there is the pernicious influence of the cinema and the cheap literature in which sex permeates.

The current advertisements trying to promote sale of under-garments, towels and bedsheets by incidently exposing the female anatomy also lead to degradation of woman as a commercialised commodity in the mind of man. Fourthly, there is the rush to the urban in search of adventure and employment. Away from the restraining influence of the families, the youngsters look for kicks, excitement and thrills which they seem to get in acts of eve-teasing. Infliction of pain on the eve acts as a stimulant to their sexual desires. Fifthly, there is the lack of fear of punishment or adverse publicity or social disgrace. The police with its insufficient strength and preoccupation with other problems of law and order and the courts with their proverbial delays and intricate legal procedures fail to bring most of the vagrants to book.

Physical Torments

Beating Roughly : Women who are married at a younger age are at higher risk of physical violence. The women who got married at younger age were more victims of physical violence by their husbands in contrast to those who got married at later age. Further, it was noted that there was a progressive decrease in the percentages of victims of physical violence from lower age at marriage category to higher age group. Out of 60 respondents who got married below the age of 18 years, 45 per cent were the victims. In contrast to this, who were married after the age of 21 years, only 24.71 per cent were the victims of physical violence.

It is also interesting to note that median age at marriage of victims of physical violence was lower than those of non-victims. It can, thus, be concluded that those women who married at lower age were at high risk of physical violence in comparison with those who got married at later age in the Indian society, although the age at marriage is increasing yet in the rural areas it still remains quite low that is, 17.81 years. Therefore, class and situational factors may play an important role in determining the age at marriage, which in turn may be associated with violence because young couples are under lot of stress to adjust to new role responsibilities.

A few studies indicate that wives of younger age group are at higher risk of abuse as compared with those of older age group because older women are not prone to file assault charges either because of traditional attitudes or because of the possibility of divorce. The results of National Family Violence Survey conducted in America indicate that all forms of marital violence occur most frequently among those under 30 years of age. The rate of marital violence among those under 30 years of age was found to be more than double the rate for the age for 31 to 50 years.

The data for the present study were tabulated to find out association between the age of the wife and her being victim of physical violence. The respondents were distributed into four age categories. There was a progressive decrease in the percentages of victims of physical violence from lower age category to higher age category. Among the victims of physical violence 45.45 per cent were below the age of 30 years. In contrast to this those who were in the age group of 50 years above, only 18.18 per cent were the victims.

Similarly, if the median age of the victims of physical violence is compared with non-victims, it was noticed that median age of victims was 35 years in contrast to 39.24 years median age of the non-victims. In short, an inverse relationship was found between the age of wives and their physical abuse. In other words, physical violence against wives of younger age group was more frequent as against those of higher age groups. The data of the present study support the findings of studies cited above.

Local Skirmishes

Wife abuse can occur at any age but the data on age indicate that wives of younger age are at higher risk of being abused. It may be due to the fact that younger couples are still learning to make adjustment with each other and addition of children in the family puts enormous demands and stresses on the younger people.

Presence or absence of children in the family is likely to affect the quality of relationship between husband and wife. Further, presence of more children in the family would create problem of management and proper training of the younger ones. Researches on the impact of children on marriages consistently show that the level of marital satisfaction and marital adjustment goes down after the birth of the first child.

An additional child would imply a decrease in time for parents to pursue their own interests. Further, each additional child increases the work load and conflicts. In the traditional societies like India, child care still remains under the domain of mothers and for any deviance on the part of child, it is the mother who is blamed. Further, more children put a lot of stress on the limited resources of the family.

Among the victims of physical violence it was found that the rate of violence against mothers who had five or more children or no child was more than double the rate for those who had one or two children. Keeping in view the number of children it was noted that there was a progressive increase in the percentages of victims of physical violence from one to two children category to women having five or more children or with no child. In short, it can be concluded that a large number of children in the family become a source of conflict resulting into violence against wife or mother.

The highest percentages of physical violence was found in those house-holds which had no child. It may be attributed to their younger age as well as wives' inability to have children because children are valued in the Indian society and those women who are unable to bear a child are ridiculed.

In the patriarchal society like India, greater importance is given to the male child. The female child is not only considered a liability because of associated dowry problems, but mothers who give birth to female children only do not get much respect in the family as compared with those who give birth to male children. Lately with the help of amniocentesis the couples would like to know the sex of the child. In case the foetus is of the female sex, they go for abortion. A study of 8000 cases of abortion showed that 7999 of them involved a female foetus. The high female foeticide reinforces the sex preferences prevalent in our society.

The victims of physical violence were almost equally divided in the categories of those who had only male or female children of both the sexes. In the present study sex of the children in the family was not found to be associated with wife abuse.

Wives living in extended and joint households are required to make adjustments with a large number of kin in contrast to those who are living in nuclear households. Further, patrilocal residence and patriarchal structure of the family places women into subservient position. The men are more likely to act as sons rather than husbands. The parents-in-law and other kinsmen continue to have greater affiliation with the sons as compared with daughters-in-law.

A number of cases have been reported where because of backbiting, the husbands have maltreated their wives. Hence presence of a large number of members in the family not only creates the problem of adjustment but they also act as instigators for wife abuse. Although there was no marked difference in the percentage of victims living in nuclear and extended households, yet among the victims a relatively higher percentage (36.67) were found to be living in joint and extended households in contrast to those living in nuclear households (32.94). Similarly, among the non-victims no marked difference was found with regard to their pattern of living arrangement. Hence, the composition of household was not found to be associated with wife abuse.

From the foregoing discussion on the demographic correlates of wife abuse, it was found that the younger age at marriage, young wives and those having no child or a large number of children were at higher risk of being victims of physical violence. However, no association was found between the sex of the children as well as living arrangement and wife abuse. Based on the results of this exploratory research, the following hypotheses can be formulated for verification in future researches.

1. The younger the age at marriage of the women, the greater is the possibility of their being battered.
2. The younger the age of wife, the greater are the chances of her being victim of physical violence.

3. The greater the number of children, a woman has the greater is the possibility of her being victim of physical violence of her husband.
4. The absence of child is likely to result in wife battering.

An individual's social milieu not only influences his social position, network of relationships and contents of learning but also his social behaviour pattern. Social behaviour is a function of the life situations which may be physical, economic, social or cultural or an interplay of these elements. It is assumed that persons having differential life situations would react differently to the same stimuli. It is, therefore, essential to explicate the role of these social variables for understanding the quality of conjugal relationship.

The social variables considered for the present study are educational and occupational status of the respondents, their social class background, their caste and religious background, their attitudes regarding traditional gender roles in the family and their value orientation in favour of use of violence for the resolution of conflict.

Formal education helps an individual to know what is happening outside one's immediate surroundings. It also facilitates him to develop rational outlook towards life. Education widens the horizon and makes the individual more knowledgeable. Education also helps an individual to get jobs of high prestige and with high economic returns. Further, higher education enhances one's social prestige. Efforts have been made to find out association between the level of education one has and the quality of interpersonal relations.

A few studies indicate that the less education a person has, the more likely he or she is to approve of and support violence. Some other studies, however, contradict their findings and on the other hand, they are of opinion that couples with the lowest educational levels are less prone to violence than those who had attained higher education. It is argued that low education level does not cause violence but it aggravates the frustration.

The reason for more violence among those who have higher education, may be that women with high education may not endorse the traditional role relationship and this may be considered as threat to the dominant position by their husbands. However, education can provide people with alternatives for resolving family disagreements. It is, therefore, expected that with the help of education, individual learns different mechanisms to resolve the conflict in the conjugal relationships.

The educational background of the victim wives indicates that those who have low educational attainment or higher educational attainment had over representation as compared with those who had moderate level of education. There is a progressive decrease in the percentage of the victims from illiterate educational category up to graduation with the exception of those who had higher education. This curvilinear distribution of victims of violence indicates that women who have no education or have higher educational attainment are more prone to physical violence by their husbands.

The women with low education designate their complete dependency because with low educational background they will not be able to have economic independence or would be engaged in occupations with low economic returns and low prestige. In the case of those who have higher education they may be in better position to gain economic independence and with the higher education they may start questioning the dominant position of their husbands. Such a threat is not tolerated by the husbands and they use physical violence as their ultimate resource to maintain their dominant position in the family.

Occupation is an important indicator of a person's position in society. It is believed that the higher the education one has, the higher the occupation one holds and the higher the prestige he gets in society. Conversely, the lower the occupation, the lower will be the economic returns and as a consequence thereof, there are likely to be higher frustrations and greater marital conflicts.

Many studies indicate that persons engaged in occupations of lower prestige are more likely to resort to physical violence against their wives to give vent to their economic stresses. It is also argued that women who stay at home and are not engaged in paid work outside their homes are at somewhat greater risk of being physically abused than those engaged in paid work.

This is probably because housewives are perceived to contribute less to family subsistence and are consequently valued less than women who are engaged in paid work outside the home. Wife beating is far less common in societies in which women have independent economic and social resources, perhaps because these resources are valuable enough to make a husband think twice before acting in ways that might force his wife to terminate the marriage.

In the sample there are only 65 women respondents who were found to be engaged in paid work. Out of these, 47.69 per cent were victims of physical violence of their husbands. On the other hand, out of those not engaged in paid work outside their homes, only 26.67 per cent were physically abused by their husbands. The results of the present study support the findings of Homung et al. who, in one representative sample, found housewives had a lower risk of violence than working wives.

The reason housewives are abused less than working wives is because keeping in view their economic dependency they may have "Learned helplessness" with the result they have developed tolerance of such violence and do not share with outsiders that they are being abused or they would endorse the traditional gender roles and would not question the authority of their husbands. Hence, they do not provoke their husbands to use physical violence to maintain their dominant position in the conjugal relationship.

On the other hand, the working wives may not accept the dominant position of the husband in family decision-making and raise questions about asymmetrical conjugal relations. Such a situation may prompt the husband to use physical force to retain his dominant position. The general contention that working gives economic independence to women, hence, they would be relatively free.

On the other hand, it is the working women who are more abused than the non-working women. The status and her physical abuse between wives' working and non-working will become more clear if the type of occupation in which women are engaged in is taken into consideration.

As the number of respondents under the working category were limited to 65 cases only, their occupations were grouped under three categories, i.e., occupations with low prestige, medium prestige and high prestige. The data reveal that the percentage of the victims goes on decreasing from low occupational prestige category to higher prestige category.

In short, there was inverse relationship between occupational prestige and physical violence, i.e., the lower the prestige of paid work, the greater was the violence against wives. The results indicate that it is not the working status per se which provides women freedom from physical violence of their husbands but it is the nature of the occupation and associated prestige and economic returns which facilitate women to be free from physical abuse.

Idea of Social Status

The concept of social class has been defined by several sociologists. They have, however, given emphasis to different attributes. One salient feature of different definitions is that members of a class group have common style of living and value orientation. Wolfgang and Ferracuti in their study of subculture of violence have even divided a class into subclasses depending upon value orientation of the members. Similarly, a number of scholars have tried to find out association between class background and family violence. One set of studies maintains a positive association between lower class and wife battering. Whereas some researchers do not endorse their findings and they have contended that wife battering transgresses the boundaries of class.

An attempt has been made to find out association between class background and wife beating. The class background of the respondents has been worked out based on education, occupation and income of the husbands of the respondents because a majority of the women respondents were not found to be working and hence, had no independent income of their own. While selecting the sample their living arrangement was taken into consideration and 50 cases from each house type were included in the sample, which were redistributed into different social classes. The class background of the respondent was also divided into lower, working, middle and high for the purpose of finding out differential behaviour pattern, i.e., wife abuse in different classes.

The data indicate that in contrast to 19.23 per cent victims of physical violence in the upper class, there were 51 .85 per cent victims in the lower class. There is a progressive decrease in the percentages of victims of physical violence from the lower through the middle to the upper class. Similarly, among the non-victims the higher per cent (80.77) belong to the upper class. In short, women belonging to the lower class were at a higher risk of being physically abused by their husbands. The results of the study indicate inverse relationship between class background and wife battering.

These findings support the contention of those researchers who found that women belonging to the lower class were at a higher risk of physical violence which was attributed to their way of life. The use and approval of physical violence in the lower class has been attributed to what Lewis calls, the culture of poverty. The concept implies that the poor people have a distinct subculture. Due to common experiences they have developed certain attitudes and behaviour pattern which have been transmitted from parents to children. These include the casual resort to physical violence, an inability to plan for the future, seeking of immediate gratification, weak impulse control and fatalistic attitude towards the future.

Davis while describing the class linked, violence contends that physical violence in the lower class families is normal, socially approved and socially inculcated type of behaviour. Similarly, Whitehurst while making a distinction between the middle and the lower class families with regard to control over violence, maintained that violence-responses were much more built into lower class subculture as a means to achieve some goals to assert independence and masculinity.

The members of the lower class are subject to a lot of economic pressures and strains and they cannot show their resentment and frustration, against those who are highly placed and hence they give vent to their frustrations at the slightest provocation by beating their wives on whom they can exert their power. On the other hand, members of the middle and upper classes have more resources and can keep their violence private and additionally, because of the sensitivity of the issue and embarrassment, the victims are not likely to admit its existence in their conjugal' relationship.

Individual's social status is determined by his ascriptive and acquired attributes. In the Indian society ascriptive attributes, like caste, determine not only his social milieu, as castes are hierarchically placed but also his opportunities to acquire new attributes. Although an individual is now theoretically permitted to achieve any position and support any ideology. Yet caste plays an important role in influencing his behaviour pattern. Keeping in view the importance of caste in the Indian society, it will be worthwhile to find out an association between caste and wife battering.

The distribution of the victims of physical violence according to their caste background indicates that respondents belonging to

of dependency are combined to find out their combined effect on physical violence.

The total dependency scores of the respondents have been arranged into three categories—low, medium and high. The data indicate that wives with higher level of dependency are at higher risk of being abused in contrast to those with lower level of dependency. In contrast to 27.42 per cent of wives with low level of dependency more were the victims of husbands' physical violence. The percentage of non-victims goes on decreasing from lower level of dependency to higher level.

Abduction and Kidnapping

Kidnapping and abduction is a heinous crime. It affects adversely the career of a large number of girls and women every year. Normally it has been noticed that the abductors and abducted victims are acquainted, rather not strangers to each other. The initial contact between the abductor and his victim frequently occurs in their own homes and neighbourhood rather than in public places. On the other hand, father is too busy with his own world.

The mother too has developed a circle outside the home. Thus, the parents do not know or even ask their sons and daughters where they spend the evenings. There is lack of parental control. The bond of love, affection and respect seems to be vanishing from Indian families.

As discussed earlier on the taking or enticing away of a girl less than 18 years of age or of a male less than 16 years of age without the consent of the lawful guardian constitutes kidnapping. Abduction is the forcible, fraudulent or deceitful taking away of a woman with an intension of seducing her to illicit sex or compelling her to marry a person against her will. Thus, "abduction" differs from "kidnapping".

The latter is committed only in respect of a minor, while the former in respect to any person. In kidnapping, the victim's consent is immaterial but in abduction, the victim's free and voluntary consent condones the crimes. In kidnapping, the offender's intention is irrelevant but in abduction, it is the all important factor. Thus, a girl of 18 or over, could only be abducted and not kidnapped; but if she is under 18 she could be kidnapped as well as abducted if the taking is by force or the taking or enticing was by deceitful means.

Different Forms

There are different circumstances and motivations leading to kidnapping or abduction. Sometimes it is politically motivated, sometimes economically and sometimes it occurs due to some personal reasons. The political kidnapping of famous filmstar Rajkumar, Veerapan attracted much attention. Economically motivated kidnapping is mainly for ransom and sale for prostitution. In this study we are chiefly concerned with the kidnapping of woman for marriage, sex satisfaction or for sale for prostitution.

Kidnapping/abduction may occur with or without the consent of the girls. Sometimes the victims "run away" from their homes willingly to marry persons of their choice and when caught their parents describe the act as an "abduction". Sometimes the victims "run away" from their homes willingly to marry boys of their own choice as they fail to get the consent of their parents and their parents knowingly report to the police, the act as an "abduction". Sometimes even married men "run away" with married girls as even after marriage their affair did not end finally. Sometimes the abduction is done by a man not getting a marriage proposal which drives him to this madness. Sometimes abduction is done by an ascetic.

Sometimes abduction of Harijan girls is done by their landlords to demoralise their men in their struggle for an improved existence. Sometimes mishap victims are kidnapped by criminals. A married woman of Mara village under Khagaria Police Station, a victim of the Mansi train disaster of June 6 was kidnapped by a notorious criminal and compelled to live a life of shame. Sometimes abduction is done due to old enemity. A 34-year-old woman of Chandpura village under Begusarai was raped and murdered after being abducted from her house. Old enemity with a fellow villager was said to be the cause of this crime. Sometimes women play major role in abduction for sale and immoral purpose and the women involved in this trade are themselves abducted women.

CASES OF LEGAL CHARACTER

Consequences of Kidnapping and Abduction : In the majority of cases abductor and the victim are known to each other. Sometimes they kidnap the girls as an adult, sometimes as a minor. Sometimes the consequences of kidnapping is rape and murder. A young unmarried girl of Manpur in Gaya was enticed away by her lover and after the rape murdered her for fear of being detected, and later her body was found in the dry bed of the river Falgu. Sometimes it ends in marriage. A young girl of Shastrinagar Police Station of Patna filed a petition in the Court of Chief Judicial Magistrate, Patna, stating that she was a major (19 years) and nobody has kidnapped her.

She also stated that she had married with her own consent and free will at Muzaffarpur and since then she was living with him as his wife. Sometimes kidnapping leads to communal tension. A former student of the T.P. College, Madhepura who had kidnapped a daughter of a noted businessman of Madhepura surrendered in the court. Both told the court that they were married to each other and demanded protection in view of the communal tension mounting in the area due to their marriage.

Sometimes parents accept the marriage and choice of their wards. The Chief Judicial Magistrate of Patna ordered the release of the couple after the girl's father had filed an affidavit before the court stating that the case of kidnapping of her daughter filed by him was done under misinformation. He said his daughter was a major and had married on her own. Another affidavit was filed by the boy's father that he had no objection to the marriage. Sometimes, the parents of the victims even after marriage do not accept the choice of the girls and lodge a kidnapping case against their husbands.

A school-going girl of Shastrinagar area at Patna returned after marrying a young man in a temple at Muzaffarpur. However, the parents of the girl did not accept the choice of the girl and lodged a kidnapping case against her husband.

Profaned Lot

A kidnapper may be any person irrespective of his age, education, religion, caste, creed, and culture. He may be a priest. More than 30 young girls were liberated from the Ashram of a Yogi at Gopalganj. According to the police the fake Yogi trapped innocent young girls, women and gents at the gun point. The wife of the temple's pujari near Sataquat Ashram was kidnapped by a frequent visitor of the temple and she was recovered from Vaishali, the kidnapper was holding a respectable position in society. A doctor of Patna Medical College Hospital was arrested by the Kadamkuan police on the charge of kidnapping, wrongful confinement and attempt of criminal assault on a minor girl.

Some armed men raided a house in Mehadia village under Arwal police station of Jehanabad, lifted a young girl after taking some household articles at the gun point and escaped. A school clerk of Madhupur was taken into custody by the local police with the co-operation of the Darbhanga police for kidnapping the minor daughter of his landlord.

A young girl of Rajendra Nagar near the Station of Patna stated before the Magistrate that she had been kidnapped and criminally assaulted by a person living in the ground floor of the house. An umarried girl of Chausa police station of Madhepura was kidnapped by a co-villager who was arrested by the Delhi police. A student of R.N. College, Hajipur kidnapped a 15- year-old girl student in collusion with some anti-social elements. A girl of 16 years of Mandi village of Begusarai ran away with her servant and was arrested at Lakhminia railway station.

A school girl of Giridh was allegedly kidnapped by her tutor about seven years ago, was recovered from a farm at Ludhiana in Punjab. A teenage school- going girl of village Jeetpur of Madhepur was kidnapped by her servant. While preparations were being made to sell the girl, the police could find her and arrested two persons in this connection. A young daughter of Munger has accused her father of trafficking in women.

Abduction is definitely related to the absence of parents' control over the victim and non-harmonious relation in the family.

But in the eyes of law kidnapping is proved on three grounds. First involves the age of the victim, second the absence of the consent of the victim and the third is the use of force and physical resistance.

Kidnapping and abduction are very common offences unleashed against minor girls or women. Minor girls are enticed away by unscrupulous persons while young women irrespective of age, fall prey to any sort of deceit or force. What is important is that one should clearly understand the offence that is made out, which would depend upon the nature of allurement or force and the age of person.

Law Applied

A person who kidnaps or abducts a woman with the intention that she may be compelled to marry another person against her will, commits an offence under Section 366 of the IPC. Even the knowledge that she may be compelled to marry or have illicit intercourse against her will, even if there is no intention, would add to the gravity of the offence and would be punishable under this section. Abuse of authority, or criminal intimidation as defined in the code, or any form of compulsion used for inducing a woman to go from one place to another with the knowledge or intention that she may be forced or seduced for illicit intercourse is also similarly punishable.

This section provides a deferrent punishment to persons who resort to the use of force or fraud, for the purpose of marriage or illicit intercourse. However, in all such cases, the intention or the knowledge has to be proved apart from the main ingredients of the offence of kidnapping or abduction as the case may be.

Minor girls have been the victims of various types of nefarious activities by anti-social elements. Sections 366A, 372 and 373 of the IPC take care of such cases where minor girls are subjected to illicit intercourse, sale or purchase. Thus, inducement of a minor girl under the age of eighteen years to go from any place or to do any act with the knowledge or intention that she will be seduced or forced to an illicit intercourse has been made punishable with 10 years imprisonment. The means used for inducement are irrelevant. The basic ingredients of the offence are that she:

(i) should be a minor girl below the age of 18 years;

(ii) she should be induced by whatever means;

(iii) inducement should be to go to any place or do any act;

(iv) there should be knowledge or intention on the part of the person that she will be seduced or forced to an illicit intercourse by another person.

This section would, therefore, help those cases where innocent girls are allured with promises of a good life and are then exploited by anti-social elements for sexual offences, prostitution, etc.

Selling or buying minor girls for the purposes of prostitution is an offence under section 372 and 373 of the IPC. The selling, buying, hiring and disposing of or obtaining possession of a minor person with the intention or the knowledge that the person will be used for prostitution, illicit intercourse, or any unlawful or immoral purpose are the essential ingredients of the offence. It is not necessary that the person should be immediately put to such an abuse.

The knowledge that such a person would be used in future for such a purpose would also constitute the offence. If a minor girl is sold, bought, lent or hired or disposed of to a prostitution or the brothel keeper or is so obtained, there is presumption that she will be used for prostitution. In other words, it is not necessary to prove the intention, as the circumstances amply point out that the girls would be used for illicit intercourse. Illicit intercourse has been given a very wide definition and would include any sexual intercourse between persons not "united by marriage" or any union which is not recognised as marriage by the personal law of the persons.

The provision made in the Indian Penal Code on kidnapping and abduction, particularly where the intention is to seduce a minor girl or force her to an illicit intercourse, provides ample safeguard against the exploitation of innocent girls and women of tender age by anti-social elements.

In spite of the various sections of IPC. that take care of such notorious activities as kidnapping and abduction, the trend of this crime is rising. According to official police records, around two out of every one lakh women are the victims of abduction and kidnapping annually in our country. But the true rate of victimization is far greater than this. Estimates have placed the figures at 2 to 10 times the official rate. This difference can mainly be explained by the reluctance of the victims' parents to report the incidents to police.

The Sinners

Trafficking of women and girls has become a highly organised and inter-state business. A gang engaged in kidnapping girls from Bihar and Assam and selling in many districts of UP has been brought to light. A gang of kidnappers engaged in supplying the girls to middle east has been noticed. A gang of kidnappers usually consists of both males and females, who operate everywhere, in rural as well as in urban area. Female kidnappers have been found to work as domestic servants who facilitate kidnapping of girls. They have been found to be very active in places of public entertainment, educational institutions, hostels, hospitals and in folk festivals, busy railway stations, bus stands etc. and entice away girls.

The gangs of kidnappers and abductors have their own secret methods of transporting girls and shuttle them to and fro, from city to city, to minimise the risk of their being rescued. The kidnapped or abducted girls are escorted by respectable looking men and women so that they cannot be checked or interrogated by the police. They have their agents at the bars, in courts, and in newspaper offices, they have friends in every political organisation and plenty of funds is given to those who can protect them from the law.

The police have in many cases extorted money from these unspeakable scoundrels. It cannot be denied that corrupt policemen with the help of dishonest politicians in power have made systematic collections from this source. Sometimes male members of the victim's family are killed or injured in a bid to save them from abduction.

We can classify the victims into four groups by taking all cases "willing" and "unwilling" victim:

1. *Forced Abduction:* This group of victims who clearly do not consent to accompany their kidnappers are forcibly abducted by the offenders.
2. *Willing Abduction:* This group of victims willingly agree to live with offenders because they (victims) intend to marry them against the wishes of their parents.
3. *Accessory Abduction:* This group of victims neither give their consent nor oppose it, thus, aiding or contributing in a secondary manner to the abduction activity. The

abduction stands in a relationship "power" over the victim because of being older, being an authority figure or some other reason. The abductor then gains access to the victim and pressurizes her to leave her house with him.

4. *Stress Abduction:* This group of victims initially agree to leave the house with "offenders" but are stopped when "something goes wrong". Usually what goes wrong is that the offender "exploits" the agreement and rapes the victim, or he brings his friends to have sexual relation with her, or sells her ornaments, or leaves her in the hotel, or at a railway station or bus stand and so forth.

Criminal Motives

The following motives may be identified for kidnapping the unmarried girls or abducting the married women:

The unmarried girls and married women may be kidnapped and abducted in the following circumstances:

1. The abduction of girls who lead an unhappy life in their parent's home. A beautiful girl kidnapped from Jharia in her statement refused to go to her parent's house for fear of being killed. Moreover, she expressed her desire to get herself married with a man of position and means. She refused to accept a constable as her husband saying he would better serve as her servant.
2. The abduction of girls whose parents refuse to marry them to the "abductors". A girl research scholar of Patna University left the hostel without any information with a boy of her own choice as she failed to get the consent of her parents.
3. The abduction of young girls with the object of selling them: A gang engaged in selling of kidnapped girls from Assam and Bihar has come to light.
4. The abduction for sexual purposes: A kidnapped girl of Kolkata alleged before the police that she was brought to

Patna for working in the house. But she was raped and was asked to entertain VIPs.

We may classify abductors in four groups on the basis of the news reported in newspapers.

1. *Accesory Abductor:* He "abducts" victim with her consent to marry him.
2. *Opportunist Abductor:* He abducts the victims only for sexual purposes on the enticement for a better life.
3. *Lover Abductor:* He is in love with the victim to the extent that he even abducts her to marry her against her own and her parents wishes.
4. *Fraud Abductor:* He abducts the victim to sell her and earn money.

PEOPLE, TARGETED

We may classify the abducted victim in five groups:

1. *Co-operative Victim:* She is a woman who willingly agrees to leave her house with the accused, being very unhappy in father's house.
2. *Accidental Victim:* She is a woman who by chance falls in the hands of a wrong person who abducts her on false pretexts.
3. *Misled Victim:* She is a female who takes the advances of a male seriously.
4. *Corrupt Victim:* She is a female who is in search of pleasure.
5. *Forced Victim:* She is a female who is forcibly abducted against her wishes.

Some of the suggestions which need proper attention are as follows:

1. It is desirable that the parents have to be watchful about their wards, both male and female. They must see

to it that they keep good company and remain usefully engaged.

2. As for the girls, they should be escorted properly in late hours or in desolate areas, they are not to be left to the care of the servants, drivers or even tutors who take liberties with them.
3. Girls and women must enjoy a status of freedom in marriage and position of respect in family and society.
4. Parental control over the children and harmonious relation in the family is necessary for a healthy society. The children both male and female should be equally given due love, affection and respect in the family.
5. Police should be informed about the missing of their wards at the earliest.

Handling the problems of kidnapping, abduction is a difficult task. It can be and ought to be solved through appropriate collective action, the victim, the parents and the police. It is not good blaming the police all the time.

12

Female Prisoners

The custodial justice to women has been one of the thrust areas of the activities of the social workers, since its inception. The visits to the jails have revealed extremely unsatisfactory conditions under which women prisoners live. While the visiting members conveyed to the concerned authorities their general observations about the living condition of women and made specific suggestions about certain hard cases, it was felt that a study should be undertaken to assess the existing conditions in the jails throughout the country.

Observations and Suggestions made by Members Inspecting the Jails :

(i) Adequate arrangements for vocational training should be made for women inmates in jail and a programme prepared for rehabilitation of released prisoners. To take an example the visiting Members came across the case of life convict in Assam who was to be released shortly but was very apprehensive of her future since she thought that her husband and society might not accept her. She wanted to acquire some professional skill to be economically independent. She had aptitude for nursing. At the suggestion of the member she was given training in midwifery and was ultimately able to make her livelihood by the profession.

(ii) Courts should ensure that female prisoners are handed over to bona fide guardians after release, so that they may not fall into the hands of imposter guardians who may force them into immoral trafficking as the some happens in many cases.

(iii) Mentally ill women should be kept separate from the other women prisoners.

(iv) Certain women prisoners had been kept in custody on the ground of being lunatic despite the fact that they were not actually lunatics. There should therefore, be an objective medical examination of such cases.

(v) The women's wing of Tihar jail was found to be overcrowded by more than four times its capacity. Construction of additional accommodation was suggested to ameliorate the condition of women inmates. It was noted that the women inmates were encouraged to engage themselves in the training of various vocations. Also, a de-addiction centre had been set up by the jail authorities. However, revamping of the training programme was suggested so that the inmates were enabled to produce marketable goods and make an earning for themselves for future security.

(vi) In the Jail in Delhi, there was a case of a smart girl who had secured the job of a police A.S.I. by impersonation but she was a Karate expert. It was suggested to the Jail authorities to engage her in some fruitful activity like imparting physical training to other prisoners. A similar approach is necessary in like cases.

(vii) In certain prisons, some women inmates were found to suffer from T.B. It was suggested that they should be separated from the others and also given proper medical treatment.

(viii) In the Central Jail in Mumbai, the Tata Institute of Social Science was conducting some useful services for the jail inmates in collaboration with the Mumbai Police such as literacy classes, creches for children, vocational training, counselling, legal guidance, placement on release, etc. This was considered as a good example to be followed.

(ix) The authorities at Sabarmati Central Jail, Ahmedabad expressed the view that the vocational training facilities for male prisoners could not be extended to female inmates as their number was too small. It was suggested that in such cases women inmates could be congregated in one or two suitable jails for making such facilities available or, alternatively provided with such other work as gardening, cooking, etc. and wages paid for the same.

(x) In several jails, regular visits by doctors are not made but they are called only when needed. Also no facilities for lady doctors or nurses exist for women prisoners. It was suggested to the concerned jail authorities that it is desirable that women prisoners are treated only by women doctors, unless the prisoners opt otherwise. However, medical examination should be provided as a matter of routine.

(xi) In the jails visited in Madhya Pradesh, it was found that most of the prisoners were tribal and had their own cultural tradition. The crimes committed by them were not pre-planned and had altogether different background. Therefore, instead of convicting them straightaway under the provisions of Criminal Procedure Code, a lenient view should be taken in the context of their socio-economic environment. It was suggested that suitable training should be given to Adivasi women prisoners in bidi making sericultre and other related industries to which they are traditionally accustomed.

(xii) Women prisoners convicted under TADA were generally found to be young school and college-going girls. It was suggested that they should be provided with facilities to continue their studies and persistently motivated to return to the mainstream of life.

Conditions in Jail

The personal visits of Members to the jails convinced the Commission that there was a serious shortfall in the delivery of services to women who are in custody in jails. The Commission therefore decided to issue a questionnaire to all the States and Union Territories calling for data/information in respect of facilities available to women inmates with regard to diet, accommodation medical aid, sanitation, education, vocational training, legal aid, recreational opportunities, provisions for children accompanying prisoners, visitorial facilities, ventilation of grievances, etc.

The information received from all over the country is being processed in the Commission and an analysis thereof will be presented before the Expert Committee with a view to formulating recommendations bearing on the conditions of women in custody and norms thereof. The Commission also thought it fit that some immediate suggestions should be preferred by the Ministry of Home affairs, Government of India, for adoption in order to secure custodial justice for women behind the bar.

While drawing up these suggestions, consideration was given also to the aspect of gender justice in the realm of criminal law and administration after taking a stock of the recommendations made by various commissions and committees on the subject, notable among which is the Report of the National Expert Committee on Women prisoners headed by justice Krishna Iyer as well as that of All India Committee for Jail Reforms and also various findings of the Supreme Court of India on the subject.

The suggestions were sent for immediate implementation as these are supposed not to entail any substantial strain on the governmental exchequer and are implementable as a short-term measure. These are given below :

1. Women shall not be arrested between sunset and sunrise and shall not be arrested expect in the presence of women. This will necessitate amendment of section 46 Cr. P.C. 1973.
2. In all cases of bailable offences, bail on her bond shall be granted forthwith by the police themselves. As far as possible in non-bailable cases also, bail should be granted unless special circumstances warrant a different course, in which case, the arrested woman shall be remanded to judicial custody with utmost expedition.
3. On arrest, the police should immediately obtain from the arrestee the name of a relative or a friend to whom the intimation of her arrest should be promptly given.
4. If consideration of arrestee's own safety and freedom from ensnarement by anti-social elements demand detention in public institutions, bail shall be refused to the women in her own interest unless she is specifically states her willingness to be thus released even after being altered to the above consideration.
5. The person of a women shall not be searched except by a women authorised by law, and in a manner strictly in accordance with the requirement of decency. Whether in custody or in transit, the arrested woman must always be guarded by a woman police or female surrogate. A relative may be permitted to accompany the female arrestee.
6. Whenever a woman is to be examined by the police or other investigative agency as a witness it should be done only at her residence; nor should she be summoned to the police or investigative station unless she expresses her preference to be examined at the station.
7. No female prisoner shall be subjected to any form of

corporal punishment or use of handcuffs fetters or isolation as a form of disciplining.

8. When women are examined in court as accused or as witnesses, due courtesy and decency shall be shown. If circumstances so demand in the interest of modesty and privacy of a woman, the trial may be held in camera or the woman may be examined on commission through women advocates.

Exclusive Custody for Women

1. There should be police stations exclusive for women and exclusive lockups under the control of women police. This will necessitate amendment of prison Act and police Act. Separated space for female arrestees in every police lockup and complete segregation of women prisoners in jail and other custody should be maintained.
2. Where such facility is not available, a female arrestee may be lodged in a special home or institution designated under any law for the time being in force to receive women. At no, time shall a woman arrestee be left unguarded by a woman guard or surrogate.

   In all places of police custody, basic amenities such as living space, water, toilet, food, medical examination and care, and provisions to meet the special needs of women shall be provided.
3. As far as possible each state should have at least one or more separate jail for women.
4. There should be separate custodial facilities for convicts and under trial women. Separate institutions or reception centres where undertrial and remanded women may be kept, should be set up in larger cities, district headquarters, and in female-crime-endemic areas. Where convicts and undertrials are currently housed in one institution they must be kept apart in separate wings until independent facilities are set up.

Visitorial Provision in Custody

1. Additional provision should be made in the existing legislation conferring visitorial rights on recognised institutions or individuals, institutional and individual accountability for lapses and excesses should also be provided for.
2. Information on women in custody should be made available to recognised social organisations and individuals on request. Persons and institutions accredited as visitors should be allowed as a matter of right, free access to police stations and records.
3. Visiting Committees to jails should be constituted in consultation with professional bodies and university department of laws, criminologists, social workers and social scientists from the neighbouring area. Visitors should be nominated on the bases of merit, public spiritedness activist record and actual time likely to be made available to the visitorial function.

A woman DIG should be appointed at state headquarters preferably from the prison service to specifically look after the work relating to women prisoners and women prison staff.

Fresh Prisoners

Women superintendents of separate prisons for women (currently six in number) should be made fully autonomous in functioning.

Advice Given

Prisoners Councils or Bandi Sabhas should be set up in all prisons to help airing prisoners grievances and difficulties.

Social Proposal

1. Socio-legal counselling cells should be set up in every prison for women inmates.

2. In exceptional circumstances when a woman arrestee is taken to a police lock-up the police should immediately give intimation to the nearest Legal Aid Committee or recognized legal service or body which must render all necessary legal services at State expense.

3. Magistrates shall inform women when first produced of their right to legal aid at state expense and direct the provision of necessary services. They shall also explain the nature and scope of the proceedings against her and her rights in it.

4. Legal aid and counselling through professional bodies assisted by para-legal and social workers should be institutionalised in respect of every prison and custodial institution.

   Law schools and schools of social work should be encouraged and permitted to render socio-legal counselling service to the inmates.

5. In the disposition of women offenders courts should mandatorally call for and give due regard to the probation officers report and to the report of medical/psychiatric examination. Where probation officers are not available, probation investigation should be entrusted to recognized and accredited institutions and individuals.

External Support

1. Released Prisoners' Aid Societies should operate in every district to provide a single-window assistance towards rehabilitation and mainstreaming of the released women prisoners.

2. Before a female prisoner is released, her relatives should be informed and where no relative exists or shows up the released prisoner should be sent to her destination with a female escort.

3. Appropriate assistance should be rendered to every female prisoner on release whether during or after completion of

sentence. For this purpose a centre for assisting released prisoners should be set up to serve as a cluster of prisons and custodial institutions on an area-wise basis. Even without the centre the prison authorities should take necessary steps to arrange the rehabilitation of the released prisoner either through the family, the relief centre or a voluntary organisation.

4. Aftercare and short-stay homes for women prisoners may be established in every state to serve those prisoners who are homeless or rejected by their families.

Children Accompanying Women in Police Custody/Jail Custody

1. When arresting a women, proper arrangements for the protection and care of her accompanying children should be the responsibility of the state. Children who need to be custodialized jointly with their mothers should enjoy rights justly needed, while in custody in terms of food, living space, health, clothing and visitation.
2. In the disposition of women to custody or otherwise, the magistrate must enquire and direct that suitable arrangement for the welfare of their children be made in a manner that protects the rights of children. While sentencing women to imprisonment or any form of custodialisation suitable orders should be made for the custody and welfare of their children.
3. Expectant mothers in custody should be shown special consideration by way of medical and nutritional care, education in child rearing and mother craft.

Friendly Attitude of Police

1. Women's Assistance Police Unit contacting cadre of men and women police with specific task of crime prevention work and assistance to women should be set up in each district.

2. In endemic female crime areas, or wherever otherwise desirable exclusive police station or booths and counters within police stations, shall be set up to deal with women needing protection of or coming in conflict with law. Such booths and police stations should be managed by an integrated cadre of men and women police specially trained and sensitized to deal with women.

On 3rd February, 1993, the Commission organised in New Delhi a conference of Inspectors General of Prisons from all over the country with a view to obtaining their views on the diverse issues relating to custodial justice as well as gender justice in the realm of criminal law administration.

The Conference discussed at length a host of issues arising out of the topic of custodial justice to women as well as gender justice in the realm of criminal law administration. It was felt that the issues deserve a more thorough probe in the light of desirability as well as to implement ability of the various suggestions emerging out of the Conference.

Moreover, the suggestions were also desired to be screened and reviewed by the Expert Committee on Custodial Justice in order that light may be shed from all angles of views and a consensus arrived at. Accordingly a sub-committee of eight persons, out of the participants of the Conference, was appointed to interact with the Expert Committee on Custodial Justice to women on all the significant suggestions and in particular about the suggested amendments to the laws in force in the realm. This culminated in formulation of recommendations by the Commission for amendment of the code of Criminal Procedure.

13

Assaulted in War

Women are often cast in terms of opposites and dichotomies. She is *shakti* (power) and a weaker sex. She is auspicious *(sumankali)* and polluted. She is the maker and destroyer. She creates but is herself polluted at the time of creation. She is the evil force but she is godly as a mother. As a young women she is sexually dangerous and vulnerable but in a married form she is harmless and passive. A devadasi is also a paradox *par excellence.*

A Devadasi is *nitya sumankali* (Kersernboom 1987:xv) i.e. auspicious forever. Under normal circumstances the state of *Sumankali* is bestowed on women who are married and whose husbands are alive. *Tali,* flowers, gold and the mark on the forehead, *pottu,* are the symbols of being *sumankali...* when the husband dies, all the symbols are removed and the widow is pronounced ritually inauspicious and kept away from events such as weddings... However in the case of the *devadasi,* she is not within the family, is never married to a man, does have relationships with many men and she is not governed by the rules of chastity and codes of restraint. But she is considered perpetually a *sumankali.* (Thiruchandran, S: 1997, 55).

Women have come out strong during the war... they have stood out as individuals or as small groups; exposing the atrocities and violations of dignity... Women, who in the midst of war pleaded and argued with the militants for their families and the whole nation... Women's history does have a triumph. There is powerlessness, disappointment and disillusion but also hope. We have done it...a little bit.

Objectively, the pursuit of truth and the propagation of honest positions were not only crucial for the Community, but were a view that could cost many of us our lives. (Dr. Rajini Thiranagama, senior lecturer, Jaffna University, assassinated by LTTE cadres on September 21, 1989).

Untypical Parts

Historically, women who took on various non-traditional gender roles in situations of social stress, conflict, war and revolution, have been "pushed back into the kitchen after the revolution" as part of a return to everyday life (Jayawardane: 1986, Enloe: 1983). Arguably, one of the primary reasons that the return to peace often meant a return to the gender *status quo* was the lack of social recognition and a culturally appropriate idiom to articulate and legitimate women's empowerment in the midst of conflict, trauma and social disruption. This is particularly the case in societies where women's roles tend to be confined by kinship ties and ideologies and displacement out of a single caste village might mean loss of caste and social status.

This paper attempts to trace languages of empowerment in the generally tragic story of displaced Tamil women's lives towards recognising and promoting positive changes to women's roles and lives wrought in armed conflict. In the Sri Lankan armed conflict, now in its 14th year, many young and middle aged women have had to take on an unaccustomed role as head of household and principal income generator after being displaced and/or suffering the loss of husbands, fathers, sons and brothers. Often the victims or witnesses of extreme violence and trauma, over time, many displaced women have also gained greater confidence, mobility and authority within their families and even their communities as they are forced to take on new, traditionally male roles due to the social disruption caused by conflict. This is particularly the case with a growing number of young Tamil war widows who are challenging conventional Hindu constructions of the 'good woman' as one who is married and auspicious *(samangali)*.

Increasingly many young widows are redefining the perception of widows (and to a lesser extent unmarried women), as inauspicious beings *(amangali)*, by refusing to be socially and culturally marginalised and ostracised because they have lost husbands. Yet very few of these women seem to have found a culturally appropriate language to articulate the transformations that they have experienced and many feel ashamed, guilty and/ or traumatised by their changed circumstances and gender roles arising from conflict.

The paper then also attempts to map civilian women's agency in moments of violent social transformation and cultural change, to configure a more complex picture of women's agency, as well as their languages of resistance and empowerment in conflict. It also takes a critical look at how the construct of the Sri Lankan Tamil woman as a double 'victim': of war, as well as Tamil caste, culture, and society in peacetime might obscure and indeed impede women's agency and empowerment in conflicts. I do not directly address the issue of militant women of the LITE who might have found questionable if not deadly liberation in the Tamil nationalist project as fighting cadres or suicide bombers partly because there already exists a fairly extensive debate on the subject (cf. Balasingham: 1983, Coomaraswarmy: n.d, De Mel: Maunaguru: 1995).

I draw from ethnographic field research conducted during several field work stints over a number of years (1996-1998) in the 'border areas' (as they have come to be termed in the media and popular culture), of the north-central province of the island which have experienced cycles of violent armed conflict, including repeated bombing and shelling of civilian populations. In particular, I draw from interviews conducted with women living in three different settings of displacement:

(1) Welfare centres or refugee camps where people are housed in sheds, schools or structures constructed by UNHCR and other relief agencies working with the government.

(2) Residents of border villages who have been displaced many times by the fighting, shelling and bombing, but chose to return to their villages rather than remain in refugee camps. These people live in constant fear of attack and displacement again but since the majority are farmers, they choose to return to their land.

(3) New settlements in the border areas of the Vanni where the Sri Lanka Government settles landless displaced families from the same province in a new plot of land. These new settlements are part of the rehabilitation and reconstruction programme in Vavuniya. In particular, I draw from interviews with young women heads of households in Siddambarapuram Camp, which is located just outside the town of Vavunia. This particular camp received a large number of displaced persons and families from Jaffna and the Vanni who had fled to India in the early nineties and were subsequently repatriated. I also draw from interviews conducted with women heads of households in the new settlement scheme adjacent to Siddambarapuram camp.

Currently there is growing recognition among those involved in humanitarian relief and rehabilitation work that women frequently bear the material and psychological brunt of armed conflict and hence there is a need for gender sensitive relief and rehabilitation work. Yet few programmes have systematically explored how relief might aid recovery from individual trauma and social suffering and facilitate women's empowerment in and through conflict. Thus many gender programmes organised by the Government's relief and rehabilitation authority and NGOs still remain within conventional development thinking rather than attempting to work out culturally appropriate and effective strategies for women's empowerment in the context of the social transformations that have occurred over years of armed conflict and displacement. The second part of this paper then deals with the impact of humanitarian relief initiatives on displaced Tamil women's lives and seeks to link relief with building and sustaining women's recovery from the traumas of war through a critique of the victim ideology that pervades many humanitarian interventions.

Preys of War, Caste, and Culture

In Sri Lanka the tendency to view women as 'victims' of armed conflict has been fuelled by a number of popular and specialist discourses, concerning several brutal rapes committed by the Sri Lanka Army, as well as the Indian Peace Keeping Forces when they controlled the conflict zones. Human rights discourse and humanitarian interventions have significantly contributed to the tendency to view women as 'victims'. For the various and systematic forms of violence that civilian women experience at the hands of armed combatants, whether state armies or paramilitary personnel in situations of armed conflict and displacement, was extensively documented and highlighted in the former Yugoslavia, Rwanda, and other parts of Africa and Asia. This process culminated in the UN resolution that established rape as a war crime and saw the appointment of a Special Rapporteur on Violence against Women . Highlighting gross violations of women's bodies and lives in situations of conflict and displacement has been part of an intervention by feminists and activists to promote women's rights as a human right internationally. Yet, the focus on women as 'victims' has arguably resulted in the elusion of how long-term social upheaval might have transformed women's often subordinate gender roles, lives and position in non-obvious ways.

But the construct of the Tamil woman as 'victim' of war also draws from another genealogy. Anthropological, sociological and literary ethnography has tended to represent Tamil women as living within a highly patriarchal caste ridden by Hindu cultural ethos, particularly in comparison to Sinhala women whose lives are seen to be less circumscribed by caste ideologies and purity/pollution concepts and practices. The figure of the LTTE woman soldier, the armed virgin or the nationalist mother stands as one of the few highly problematic exceptions to the representation of the Tamil woman as a victim of her culture and caste.

Of course the representation of Tamil woman in relation to caste and family is not entirely monochrome in the anthropological literature which is split on the subject. Many anthropologists have also emphasised strong matrilineal tendencies in Sri Lankan Tamil society, where women inherit property in the maternal line according to customary The *sawalamai* law and enjoy claims on natal families, in contrast to the rigidly patriachal cultures of North India where patrilineal descent and inheritance is the norm (cf. Wadley: 1991). Feminist ethnography, on the other hand, has emphasised the subordinate status of Tamil women in the Hindu caste structure, while frequently noting the split between the ideology of *Shakti* or female power as the primary generative force of the universe (also associated with the pantheon of powerful Hindu goddesses) and the reality of women's apparent powerlessness (Thiruchandran: 1997).

Both schools however emphasise the generally restrictive nature of the Sri Lankan Tamil Hindu caste system on women and often tend to see caste and gender relations as culturally rather than historically determined. Women have rarely been centred in debates on caste and when they have been, they are more often than not constructed as victims rather than agents of culture.

More recently anthropologists have argued that colonialism permeated by British Victorian patriarchal culture eroded the status of women in the South Indian societies that follow the matrilineal Dravidian kinship pattern, where property is passed in the women's line, from mother to daughter—a practice which usually indicates the relatively high status of women in society.

Rather, they highlight how colonial legal systems might have eroded the rights and freedoms that women had under customary law, particularly in matrilineal societies, while emphasising the historically changing circumstances of family, kinship, caste and gender relations. In this vein, this paper explores how fifteen years of armed conflict and displacement might have altered the structure of the family, caste and gender *status quo* among displaced Tamils in the border areas affected by the conflict.

Conflict of Arms

Since 1983 when Sri Lanka's ethnic conflict transmuted into a dirty war perpetrated by a number of armed forces and groups, civilians in the border areas have lived amidst overlapping regimes of terrifying security. Between the major contenders in the war—the Sri Lanka government's military regime of passes and check points and the LTTE's parallel security regime—civilian men and women also have to contend with the sub regimes of several other armed groups—the Eelam Peoples Revolutionary Front (EPRLF-East coast) and Rafik group, People's Liberation Organisation of Tamil Eelam (PLOTE -Vanni), Eelam People's Democratic Party (EPDP- Jaffna) for fifteen years of war has generated a number of armed para military groups who seem intent only on retaining the power they wield at gun point. Many of these paramilitary groups which are bank rolled by the Sri Lanka government and work with the Army to combat the LTTE maintain regimes of terror and torture in the areas they control. All these groups, mainly youth, carry guns.

The paramilitaries remain outside the authority and discipline structure of the Government's armed forces which are marginally better trained and better aware of humanitarian law. Thus, the paramilitary cardre tend to have a relatively freer reign than government forces to terrorise civilians, torture them and extort money at gun point. At the national level, several leaders of paramilitary groups are installed as members of Parliament and support the ruling government. These groups have also developed systems of taxation of civilians by virtue of their control over the main transport routes and the movement of persons and goods through an economy of terror, scarcity and fear. In the Sri Lankan conflict, the LTTE pioneered this system of taxation on the movement of goods and trafficking in persons. Since then, the Army has resorted to similar practices. Where the army issues passes and identification papers, there is a high degree of corruption. Residents of high security areas complain of being asked to pay large sums of money to army personnel before they are issued with these papers.

Violence against women in this context is the stuff of rape, trauma and disappeared persons, torture, assassination, and the gendered politics of body searches at check points usually conducted by armed youth who have been trained in the arts of terror, torture and the degradation of their victims. Several instances of check point rape by the Sri Lankan government's security forces have occurred, though rape has not been practised as a systematic policy for ethnic cleansing by any groups in the conflict, unlike in Bosnia. Women suffer particularly from the poor security situation in the border areas.

Their mobility and thus ability to go out to work is severely curtailed due to fear of body searches and check point rape, not to mention anxiety about being caught in crossfire. Mothers are often fearful for their daughter's safety and sexual vulnerability and tend to confine them to the home or refugee camp. Simultaneously, a sexual service industry has developed in Anuradhapura area where soldiers return from the conflict areas, with many homeless and displaced women engaging in prostitution.

The fear of checkpoint rape is a constraint on women's ability to move around and venture out of their immediate locale for work or any other purpose. Conditions are considerably worse for displaced women who are forced to live in refugee camps where privacy is minimal or non-existent and levels of generalised violence, alcholism and domestic violence are high.

Replacing Gender and Caste Hierarchies

Yet, displacement and camp life had also provided spaces for empowerment for several Tamil women who had taken on the role of head of household for various reasons. In this section some of the processes of transformation in young single and widowed women's lives are outlined, women we met at the Siddambarapuram camp and adjacent new settlement scheme. Siddambarapuram was located a few miles outside Vavuniya, the largest town in the north central Vanni region. It had received a large influx of refugees from the north. In many ways the facilities, location and environmental/ climatic conditions at that camp and the adjoining new settlements were exceptionally propitious. The relative prosperity of the locale and its residents was evident in the fact that the market in the camp was a vibrant and happening place that had become a shopping centre for nearby old (purana) villagers as well. At Siddmbarapuram the sense of independence, empowerment and mobility of many women heads of household was tangible and remarkable in contrast to other women we met in camps in less propitious settings. This is explainable in terms of the camp's location close to the larger town of Vavuniya where women could find employment, particularly in the service sector. This is of course not an option for displaced women in other less conveniently located camps.

The Siddambarapuram Camp was initially constructed as a transit camp by UNHCR for refugees returning to Jaffna from India in 1991, who were subsequently stranded when the conflict started again in what is known as the second Eelam war. Many of the people in the camp had been residents for more than five years. One of the oldest refugee camps in Vavuniya, in many respects the camp was exceptionally well located and serviced. Several young Tamil widows we interviewed in the camp and the adjoining new settlement noted that while they had initially had a hard time adjusting to displacement, camp life and the burdens of caring for their young families, they also had gained freedom to work outside the household and increasingly enjoyed the role of being the head of the household and its principal decision maker.

Many women said that they had little desire to remarry, mainly due to anxiety that their children might not be well cared for by a second husband. Several women commented that previously their husbands would not permit them to work outside the household, even if they had done so prior to marriage. Of course one of the principal reasons for these women's newly found sense of control was the fact that they were able to and had found employment outside the household and the camp. Their sense of independence was evident in the defiance with which they wore the red pottu, the auspicious mark of the married Hindu women, despite being widows or women whose husbands had abandoned them. The demographic fact of a large number of young widows who were unwilling to take on the role of the traditional Hindu widow, who may not participate in auspicious social rituals such as wedding ceremonies and who are generally socially ostracised, indicates that there is space for redefinition of what it means to be an unmarried or widowed woman in the more orthodox Hindu tradition.

To a great extent the erosion of caste ideology and practice particularly among the younger generation in the camps had contributed to women's mobility and sense of empowerment. For, caste has historically provided the mainstay of the Hindu Tamil gender status *quo* since caste belonging often determines women's mobility and seclusion particularly among the high castes is a sign of high status. Unlike in Jaffna where village settlement was caste and region based, in the camp it was difficult to maintain social and spatial segregation, caste hierarchies and purity pollution taboos for a number of reasons. This is particularly true for members of the younger generation who simply refused to adhere to caste inhibitions.

As one mother speaking about the disruption of caste hierarchies in displacement observed: "because we are poor here as displaced people, we only have two glasses to drink from, so when a visitor from another caste comes we have to use the same glass. Now my daughter refuses to observe the separate utensils and she is friendly with boys we wouldn't consider at home. Everything is changing with the younger generation because they are growing up all mixed up because we are displaced and living on top of each other in a camp". This mother went on to detail how it was difficult to keep girls and boys separate in the camp situation. She thought that the freer mingling of youth meant that there would be more inter-caste marriages and hence an erosion of caste. Presumably this also means that girls had more choice over who might be their partners.

The reconstitution of displaced families around women who had lost male kin curiously resonates with an older gender *status quo:* that of the pre-colonial Darvidian matrilineal family and kinship system where women remained with their natal families after marriage and were customarily entitled to lay claim on the resources of the matri-clan and hence enjoyed a relatively higher status in comparison with strictly patrilineal societies. For as Binna Agarawal has pointed out in "A Field of One's Own" (1996), the existence of matrilineal systems where matrilineal descent, matri-local residence, and/or bilateral inheritance is practiced is usually an indicator of the relatively higher status of women when compared to the status of women in patrilineal groups. Similar observations concerning the status of women in matrilineal communities have been made by anthropologists who have studied the Nayars of Kerala as well as the Sinhalas, Tamils and Muslims of the east coast of Sri Lanka where matrilineal inheritance is the norm (Yalman). These are also societies where social indicators have been consistently good, with high levels of female literacy, education and health care in South Asia.

During the colonial period in Sri Lanka there was however a general erosion of the matrilineal inheritance and bilateral descent practice, despite general provisions being made for customary common law for indegenous communities (Thesavallamai, Tamil customary law, Kandian Sinhala law as well as Muslim Personal law). In the same period the modernising tendency to the nuclear family enshrined in secular European, Dutch and British law, also privileged male inheritance, thereby reducing the power of women within their families.

The switch from matrilineal, matrilocal, to virilocal forms of residence and inheritance, where women take only movable property to their affinal household might also be traced to various post-colonial land distribution schemes wherein title deeds for land were invested in male heads of household, with the injunction against the further division of land due to land fragmentation, which set a precedent for male inheritance of the entirety of the family's land. The result has been the tendency towards male primogeniture—with the eldest son inheriting the land and daughters being disinherited from land ownership.

Unfortunately similar pattern of title deeds being invested in male heads of households is still evident in the new settlement and land distribution schemes for landless displaced populations which are taking place in Vavuniya under the rehabilitation and reconstruction project. In these projects it is only where the male head of household is presumed dead that title deeds are invested in women. Women whose husbands have left them or whose where abouts cannot be ascertained are not deemed eligible for land grants.

Frightening Widowhood

Nevertheless a generation of young Tamil war widows who have been displaced to and in the border areas for many years seem to be increasingly challenging conventional Hindu constructions of widow hood as a negative and polluting condition which bars their participation from many aspects of community life. Consciously or unconsciously, they appear to be redefining conceptions of the "good woman" as one who lives within the traditional confines of caste, kin group and village. Many of these young women who have lost husbands to death, displacement or family fragmentation in the course of armed conflict and flight from bombing and shelling, increasingly refuse to erase the signs of *sumankali* (particularly the auspicious red pottu) they wore when married and refuse to be socially and culturally marginalised and ostracised because they lack husbands and children.

Displacement along with the fragmentation and reconstitution of families around women in a conflict where men frequently have had to flee to avoid being killed or inducted by the armed groups, appears to have provided a space to redefine traditional Hindu Tamil perceptions of widows and single women as inauspicious beings. As they struggle with new gender roles and identities, many of these young widows who refuse to wear the prescribed garb of widowhood appear to break with the ideology of Kannaki *(Paththini)*, the exemplary faithful wife and widow of Tamil mythology and ideology. Rather, they seem to evoke the sign of the *devadasi - Kannaki's*, alter ego—who transcended conventional gender roles; the professional woman married to immortality for her talent and skill, most familiar to South Asian audiences in the name of the famed dancer and courtesan, Madhavi of the first century Tamil Hindu-Buddhist epic, *Sillapaddikaram*.

With the exception of the young Tamil widows, women who have found more freedom in the conflict, women still seem to lack a language to articulate this process of transformation and regeneration and clearly feel guilty about expressing their new found confidence. Only one woman directly told me "it is a relief now that he (her husband) is not with me. He used to drink and beat me up".

Clearly the process of empowerment is not transparent, unambivalent, or free of guilt and this was evident in many young widows uncertainty about whether they should return home if and when the conflict ended. For them displacement clearly constituted the space of ambivalence: a place of regeneration and the hope for a future unfettered by the past loss and trauma. They were also concerned that a return home would mean a return to the pre-war caste and gender *staus quo.* Of course, anxiety about return was also related to qualms about personal security and trauma. Anxiety about return was clearest among young women heads of households at Siddambarapuram, who had integrated to the local economy and among those who had previously been landless.

Altering Position

Many internally displaced women who have given up the dream of return are in the paradoxical position of being materially and psychologically displaced by the humanitarian interventions and human rights discourses and practices that define them as victims who need to be returned to their original homelands for their protection and for the restoration of national and international order and peace . For, the assumption of return is a fundamental premise of State, international and NGO policies vis-a-vis internally displaced people. The fact is that these policies might be contributing to prolong the conflict and a cause of trauma for people who fled their homes over five years ago. This is particularly true of women for whom restrictions on mobility are difficult. Many of these women who wish to settle in the place where they have found refuge are being kept dependent on relief handouts rather than being assisted to build new lives and livelihoods. Thus, ironically, relief might be prolonging the trauma of the very people it is supposed to assist.

Under these circumstances, an approach which conceptualises humanitarian work as part of a development continuum with gender-sensitive post/conflict intervention is especially necessary in instances where armed conflicts have lasted for several years with communities experiencing cycles of war and peace and displacement. Ironically, for some women, the conflict has provided windows of opportunity for greater personal and group autonomy and experiments with identity and leadership, for others there is only trauma. Certainly this has been the case for many displaced Tamil women, many of whom have lost husbands and sons in the conflict. It is hence important that relief aid should be conceptualised to sustain women's empowerment and leadership roles that initially arose as an effect of conflict within an altered family structure.

Tasks from Humanitarian Viewpoint

Unlike in Afghanistan where the situation of women has unambiguously deteriorated due to conflict and the victory of the Taliban, in Sri Lanka, the evidence suggests that despite many women's experience of traumatic violence and displacement, some changes to the gender *status quo* wrought by armed conflict might have empowered women, whose freedom and mobility were restricted by patriarchal cultural mores, morality and convention in peace time. Several women who have faced the traumatic loss and scattering of family members due to displacement, conflict, and the break down of family structures have also assumed new roles which were thrust upon them as a result of the disruption of peace time community organisation, social structures and patriarchal values. Yet the purpose of this paper is not to suggest that this is a general story which might be told of women living in conflict and displacement. Rather this paper has attempted to focuses on civilian women's agency at moments when they seem most victimised, to excavate some hidden moments and routes of women's empowerment in the generally tragic story of displaced women's lives in Sri Lanka.

The victim ideology which pervades relief and rehabilitation as well as social health and trauma interventions for women in conflict situations needs to be problematised especially as it may be internalised by some women with—damaging consequences. Clearly, non-combatant women who have found spaces of empowerment in the conflict need sustained assistance to maintain their new found mobility and independence in the face of sometimes virulently nationalist assertions of patriarchal cultural tradition and practices during the conflict and in the period of post-war reconstruction. The return to peace should not mean a return to the pre-war gender *status quo.* It follows that humanitarian and development interventions should be directed to creatively support and sustain positive changes to the status of civilian women living in conflict. The need to conceptualise relief as part of a development continuum is particularly evident on the gender issue. It has taken long enough to put women on the development agenda and in situations of emergency and conflict, women tend to be once again marginalised, as quick responses become the primary agenda. Displaced women should receive priority in land grants.

It is argued elsewhere that nationalist women and women combatants in nationalist struggles waged by groups like the LTTE, or the nationalist women in Ireland or Palestine, are imbricated in ultra-conservative "nationalist constructions of women" and tend to subordinate their gender identities to the nationalist cause (Rajasingham 1995). Suicide bombing is but the extreme version of this phenomenon which might, in Durkheimian terms, be glossed as altruistic suicide, when individual autonomy and personal agency is completely subsumed in the national cause. The question might well be raised as to whether women would be more given than men to altruistic suicide, given their socialisation in patriarchal Asian cultures where girl children and women are more often than not taught to put themselves second and their male folk, family, and community honour first. Clearly, non-combatant women are differently imbricated in nationalist discourses and the return to peace time (which entails the reassertion of the gender *(status quo)* is as problematic for them as it is for combatant women, but for different reasons.

14

Sexual Exploitation

The Oxford Dictionary defines the word rape as "forcible or fradulent sexual intercourse imposed on women". In the words of Susan Brown Miller, "Rape is the only crime for which the victim cannot have a revenge." It represents as "act of violence and humiliation in which the victim experiences not only overwhelming fear for her very existence, but an equally overwhelming sense of powerlessness and helplessness that hardly a few others events in ones life can parallel" (Hilberman, 1976).

Defining Rape

The word rape in many Indian languages, is *balaatkar* derived from the root *bal* meaning strength, basically in a physical sense. But it is also a beastly crime because the time and place where the rape is committed, finds the victim defenceless, weak, alone, or vulnerable. In other words, at that particular moment she is in no position to defend herself against physical assault. Rape for a woman should simply mean a criminal invasion into personal integrity. Seen from the angle of the patriarchal society, it has primarily meant an assault on the legally recognised male rights of possession where he has the right of possession of an unblemished woman. The Hindi phrase for rape is *Izzat lootna* which literally translates as "the robbing of honour".

Notions in Law

According to Section 375 of the Indian Penal Code, rape is committed when a man has sexual intercourse with a woman: (i) against her will, or (ii) without her consent, or (iii) with her consent, when her consent has been obtained by putting her or any person in whom she is interested, in fear of death, or of hurt, or (iv) with her consent, when he by deception, makes her believe that he is her lawful husband, or (v) with her consent, given on account of her unsoundness of mind, or intoxication, when she is incapable of understanding the consequences of her consent, or (vi) with or without consent, when she is under 16 years of age.

'Against her will' means an act is done against a woman's will when she is fully conscious and capable of consenting and a decision-making power and is aware of what is being done and resists or objects to it. 'Without her consent' means that she is insensible and incapable of rational consent, due to fear, shock or intoxication or any other cause.

Rape is the most calculated, cold blooded, deliberate and heinous of crimes committed by one human being on another by virtue of the simple and biological fact that the one who commits rape is physically stronger than his victim. Being by no means accidental or committed in the heat of the moment on a passionate impulse, there is no anger or vengeance involved either.

In a rape, the aggressor is a man, the rapist and the aggrieved party is also a man, the father or the husband and the woman being the damaged property. The woman is the victim and it is she who has to carry the stigma for the rest of her life. The social and religious values make her an outcaste, an untouchable and a disgrace to her family. It is an exceptional crime where harassment, guilt, shame and social disapproval are attached to the victim, not to the offender. Society at large looks down on a victim with suspicion. The woman is made to feel guilty as myths about rape such as "no woman can be raped unless she wants", dressed like that she was asking for it, or "women like being raped", etc. are current in society. This makes it even more difficult for the victim to reveal her tragedy. Often men consider women tempting in any dress good or bad. When she is alone, she can be taken as inviting man and she can be considered flirting when she is socialising.

All women perpetually suffer from the fear of being raped irrespective of her age, health, appearance, mental state, shelter and relations. No woman is immune from being the victim of rape.

The scourage of rape continues to wreak havoc on the nation's thousand of innocent women. Various examples have been gathered, the rape case reported in newspapers that high class men or men in power rape Harijan women.

- Two Harijan girls were allegedly raped, their huts were demolished and a well was polluted by landlords in separate incidents in the interior of Nawada district.
- Teachers rape their students, three minor girls were raped by their teacher in mohalla Machharhatta of Barh Bazar.
- Sometimes the colleagues, residents of Myar village under Noorsarai P.S. witnessed the rape of a female teacher at the Myar Middle School by her male colleagues in the school building.
- Students rape their fellows. A young girl, victim of an attempt of rape in the hostel of a local college of Patna, was handed over to her parents by the Pirbahore police after medical examination.
- Doctors rape their patients in hospital and nursing home. Two doctors of Nalanda Medical College Hospital were

arrested by Sultanganj police on the charge of criminally assaulting a female patient; Employees rape their co-workers. A nurse of Sadar Hospital, Giridih was criminally assaulted by two employees of the hospital.

- Prison staff rape their undertrials. A Harijan woman undertrial prisoner was allegedly raped to death by the jail staff in Giridih.
- Landlords rape their tenants. A twelve-year-old girl in Barmasia locality of Giridih district was assaulted and raped by her landlord as the parents of the victim were out of the town.
- Tenants rape their landlords. A middle-aged woman of Tekari road, Sultanganj area of Patna was raped by one of her tenant.
- Masters rape their maid servants. A 15-year-old girl working as a maid servant in the lodge in Dhaneshwar Ghat Mohalla under Bihar Sharif Police Station was raped by some students.
- Domestic servants rape the housewives. A domestic servant was arrested by the Bankmore Police of Dhanbad on the charge of criminally assaulting a housewife when the other family members of the house were out.
- Old men and young men alike enjoy the pleasure of sex out of wedlock and even women suffering from T.B. and other ailments undergoing treatment become victims. A poor, sick woman was gangraped by some identified people in village Berhna under Police Station of Patna while she was relaxing under the shade of a tree. A girl of 17 years, living with her sick mother in the hospital of Chaibasa was raped by unknown persons, after disconnecting electric line. A pregnant woman of Sinhpur village under Kasmar Police Station of Bokaro was brutally beaten by three miscreants when the victim resisted their attempt to rape her. An adivasi minor blind girl of Lakha

village under Mofussil Police Station was gangraped by three identified persons. An Adivasi woman under treatment for leprosy at Nav Kusth Ashram of Bhagalpur was gang raped by four criminals. Their physical appearance need not be always attractive.

- Sometimes the rape victims are reported to be baby girls. A man was arrested at Jamshedpur on the charge of raping a three-year-old girl.
- Old women have also been raped.
- An old woman of Agrer village under Sasaram block of Rohtas district was raped in her house by some goondas in a drunken state when his husband was out of station. Later on she was strangulated to death.
- Women may not be safe even in their families. A 20-year-old woman was raped and murdered by her father-in-law at Sheonar village of Mokameh.

Rape of women cuts across barriers of caste, class, education, looks, age and status. The rapist may be any person—a holyman, a doctor, a teacher, a servant, a landlord or a farmer, a student, a neighbour or a co-villager, a relative or a criminal. Therefore, the rapist is one among ourselves. He has no distinct identity. There are an umpteen numbers of instances and a plenty of evidence to show that rapist may be no stranger to the victim and the offence could just as easily occur in family setting—offices, educational institutions, hospitals and even homes. The aggressor could even be a boy friend or acquaintance. He could be an employer, or landlord who wields power, a neighbour or a member of the family.

Sexual harassment is unknown in the dingy corridor and cubicles of office and factories in metropolitan and industrial towns. Working women are harassed by their bosses and colleagues. Those who come from cultured families and also have some financial means give up their job as a protest. But women who come from the lower middle-class and are sole supporters of a family or their income is an indispensable supplement to their husband, bear their boss's sexual overtones silently. It is a mistake to assume that all rapists are perverts, normal men do rape. There are the cases male members of the victim's family have even lost their lives in a bid to save the female members from being raped.

It would be more precise to state that rape is mostly used to express or to assert class power or as an instrument of class oppression. Rape an assertion of male power as a terrorising instrument of punishment, is indulged in by the elite, by the guardians of the law and order on woman from the rural areas, woman from the scheduled castes and tribes. Why is it that educated women are raped less frequently than illiterate and ignorant women? Why is it that high caste women are raped very rarely. A 19-year-old girl was gang raped by a number of Harijans in village Neura of Barh subdivision in broad day light and the rapists prevented the victim's family from going to the police station and in their bid to do so they opened several rounds of fire.

While low caste tribal woman and women from minority communities who are also poor are raped quite often? And finally, women from the upper, middle and affluent classes are hardly raped while women from the economically poor classes are subjected to rape every other day. Rape among the middle and upper classes is another taboo subject. Even among middle class women, the general attitude towards rape is that it is something which happens to lower class women, something the rest of society is protected from by virtue of caste or class. In parts of the country even today, landlords demand 'first night' privileges. It is the common allegation in rape case where the authority is the offender and helpless, poor women are the victims that these women are of loose moral character.

The question is: how can the investigating authorities make any positive conclusions about the moral character of any woman, whether she is raped or not, without having any knowledge about her lifestyle except the fact that she is poor, illiterate and belongs to a backward and oppressed community? Even if the women who have been victimised are women of loose morals, what has character got to do with a man's right to rape her? These questions remain unanswered in this male dominated society. It may be known that — a woman is a woman just as man is a man. One human being's moral or immoral or amoral stand does not in any way justify another person's humiliation of her or him, sex notwithstanding. If one were to reverse the theory, then what would women do with men who have loose morals? But women cannot do anything specially if they are poor, illiterate and belong to the backward classes as long as it is the men who man the law and judicial machinery of the country.

Rape is one language often used by two groups of warring men to get even with each other, not considering that the people who are used for this, are flesh-and-blood thinking and living beings because they are women. Rape is not always necessarily for the perverted sense of sexual pleasure of man as was commonly believed for ages together. Brownmiller states that populations have been terrorised by rape : (i) in the two World Wars, (ii) in the wars of Bangladesh and Vietnam, (iii) during partition riots in India in 1947, when there was mass rape of both Hindu and Muslim women. Rape, therefore, has been systematically and calculatedly used as an instrument of intimidation in India, not only for women, but also to humiliate and demoralise the men. After the assassination of Indira Gandhi, about 2000 women were raped in Delhi in the riots following her death.

Rural-urban difference in the incidence of rape in Bihar revealed the following trends:

(i) Percentages of rape in rural areas were slightly higher compared to urban areas in all the years except 1981 and 1988.

(ii) In urban areas higher rate of incidence was in 1981 and 1988 when the percentage of incidence was 50.61 and 51.05 respectively.

(iii) Both rural and urban areas demonstrated decreasing as well as increasing tendencies in the rate of rape cases.

The data were further analysed to examine the difference between rural and urban areas within each region.

Studies in Bihar indicate that the incidence of rape was always higher in urban compared to rural areas except in Adivasi region where the incidence was double in number in rural areas compared to the urban areas during the same years in the four regions. When the rape cases were analysed region-wise, the rural-urban differences became more vivid as well as region-specific. In Magahi, Maithili, and Bhojpuri region urban areas contributed more towards the incidence than the rural one. On the other hand, in the Adivasi region it was rural side which reported higher rate of rape cases.

DIFFERENT CATEGORIES

Rape of Dalit and Tribal Women : It is an all-pervasive fact that Dalit and tribal women are oppressed by society at large; rape is simply being used an instrument to oppress women. Dalit and tribal women are raped for a variety of reasons not least of which is the fact that they are vulnerable women and raping them is not likely to result in any punishment. They are also raped as a way of demoralising them in their struggle for an improved existence. For the last two decades Bihar has seen many gruesome violence taking place in different parts of the state. The incidents at Belchi, Pipra, Parashbigha, Arwal, Kansara, and Gua are some of the most prominent ones, where women had been targets of rape and molestation. A big demonstration by about 5000 tribal including women was held in front of the office of the Deputy Commissioner demanding immediate action against the policemen who had allegedly misbehaved with tribal women while they were on their traditional 'Janishikar'.

Rape on the Job : The rape of working women is a national scandal which is at least as widespread as custodial rape, yet it does not receive as much attention. They are harassed by their bosses and male workers. Domestic servants are molested by employer or the relatives or friends of employers. The headmaster of an English medium school at Bhurkunda, 30 km from Ramgarh Cantt was taken into police custody for raping a lady teacher of his school. A nurse of Sadar Hospital, Giridih was criminally assaulted by two young employees of the hospital.

Rape by Strangers : Women are not safe anywhere, may it be the street or the fields or even her own home.

A married woman of Chandi mohalla of Barh was brutally assaulted by six youths at her residence as the other members of the family were out. A Harijan girl of village Musapur under Sarairanjan police station of Dalsingsarai was raped and murdered by identified persons in her house while she was sleeping with her mother.

Rape of Minor : Rape of minor is particularly horrifying and now it has become a common crime. Newspapers regularly print accounts of the rape of minor girls. One person of Jamshedpur was taken into custody on the charge of raping a three-year-old girl. A five-year-old girl was lured away from a Ganesh Puja pandal and raped by an unidentified man and she was taken to the intensive care unit of the Tata Main Hospital in an unconscious state.

Rape in Journey : Women are not safe even while travelling. A minor girl waiting for a particular bus at the Harding Park bus stand of Patna was taken to a lonely place by a worker of a transport agency on the pretext of guiding her to the said bus and was raped. Two women train passengers were kidnapped from North Eastern Railway Dighwara station and allegedly gangraped.

A young woman passenger was criminally assaulted in a compartment of the Munger-Jamalpur local train after locking the gates and her husband who tried to resist them was thrown out of the running train.

Rape of Sick : Even women suffering from T.B. or other ailments undergoing treatment, pregnant, blind women and women suffering from leprosy are the victims of rape.

A sick women of Patna who went to a hospital for her treatment was allegedly raped by three persons.

A pregnant women was brutally beaten by three miscreants when she resisted their attempt to rape her.

An Adivasi minor blind girl was gangraped by three youngsters.

An Adivasi woman under treatment for leprosy was gangraped by four criminals.

Rape within Family : Women are not safe even in their own family. A 20-year-old woman was raped and murdered by her father-in-law of Sheonar village in Mokameh. A young married woman deposed before the Judicial Magistrate that her father-in-law entered her room and committed rape on her and it was why she stabbed him.

Thus, it is observed that women are raped at work, on the street, in the fields, at bus or railway platform, in train, in school, in their homes by men who are their employers or employees, their acquaintance, their neighbours, their relatives, and their in-laws. It is not only Dalit women who are victims and not only landlords who are rapists.

There may be at least three categories of rapists. There is one whose assault is the explosive expression of a pent-up sexual impulse; he is motivated by sex desire only. In such cases the rapists has no respect of age or looks. The second group is motivated by an impulse to punish and hurt the victim, rather than sex desire. Gang rapes by dacoits after committing a dacoity, rapes on Harijan women, rapes on women during communal riots, rapes due to family dispute and gang rape by policemen all come under this group. And there is a third group of rapist, the aggressive criminals, who is out of pillage and rob, like the soldiery of a conquering army.

Gebhard in a psychological study of rapists found the following five categories of rapists:

(i) *Sadists :* Who have a past history of violence, a strong hostility to females, and who obtain sexual satisfaction only when it is accompanied by physical violence.

(ii) *Moral Delinquents :* Who are not hostile to females, use force to get what they want and commit rape to satisfy sexual desire without taking interest in victim.

(iii) *Explosives :* Who are normally "upright" citizens. A disturbed family background usually underlies the behaviour of these offenders.

(iv) *Drunken Variety :* Who after drinking delude themselves into thinking that a female is trying to seduce them.

(v) *Double Standard :* Who divide females into "good" and "bad" and rationalize the use of force, if necessary, on "bad" girls.

Hunting down the Rapist

The sex, instinct, indeed had been a very powerful motivation since the times immemorial. In a way, every man in this world is a sexual criminal at the unconscious level. But what matters is the action. People who translate their latent feelings into action give way to the doctrine that pleasure is the chief god. Through psychoanalytic studies, it has been revealed that the rapists are persons with poor judgement and inadequate impulse control. They lack the power of reasoning which leads them to sexual perversion. A man with a well developed personality and a strong moral standard would never indulge in such activities.

Rape is also attributed to unhappy family life which may be due to various incapabilities such as potency, temperament, habit and economic conditions, as a result of which marital life turns annoying and frustrating. Broken homes and constant friction in family turns children into sex delinquents.

Pornographic literature and the modern movies depicting crude rape and bathing scenes are also contributing to the desire to rape among adolescents and youth. Disregard of moral values and lack of religious sanctions also give rise to urge of rape.

Sex crimes also occur due to psychological factors like desire to rape, exhibition of potency, experience of pleasure in the pain of others (Sadism), taking revenge on a woman and like. A major study of forcible rape (Amir, 1971) has shown that in 85 per cent of all reported rapes there was some form of overt violence such as beating or choking. It may be stated that rape is an act of aggression and violence and it is committed by persons who are not motivated by sexuality; rather they are motivated primarily by power, hostility and the urge to brutalise, humiliate and debase their victims.

According to Mackellar (1975), "The man who rapes does so because he lacks a better means for making the point, 'I am a man,' while Bart (1975) has stressed the anger in rape: "Psychiatrists say a gun is a substitute phallus. Rape is a power trip, not a passion trip. The rapist is more likely to rape in cold blood, with contempt and righteousness, than with passion".

Thus, rape is a universal phenomenon. Its etiology is complex and the manifestations are extremely varied according to time, place and person. It also varies with historical periods, modes of life, economic conditions and social attitudes.

Method of Working

The victims of rape are victimized in sundry ways and rape is pregnant with momentous consequences for its victim. We may distinguish three ways of victimization of, and three types of consequences for, the victim of the rape: psychological, physical and social.

Psychological Victimization : Psychological victimization of the victim and its consequences can be understood in three phases of rape: before, during and after rape.

The fear of rape troubles all women, it is a source of mental anxiety to the victim. Research on the fear of crime and on public opinion, about crime shows that the very possibility of being victimised troubles many people. Freedom from criminal victimisation is a social good, much like any other social good of a just society.

Rape affects all women whether or not they are actually victimized. According to Griffin (1970) who verbalizes as follows, the experience of many women: "I have never been free of the fear of rape. From a very early age I, like most women, have thought of rape as part of my natural environment something to be feared and prayed against like fire or lightning". Women are under perpetual fear of being raped which induces a continuing state of psychological stress in women due to which they resort to several safety precautions which, in turn, seriously restrict their freedom, such as not moving alone, or avoiding to go to certain places, or going out with certain men. Several studies attest to these consequences of the fear of rape on all women, all the time, everywhere, who may not have been victimized but who, nonetheless, are subjected to the threat of rape and to the concomitant forces of social control.

The actual commission of rape is a "crisis situation" full of stress and strain for a victim thus far leading a normal life. And it is a strange sudden crisis—a crisis with which the victim must deal herself. If she surrenders sexually, then her life is spoilt personally and socially, and if she resists, then she runs the risk of being destroyed physically at the hands of the rapist.

The post-rape period poses a more lingering as the ordeal for the rape victim. The terror of the criminal justice system, social stigma, and the physical injury, combine together to cause psychological malaise beyond description. In her post-rape life, she begins to nurture distrust in men and society, confronts difficulties in her sexual adjustment, and suffers from a host of psychological disturbances, including fear, insomnia, anxiety, dreams, hallucinations and others. Many a time, the victim reconciles with the mental trauma caused by her by taking refuge in suicide.

Physical Victimization : In the process of preventing the rapist from raping the victim incurs a wide variety of physical injuries, depending upon the location and the extent of resistance put up. The injuries from the physical attacks of the rapist are on various parts of the body, throat, neck, cheeks, thighs, legs, arms and genitalia. And injuries themselves are varied 'scratches, bruises, at times being knifed or shot at.

Varieties of physical complaints and complications begin to appear in post-rape period: physical pain in different parts of the body, skeletal muscle tension, gastro-intestinal irritability and genito-urinary disturbances, to cite a few.

The victim's large number of complicated physiological problems warrant immediate medicare. For instance, there is a possibility of contracting venereal diseases and conceiving, besides other physical injuries in course of her struggle to resist the occurrence of rape. It is the victim alone who has to bear the cost of the medicine, besides bearing the physical pain and mental agony. Needless to say, the hospitals lack physicians with special training in handling physical and emotional complications which rape victims are exposed to. Furthermore, the hospitals are not adequately equipped to treat even the physiological damages, what to speak of psychological treatment, facilities which are practically non-existent throughout the length and breadth of the country.

Social Victimization

The Victim's Plane : Rape has several far-reaching social implications both for the victim and for the society. Although it involves a limited number of men and women on the face of it, rape is basically a social problem (Rose, 1977) of great magnitude. On the victim's plane, the implications of rape depend upon whether she is married or unmarried, child or adult, having first sexual experience or not. In case the victim is unmarried, it creates problems in the settlement of her marriage if it becomes public. And, if she is married, there is a possibility of a breakdown of the marriage. Even if the marital life continues, or marriage of the unmarried happens to be solemnized, the sword of the fear of rape being divulged, and consequently being disturbed when it becomes known it always hang over the head of the rape victim. And, if per chance the rape remains concealed throughout, the psychological stress caused by sexual assault remains for ever.

The volume of physiological pain due to sexual assault differs to different age groups of the victims but psychological complications also vary. The severity of the impact of rape felt by the victims varies depending upon whether the victim is a child or a younger or older or an adult.

In all these, and many other ways rape has a chain of negative consequences in the life of the victim as a wife, a daughter, betrothed, a beloved, a child, parent, working women, and so on. In this manner, rape threatens the very existence of the victim in society.

The Social Plane : Rape is one instance where the atrocities of men against women become naked. Rape is in fact, not the rape of women but the rape of morality and the noble ideals of the society as a whole. The rapist remains a man and, at times, he is honoured in society, whereas, the victim of the same rapist is treated as a 'bad' women. In a male- dominated society, females are subjected to all sorts of subjection—physical, social and psychological. On the social plane, the threat of rape serves as a weapon in the hands of men and the society. They dominate to maintain social control of women by keeping them in a state of perpetual anxiety and by encouraging the self imposition of behaviour restriction in quest for safety (Riger and Gordon, 1981: 71-92). Rape is a crisis for the victim's family members and friends who also need emotional support (Krishna, 1988). If the rape is her first sexual experience, she may find herself quite confused about the relationship between sexuality, violence and humiliation. On attempting to leave her house and have an independent identity, her sense of adequacy is challenged by her feeling that she really cannot take care of herself. The women who have an ongoing sexual relationship may prefer not to disclose it to their man/men for fear of disrupting the relationship.

Rape of women is simultaneously a crisis for the victim's family. The very feeling that a woman of the family has been raped is a kind of shock, difficult for a family to bear. In such a crisis situation, the family members become emotionally disturbed. The prestige of the family in society is lowered, if such cases become public through the court or otherwise. In many cases, raped wives and daughters are not accepted by their husband or parents as the case may be. Many a time they are thrown in the lap of prostitution. Even if the victim survives the shock and remains in the family, social stigma labels her as a 'bad' woman throughout her lifetime.

Rape cannot be consummated until after force and prolonged resistance have been overcome. So if there is no outward evidence of resistance such as a black eye, bruise or scratch, there evidently was no resistance. Right from the beginning the victim is subjected to embarrassing queries which hinge on whether she had resisted sufficiently, and generally the accused gets the benefit of doubt. Rape is a personal crisis in the sense that the victim must deal with the impact and meaning of the event for herself. The stereotype that a woman should always attempt to prevent the rape through struggle leaves women in a double mind. If they do not struggle, they have a very hard time in court. If they do struggle, they run the risk of incurring even more injuries at the hands of the rapist.

Rape involves at least two major crisis for the women. The first is the rape itself. The second is her experience of going through the medical examination and the criminal justice system, with her appearance in court being the most painful part. While it is difficult to provide all the long-term psychological problems of the victim, some of the issues which seems to re-emerge at a later date are mistrust and avoidance of men, sexual disturbances, phobic hallucination, delusions, insomnia, terrifying dreams, anxiety and depression often precipitated by seemingly trivial events which symbolise the original trauma. Due to sexual repulsion and fear there is a decline of interest as well as withdrawal from one's partner. Post-rape adjustment is one of the most important psychological problems, which must be tackled properly in time by counselling. Psychologically problems are more severe when the rapist is a near relative. There is no law that can obliterate the trauma with which she must live.

What the Time Warrants?

The evidence of resistance required in case of rape victim is not required for dacoity, etc. The rape victim is subjected to embarassing questions. The social stigma attached to such cases is deterrent enough to reporting such cases. Under Rule 228(A) of the Act, the identity of the victim and all details of the rape itself will be kept in the strict confidence of the trying court. The entire legal proceedings will be held in camera.

Values and attitudes regarding rape should be changed. When a woman is raped, why should she be held guilty. The man has committed the rape on her person should be held responsible for the shameful act. Why should her identity remain secret? Why should she feel ashamed or guilt or both? Because she is the subordinate and less important sex? Because if she is unmarried, her chances of a good marriage may be lost for ever? Because she has lost her virginity if she is unmarried, and her chastity if she is married and these two things are held at the premium in a society where social values are decided by the males?

Thus, social attitudes towards the victims need to be changed. Thousand of girls and women are victimised by society for no fault of their own. Taking unfair advantages of the social stigma, the rapist lead the victim to prostitution. Forms and values of the society should not be misinterpreted for the cause of women. If a sexually active man is perceived as a sexually active man; a sexually active woman should also be perceived as a sexually active woman, not as a bad woman. The objective 'promiscuous' should not be applied only to her. The problems cannot be solved adequately unless we change the Victorian attitude of male dominated society.

The Proposals

Some of the suggestions which need proper attention are as follows:

1. The accused should not be permitted to question the victim regarding her character or previous sexual relations with any other person.
2. Rape victims should not be maltreated at the hands of the police whose assistance has been sought during the crisis. They should not be submitted to the countless questions about her own sexual mores and behaviour by the police investigator.
3. The victims should be thoroughly examined by an expert doctor and immediate cure of physical injuries, prevention of veneral disease, and prevention of pregnancy should be taken.
4. It is advisable that the burden of proof be shifted from the victim to the offender. Let him prove that he did not rape her. Let it not be the woman's burden to prove that she was criminally assaulted.
5. In recent years, cases of false accusation have come to notice for the purpose of blackmailing the accused to extort money or women offenders, during arrests and search, to level false charges of rape against policemen. Therefore, when women are involved in a crime she must be arrested and searched by a woman police officer. Report of rape victims should be recorded by women police officers and women investigators are to be appointed to investigate such cases.

6. The burden of stigma should not be attached within the victim and his family rather it should be shifted from the victim to the offender.
7. Victims of the rape deserve emotional support and sympathy by family members for post-rape adjustment rather than being disowned by them.
8. No woman should be arrested between sunset and sun rise.
9. Sex education should be imparted to adolescents and youths in order to prevent the crime against women. Parents should not feel ashamed in discussing sex with their children.

Our study of rape shows that the status of women continues to be low, and crime continues to be directed against them. Changes must be brought in the mind, heart and behaviour of men and women in the various compartments of our culture and in our social institutions so that the age-old sex anarchy of rape of women is removed.

15

Law, the Protector

Directive Principles of the Constitution

One of the directive principles of state policy prescribes that the state should direct its policy towards securing equal pay for equal work for both men and women. Although the directive principles are fundamental in the governance of the country and are to be applied in enacting legislation, they are not judicially enforceable. In this context, one of the provisions of the Constitution is of special significance.

After having laid down that the state shall not discriminate against any citizen on grounds of sex, among other things, it provides that nothing in this article shall prevent the state from making any special provision for women and children. So there is a Constitutional provision in India permitting the state to discriminate in favour of women, if such discrimination is found necessary.

Child marriage, especially of the female infant, was common; widow marriage was prohibited, even if she succeeded in escaping from the funeral pyre of her deceased husband where she was expected to be burnt alive; a divorce was generally looked down upon and her remarriage was socially disapproved.

If some of these attitudes still persist it is not because legislation has lagged behind, but because law has not succeeded in playing its role of social engineering and changing certain deeply-rooted social attitudes. During the last two decades a number of laws were adopted with a view to ensuring equality of status and opportunity for women. But it appears that in practice this equality eludes the Indian woman's grasp.

In what follows, an attempt is made to examine some of the more important legislation enacted by the Central legislature in India to ameliorate certain unhappy conditions in which women, particularly Hindu women, found themselves. Occasionally, there is talk about ameliorating the conditions of Muslim women, but political consideration stand in the way of doing anything substantial towards that end. Muslim personal laws are considered to be part of the religion of Islam and government generally considers it necessary not to interfere directly in matters regarded as religious.

With a view to preventing child marriages, especially the giving away of infant girls in marriage, the Child Marriage Restraint Act was passed in 1929 declaring it an offence for a man to marry a girl under fifteen years of age. Any person who performs a marriage where the bridegroom is below 18 years or the bride below 15 years commits an offence, as also parents or guardians of the bridegroom or the bride.

Socially Propelled Legislation

This socially motivated legislation has been made relatively ineffective by stating that a marriage celebrated in violation of the stipulation regarding age would nevertheless be valid. The same restrictions regarding marriageable age are found in the Hindu Marriage Act, 1955. There is a Dowry Prohibition Act also in the Indian statute book which prohibits the giving or taking dowry. But this again is ineffective in practice mainly because any dowry given may be construed as "presents" which are not prohibited by law if made at the time of marriage.

In the case of both these statutes the teeth of the legislation are practically blunted both by loopholes within the law and by the resistance of social structures and attitudes to change. Certain conservative section of the community regard child marriage a good, if not a proper, thing and would prefer to pay a fine rather than keep their infant sons and daughters unmarried.' A large number of young men and their parents consider dowry a legitimate stepping stone to higher rungs in the social ladder, and possibly a passport to domestic comfort if not happiness.

Two years before the adoption of the Hindu Marriage Act, which inter alia provided of divorce, the Special Marriage Act, 1954 was enacted. There is a provision in the Special Marriage Act for obtaining a decree of divorce by mutual consent, provided the parties have lived separately for a year and three years have elapsed since the date of marriage.

Apart from the common grounds on which either party to the marriage may obtain dissolution of a marriage performed or registered under the Act, the wife may sue the husband for divorce on the ground that he has committed rape, sodomy or bestiality. Persons married under the Act with the result that they would now be governed by its provisions.

Those who marry under the Act or whose marriages are registered under it are, in matters of inheritance, governed by the Indian Succession Act, 1925. When a man to whom the Indian Succession Act applies dies leaving a widow and lineal descendants, the widow is entitled to one third of the property of the deceased and the lineal descendants to two-thirds. Under the Act, in the case of Christians, a widow in the absence of lineal descendants will get the entire property of the husband, provided its value does not exceed Rs. 5,000.

If it does, she will receive Rs. 5,000 and a share in what remains along with the kindred of the deceased according to the specific rules laid down in the Act. Some persons, especially women, prefer to be married under the Special Marriage Act because of its beneficial provisions regarding divorce and interstate succession. We shall advert to this later.

It may be said in general that the right of a wife to obtain a divorce in India is much more restricted than that of the husband under customary law; however, in certain Hindu communities, as also among most tribal groups, it is possible for the husband and the wife to obtain divorce without resource course to court.

They are only required to follow some customary practice, like making a declaration before the elders of the community or the headman of the tribe that they no longer desire their marital relationship to continue.

It is well known that among Muslims, while the husband can unilaterally and without assigning any reason divorce his wife by pronouncing *talaq* (that is by uttering the words, "I divorce you") three times, the wife has to get a judicial pronouncement of divorce on specified grounds.

It is, however, possible for the wife to have the power of divorce delegated to her by the husband at the time of entering into the marriage contract. For instance, it may be stipulated that if he takes a second wife, she should have the option of repudiating her marriage. Such delegation is, however, uncommon. Considering the fact that the Constitution makes provision for equality of the sexes, it may be desirable to give judicial recognition to *fasaq* by means of which a Muslim wife may unilaterally repudiate her marriage. An opportunity for such recognition was lost when the Kerala High Court in 1975 ruled that the right of Muslim women to obtain divorce is exclusively governed by the Dissolution of Muslim Marriages Act, 1939 and that it is not permissible to go beyond it.

PROVISIONS OF DIVORCE

The divorce provisions of the Hindu Marriage Act, 1955 maintain equality of the sexes in the matter of grounds for divorce. The Act applies to Hindus, Buddhists, Jains and Sikhs. In the provisions of the Indian Divorce Act, which applies to Christians there is some discrimination between the sexes in the matter of grounds for divorce.

A single isolated act of adultery on the part of the wife is a valid ground for granting a divorce on the petition of the husband but, if a wife has to be successful in her petition for divorce, she has generally to prove against her husband not only adultery, but also an additional ground such as desertion or cruelty.

Commission of rape, sodomy or bestiality by the husband can also be ground for obtaining a decree of divorce. This Act was modeled after English enactments for matrimonial reliefs adopted about the middle of the last century. Over a hundred years later, the United kingdom prescribed by legislation a single valid ground for divorce, that is, irretrievable breakdown of marriage.

If in 1869 the idea was that Indian Christians would do well to follow in the footsteps of the British in obtaining matrimonial reliefs, is there any valid reason to assume that they should be governed by rules different from those applicable to the British after the passage of a century.

If irretrievable breakdown of marriage is made the only ground for judicial declaration of divorce applicable to all communities and religious groups in India there will be equality of treatment not only between men and women but also between various religious groups.

Perhaps one has to wait for the adoption of a uniform civil code for such unification of laws. In the meantime, the Indian Divorce Act could be amended making grounds for divorce identical for both men and women, preferably adopting the provision regarding irretrievable breakdown of marriage as the sole ground of divorce as laid down in the (British) Divorce Reform Act. 1969.

During the pendency of a suit under the Indian Divorce Act, a wife may apply for alimony and the court may grant an amount not exceeding one-fifth of the husband's average net income. While passing a decree for divorce or judicial separation, the court may order the husband to pay a lump sum or make periodical payments for life to the wife, taking into account her fortune, the means of the husband and the conduct of the parties.

There are similar provisions for the benefit of the wife in the Parsi Marriage and Divorce Act, 1936. The spirit of equality envisaged in the Constitution finds clear expression in the Hindu Marriage Act, 1955.

It makes provision for the grant of expenses of matrimonial suits and a monthly allowance for the support of either spouse during the pendency of legal proceedings, provided the spouse applying for the expenses and allowances has not sufficient income to support himself or herself.

The Act also has a provision for making an order for permanent alimony or maintenance in favour of either of the spouses. On remarriage the spouse loses his or her right to maintenance. Further, if the recipient of the alimony is the wife, she is required to remain chaste; if maintenance is granted to the husband, he is enjoined from having sexual relations with any other woman.

In spite of the provisions for divorce contained in the Act of 1955, it is not often that recourse is to them : this is because Hindu social values in general are opposed to the concept of divorce. As Kapadia puts it, "the principle of divorce is alien to the social pattern" with the result that "the norm accepted by law has not been accepted in practice". Whereas prior to 1955, divorce was considered absolute anathema by women of the higher castes, after the passing of the Act, it is the women of the upper classes and higher castes as well as the rich and educated in urban areas who petition the courts for divorce. Probably, the illiterate women in the rural areas do not even know that there are legal provisions for divorce apart from those enshrined in the customary law of certain communities or tribes.

Marriage under the Special Marriage Act has the effect of making the provisions of the Indian Succession Act applicable to the parties. These provisions were more beneficial to women, be they Hindus, Muslims Indian Christians of Pondicherry or Indian Christians in those areas of Kerala which formerly comprised the princely states of Travancore and Cochin, provided they were not governed by matrilineal custom.

Before the adoption of the Hindu succession Act in 1956, when a woman succeeded to the divided property of a deceased Hindu male, she took only a limited interest. A woman was denied her legal capacity in a Hindu joint family.

The Hindu Succession Act, 1956, which applies to Hindus, Buddhists, Jains and Sikhs determines their share on the basis of consanguinity or affinity without any discrimination on the ground of sex. It gives a woman full ownership in the property inherited or acquired by her.

The widow, the mother and the daughter now not only inherit property along with the son but also take an equal share with him. A Parsi woman takes only half the share that her brother gets in their father's property. A similar half share is the lot of Muslim women as well. Though the Indian Succession Act is generally applicable to Christians, there are various regions in the country where the Act is not applied.

There are also certain Christian Communities to which it not made applicable. Certain tribal Christian communities and those who follow matriliny are outside the purview of the Act. As the Act is not extended to the Union Territory of Pondicherry, Indian Christians in the territory are governed by traditional Hindu law (that is, Hindu law as it was in force in the region before certain changes were effected by the Indian Parliament in 1955 and 1956) in the matter of inheritance with all the disadvantages and disabilities which that law imposed on women.

In the erstwhile princely states of Travancore and Cochin, there are in operation local enactment relating to succession among Christians which appear to discriminate against women. Under the Travancore Christian Succession Regulation, 1916 the share of the widow in the estate of the husband is a life interest, terminable on her death or remarriage, except where she gets the whole estate in the absence of certain specified relatives of her deceased husband.

Christian Succession Act : Under the Cochin Christian Succession Act, 1921 the widow gets share equal to two-thirds of the share of a son if the deceased is survived by a son or lineal descendants of a son.

The Travancore Regulation seems to discriminate against daughters who can take only one-fourth of the value of the share of a son or Rs. 5,000 whichever is less. The Regulation does not apply to the small body of Indian Christians in the taluk of Neyyattinkara of the erstwhile princely state who follow Marumakkathayam (matrilineal descent).

The Roman Catholic Christians of the Latin rite and certain non-Catholic Christians living in a few southern taluks of Travancore follow their customary usage, and among them male and female heirs of an intestate share equally in his property. Under the Travancore Regulation, the maternal relatives are excluded from succeeding to the intestate if there are paternal relatives surviving him, whereas in the Cochin Act no maternal relatives are included among the heirs.

The areas where these two enactments are still in force are remarkable for a high female literacy rate and a large number of highly educated women. Nevertheless the fact remains that these women, if they happen to be Christians to whom these enactments apply, have a right to only a quarter of the share of a brother in the property of their deceased father. Would these educated women and their literate sisters think of reverting to matriliny which was once prevalent in these areas? At the moment they do not appear to be eager to effect any change.

The Hindu Minority and guardianship Act, 1956 also bestowed a few additional rights on Hindu women. It provides that though the father may appoint by will a guardian for his minor children, any such appointment will not take effect during the lifetime of the mother if she survives the father. It will take effect only on her death, provided she has not appointed a guardian by her own will.

A Hindu mother is entitled to act as the natural guardian of her minor children if the father ceases to be a Hindu or renounces the world by becoming a hermit or ascetic. The Hindu widow and the Hindu mother, entitled to act as natural guardians of their minor children, are empowered under the Act to appoint guardians for them by will.

In 1956 substantial changes were effected in the law of adoption applicable to Hindus. The Hindu Adoption and Maintenance Act, 1956 has invested the Hindu woman with certain rights of adoption which she had not enjoyed before. Previously an adoption could only be to a male but, under the Act, a woman is competent to adopt to herself a son or a daughter.

Again, under the Act, a married man cannot, except under certain special circumstances, make an adoption without the consent of his wife. Under the earlier law her consent was immaterial but under the present law, her consent is unnecessary only when she has renounced the world or has ceased to be Hindu or has been judicially declared to be of unsound mind. A Hindu woman who is not of unsound mind and who is not a minor is now competent to adopt a son as well as a daughter, provided she is a spinster, divorcee, or widow or one whose husband has finally renounced the world or has ceased to be a Hindu or has been judicially declared to be of unsound mind.

In general, during coverture it is only the husband who can adopt. If the woman wants to adopt a son, she should not have a Hindu son, son's son or son's son's son living at the time of the adoption should be younger to her by at least twenty one years.

If she intends adopting a daughter, an essential condition is that she should have no Hindu daughter or son's daughter living at the time of the adoption. Corresponding requirements have also to be observed by the man who wishes to adopt a son or daughter.

The wife has a right to maintenance for life. She may not forfeit this right even if she lives separately from her husband on certain specific grounds such as the husband's cruelty, desertion, keeping a concubine or having another wife, his suffering from a virulent form of leprosy, his conversion to another religion or any other cause justifying her living separately. She, however, forfeits her right to maintenance if she is unchaste or ceases to be a Hindu.

FACTORIES ACT

The Factories Act, 1948 empowers state governments to prohibit employment of women in dangerous operations. A few enactments lay down the general rule that women should not be permitted to work between 7 p.m and 6 a.m., but this rule is relaxable in certain circumstances. Provisions for maternity benefits for women have been incorporated in the Employees State Insurance Act, 1948 and a number of state enactments.

While maternity benefit in coal mines is governed by the Maternity Benefit Act, 1961 women workers in factories and plantations are entitled to maternity leave according to the maternity benefit enactments of different states. Both the Factories Act, 1948 and the Plantations Labour Act, 1951 make it obligatory for factories and plantation employing not less than fifty women to provide creches.

In spite of these statutory benefits and the Constitutional directive regarding equal pay for equal work, women agricultural labourers generally get 10 to 60 per cent less in wages than men for the same work.

It is not infrequent that, when the husband becomes a "bonded labourer" for the landlord or the labour contractor, the wife also becomes similarly "bonded" with the not unusual result that she is made vulnerable to exploitation including trafficking for immoral purposes.

Only 13 per cent of Indian women, according to the 1971 Census, may be regarded as workers, i.e. those who are engaged in some form of economic activity. About 80 per cent of these working women are engaged in agriculture. Only 12 per cent of the total employees in central and state administrative services and public sector undertakings are women. This may not be unrelated to their education or lack of it.

Only 18 per cent of Indian women are literate. Though one of the directive principles of the Constitution requires the state to provide free and compulsory education for all children under 14 years of age the directive is generally followed with callous disregard of its spirits and its significance for the country. Coupled with the general apathy to women's education, this indifference to put in practice a Constitutional directive results in greater social and economic deprivation for girls than for boys.

At the primary school level while 97 out of 100 boys attend school, the corresponding figure for girls is 62. Further, out of 100 girls who enter the first grade only 26 go up to the fifth grade. It is only about 2 per cent of women who are able to benefit by the opportunities provided for higher education. In 1971-72, 36 girls only were under instruction at various levels of education compared to a hundred boys. If in 1971 about 18 per cent of women were literate, this may appear to compare well with only 8 per cent literacy for women on the eve of independence in 1947, but an increase of 10 per cent in the not too short span of about three decades is hardly something that should make us complacent.

There are certain other types of social legislation which seek to protect interests and benefits that are of special concern to women. The Suppression of Immoral Traffic in Women and Girls Act. 1956, as its title indicates, is intended to protect helpless women and girls from a typical mode of exploitation not altogether unknown in the country.

The same year saw the enactment of another piece of social legislation: the Women's and Children's institutions (Licensing) Act, 1956. This was later on superseded by the Orphanages and Other Charitable Homes (Supervision and Control) Act, 1960.

The object of the enactment was to regulate the activities of these institutions and to prescribe a proper standard to which the treatment and the training of the inmates should conform. Such a measure was found necessary because, while there are many good and properly-managed charitable institutions, there are many others run with the objective of exploitation as their main and sustaining inspiration.

The Medical Termination of Pregnancy Act, 1971 may also be mentioned in the context of social legislation relative to women. The enactment seeks, among other things, to protect women's interests.

It has a few provisions which, it is clear, were enacted with the sufferings of women in the legislator's mind. It provides that a pregnancy may be terminated where the length of the pregnancy does not exceed twenty weeks, if two medical practitioners are of the opinion that the continuance of the pregnancy would involve a risk to the life of the pregnant woman or of grave injury to her physical or mental health.

Two explanations are offered in the enactment itself of what constitutes grave injury to the mental health of the pregnant woman. The first explanation reads: when any pregnancy is alleged by the pregnant woman to have been caused by rape, the anguish caused by such pregnancy shall be presumed to constitute a grave injury to the mental health of the pregnant woman.

In this case the "anguish" is perhaps palpable. The second explanation is more intriguing in that "anguish" is given an extended application. It states:

Where a pregnancy occurs as a result of failure of any device or method used by any married woman or her husband for the purpose of limiting the number of children, the anguish caused by such unwanted pregnancy may be presumed to constitute a grave injury to the mental health of the pregnant woman. Though the promotional slant of the government's family planning programme may be perceptible in this explanation, it is evident that Parliament cannot be blamed for any lack of solicitude for the largest minority in the country.

Another Provision of the Act : This solicitude may be even more evident in another provision of the Act which stipulates that in determining whether the continuance of a pregnancy would involve grave risk to the health of a pregnant woman, account may be taken of her actual or reasonably foreseeable environment. This enactment has been hailed as "a major landmark in India's social legislation", and "a far-reaching measure assuring the women of India freedom from undesirable and unwanted pregnancies.

From a study of the ameliorative legal provisions relating to women and the actual situation in which they find themselves, it is clear that something more than legislation is required. Perhaps that first thing to be attempted is to make women aware of their rights, however this is done. It is also necessary to change the attitudes of both men and women, of society in general, to social objectives sought to be achieved by legislation. A radical change in the attitudes of women induced by an awareness of their rights, which are constitutionally guaranteed and legally protected will be the first step in the complex process of transforming the social structure so that women may enjoy full equality with men in every sphere of life.

Suggestions of the Convention on the Elimination of all Forms of Discrimination against Women : Noting that the Charter of the United Nations reaffirms faith in fundamental human rights, in the dignity and worth of the human person and in the equal rights of men and women.

Noting that the Universal Declaration of Human Rights affirms the principle of the inadmissibility of discrimination and proclaims that all human beings are born free and equal in dignity and rights and that everyone is entitled to all the rights and freedoms set forth therein, without distinction of any kind including distinction based on sex.

Noting that the States Parties to the International Covenants of Human Rights have the obligation to ensure the equal rights of men and women to enjoy all economic, social cultural, civil and political rights.

Considering the international conventions concluded under the auspices of the United Nations and the specialized agencies promoting equality of rights of men and women.

Noting also the resolutions, declarations and recommendations adopted by the United Nations and the specialized agencies promoting equality of rights of men and women.

Concerned, however, that despite these various instruments, extensive discrimination against women continues to exist.

Recalling that discrimination against women violates the principles of equality of rights and respect for human dignity, is an obstacle to the participation of women, on equal terms with men, in the political, social, economic and cultural life of their countries, hampers the growth of the prosperity of society and the family and makes more difficult the full development of the potentialities of women in the service of their countries and of humanity. Concerned that in situations of poverty women have the least access to food, health, education, training and opportunities for employment and other needs.

Convinced that the establishment of the new international economic order based on equity and justice will contribute significantly towards the promotion of equality between men and women.

Emphasizing that the eradication of apartheid, all forms of racism, racial discrimination, colonialism, neo-colonialism, aggression, foreign occupation and domination and interference in the internal affairs of States is essential to the full enjoyment of the rights of men and women.

Affirming that the strengthening of international peace and security, the relaxation of international tension, mutual cooperation among all States irrespective of their social and economic systems, general and complete disarmament, in particular nuclear disarmament under strict and effective international control, the affirmation of the principles of justice, equality and mutual benefit in relations, among countries and the realization of the right of peoples under alien and colonial domination and foreign occupation to self-determination and independence, as well as respect for national sovereignty and territorial integrity, will promote social progress and development and as a consequence, will contribute to the attainment of full equality between men and women.

Convinced that the full and complete development of a country, the welfare of the world and the cause of peace require the maximum participation of women of equal terms with men in all fields.

Bearing in mind the great contribution of women to the welfare of the family and to the development of society, so far not fully recognized, the social significance of maternity and the role of both parents in the family and in the upbringing of children, and aware that the role of women in procreation should not be a basis for discrimination but that the upbringing of children requires a sharing of responsibility between men and women and society as a whole.

Aware that a change in the traditional role of men as well as the role of women in society and in the family is needed to achieve full equality between men and women.

Principle Implementation

Determined to implement the principles set forth in the Declaration on the Elimination of Discrimination against Women and, for that purpose, to adopt the measures required for the elimination of such discrimination in all its forms and manifestations, Have agreed on the following :

Article I : For the purposes of the present Convention, the term "discrimination against women" shall mean any distinction, exclusion or restriction made on the basis of sex which has the effect or purpose of impairing or nullifying the recognition, enjoyment or exercise by women, irrespective of their marital status, on a basis of equality of men and women, of human rights and fundamental freedoms in the political, economic, social, cultural, civil or any other field.

Article 2 : States Parties condemn discrimination against women in all its forms, agree to pursue by all appropriate means and without delay a policy of eliminating discrimination against women and, to this end, undertake:

(a) To embody the principle of the equality of men and women in their national constitutions or other appropriate legislation if not yet incorporated therein and to ensure, through law and other appropriate means, the practical realization of this principle;

(b) To adopt appropriate legislative and other measures, including sanctions where appropriate, prohibiting all discrimination against women;

(c) To establish legal protection of the rights of women on an equal basis with men and to ensure through competent national tribunals and other public institutions the effective protection of women against any act of discrimination;

(d) To refrain from engaging in any act or practice of discrimination against women and to ensure that public authorities and institutions shall act in conformity with this obligation;

(e) To take all appropriate measures to eliminate discrimination against women by any person, organization or enterprise;

(f) To take all appropriate measures, including legislation, to modify or abolish existing laws, regulations, customs and practices which constitute discrimination against women;

(g) To repeal all national penal provisions which constitute discrimination against women.

Article 3 : States Parties shall take in all fields, in particular in the political, social, economic and cultural fields, all appropriate measures, including legislation, to ensure the full development and advancement of women, for the purpose of guaranteeing them the exercise and enjoyment of human rights and fundamental freedoms on a basis of equality with men.

Article 4

1. Adoption by States Parties of temporary special measures aimed at accelerating de facto equality between men and women shall not be considered discrimination as defined in the present Convention, but shall in no way entail as

a consequence, the maintenance of unequal or separate standards; these measures shall be discontinued when the objectives of equality of opportunity and treatment have been achieved.

2. Adoption by States Parties of special measures, including those measures contained in the present Convention, aimed at protecting maternity shall not be considered discriminatory.

Article 5 : States Parties shall take all appropriate measures:

(a) To modify the social and cultural patterns of conduct of men and women, with a view to achieving the elimination of prejudices and customary and all other practices which are based on the idea of the inferiority or the superiority of either of the sexes or on stereotyped roles for men and women;

(b) To ensure that family education includes a proper understanding of maternity as a social function and the recognition of the common responsibility of men and women in the upbringing and development of their children, it being understood that the interest of the children is the primordial consideration in all cases.

Article 6 : States Parties shall take all appropriate measures, including legislation, to suppress all forms of traffic in women and exploitation of prostitution of women.

Article 7 : States Parties shall take all appropriate measures to eliminate discrimination against women in the political and public life of the country and, in particular, shall ensure to women, on equal terms with men, the right:

(a) To vote in all elections and public referenda and to be eligible for election to all publicly elected bodies;

(b) To participate in the formulation of government policy and the implementation thereof and to hold public office and perform all public functions at all levels of government;

(c) To participate in non-governmental organizations and associations concerned with the public and political life of the country.

Article 8 : States Parties shall take all appropriate measures to ensure to women, on equal terms with men and without any discrimination, the opportunity to represent their Governments at the international level and to participate in the work of international organizations.

Article 9

1. States Parties shall grant women equal rights with men to acquire, change or retain their nationality. They shall ensure in particular that neither marriage to an alien nor change of nationality by the husband during marriage shall automatically change the nationality of the wife, render her stateless or force upon her the nationality of the husband.
2. States Parties shall grant women equal rights with men with respect to the nationality of their children.

Article 10 : States Parties shall take all appropriate measures to eliminate discrimination against women in order to ensure to them equal rights with men in the field of education and in particular to ensure, on a basis of equality of men and women :

(a) The same conditions for career and vocational guidance, for access to studies and for the achievement of diplomas in educational establishments of all categories in rural as well as in urban areas; this equality shall be ensured in pre-school, general, technical, professional and higher technical education, as well as in all types of vocational training;

(b) Access to the same curricula, the same examinations,

teaching staff with qualifications of the same standard and school premises and equipment of the same quality;

(c) The elimination of any stereotyped concept of the roles of men and women at all levels and in all forms of education by encouraging coeducation and other types of education which will help to achieve this aim and, in particular, by the revision of textbooks and school programmes and the adaptation of teaching methods;

(d) The same opportunities to benefit from scholarships and other study grants;

(e) The same opportunities for access to programmes of continuing education, including adult and functional literacy programmes, particularly those aimed at reducing, at the earliest possible time, any gap in education existing between men and women;

(f) The reduction of female student dropout rates and the organization of programmes for girls and women who have left school prematurely;

(g) The same opportunities to participate actively in sports and physical education;

(h) Access to specific educational information to help to ensure the health and well-being of families, including information and advice on family planning.

Article 11

1. States Parties shall take all appropriate measures to eliminate discrimination against women in the field of employment in order to ensure, on a basis of equality of men and women the same rights in particular;

   (a) The right to work as a right of all human beings.

   (b) The right to the same employment opportunities, including the application of the same criteria for selection in matters of employment;

(c) The right to free choice of profession and employment, the right to promotion, job security and all benefits and conditions of service and the right to receive vocational training and retraining, including apprenticeships, advanced vocational training and recurrent training;

(d) The right to equal remuneration, including benefits, and to equal treatment in respect of work of equal value, as well as equality of treatment in the evaluation of the quality of work;

(e) The right to social security, particularly in cases of retirement, unemployment, sickness, invalidity and old age and other incapacity to work, as well as right to paid leave;

(f) The right to protection of health and to safety in working conditions, including the safeguarding of the function of reproduction.

2. In order to prevent discrimination against women on the grounds of marriage or maternity and to ensure their effective right to work, States Parties shall take appropriate measures:

(a) To prohibit, subject to the imposition of sanctions, dismissal on the grounds of pregnancy or of maternity leave and discrimination in dismissals on the basis of marital status;

(b) To introduce maternity leave with pay or with comparable social benefits without loss of former employment, seniority or social allowances;

(c) To encourage the provision of the necessary supporting social services to enable parents to combine family obligations with work responsibilities and participation in public life, in particular through promoting the establishment and development of a network of child-care facilities;

(d) To provide special protection to women during pregnancy in types of work proved to be harmful to them.

3. Protective legislation relating to matters covered in this Article shall be reviewed periodically in the light of scientific and technological knowledge and shall be revised, repealed or extended as necessary.

Article 12

1. States Parties shall take all appropriate measures to eliminate discrimination against women in the field of health care in order to ensure, on a basis of equality of men and women, access to health care services, including those related to family planning.
2. Notwithstanding the provisions of paragraph 1 of this Article, States Parties shall ensure to women appropriate services in connection with pregnancy, confinement and the post-natal period, granting free services where necessary, as well as adequate nutrition during pregnancy and lactation.

Article 13 : States Parties shall take all appropriate measures to eliminate discrimination against women in other areas of economic and social life in order to ensure, on a basis of equality of men and women, the same rights, in particular:

(a) The right to family benefits;

(b) The right to bank loans, mortgages and other forms of financial credit;

(c) The right to participate in recreational activities, sports and all aspects of cultural life.

Article 14

1. States Parties shall take into account the particular problems faced by rural women and the significant roles which rural

women play in the economic survival of their families, including their work in the non-monetized sectors of the economy, and shall take all appropriate measures to ensure the application of the provisions of the present convention to women in rural areas.

2. States Parties shall take all appropriate measures to eliminate discrimination against women in rural areas in order to ensure, on a basis of equality of men and women, that they participate in and benefit from rural development and, in particular, shall ensure to such women the right:

   (a) To participate in the elaboration and implementation of development planning at all levels;

   (b) To have access to adequate health care facilities, including information, counselling and services in family planning;

   (c) To benefit directly from social security programmes;

   (d) To obtain all types of training and education, formal and non-formal, including that relating to functional literacy, as well as, inter alia, the benefit of all community and extension services, in order to increase their technical proficiency;

   (e) To organize self-help groups and cooperatives in order to obtain equal access to economic opportunities through employment or self-employment;

   (f) To participate in all community activities;

   (g) To have access to agricultural credit and loans, marketing facilities, appropriate technology and equal treatment in land and agrarian reform as well as in land resettlement schemes;

   (h) To enjoy adequate living conditions, particularly in relation to housing, sanitation, electricity and water supply, transport and communications.

Article 15

1. States Parties shall accord to women equality with men before the law.
2. States Parties shall accord to women, in civil matters, a legal capacity identical to that of men and the same opportunities to exercise that capacity. In particular, they shall give women equal rights to conclude contracts and to administer property and shall treat them equally in all stages of procedure in courts and tribunals.
3. States Parties agree that all contracts and all other private instruments of any kind with a legal effect which is directed at restricting the legal capacity of women shall be deemed null and void.
4. States Parties shall accord to men and women the same rights with regard to the law relating to the movement of persons and the freedom to choose their residence and domicile.

Article 16

1. States Parties shall take all appropriate measures to eliminate discrimination against women in all matters relating to marriage and family relations and in particular shall ensure, on a basis of equality of men and women:
   - (a) The same right to enter into marriage;
   - (b) The same right freely to choose a spouse and to enter into marriage only with their free and full consent;
   - (c) The same rights and responsibilities during marriage and at its dissolution;
   - (d) The same rights and responsibilities as parents, irrespective of their marital status, in matters relating to their children; in all cases the interests of the children shall be paramount;

(e) The same rights to decide freely and responsibly on the number and spacing of their children and to have access to the information, education and means to enable them to exercise these rights;

(f) The same rights and responsibilities with regard to guardianship, wardship, trusteeship and adoption of children, or similar institutions where these concepts exist in national legislation; in all cases the interests of the children shall be paramount;

(g) The same personal rights as husband and wife, including the right to choose a family name, a profession and an occupation;

(h) The same rights for both spouses in respect of the ownership, acquisition, management, administration, enjoyment and disposition of property, whether free of charge or for a valuable consideration.

2. The betrothal and the marriage of a child shall have no legal effect, and all necessary action, including legislation, shall be taken to specify a minimum age for marriage and to make the registration of marriages in an official registry compulsory.

Article 17

1. For the purpose of considering the progress made in the implementation of the present Convention, there shall be established a Committee on the Elimination of Discrimination against Women (hereinafter referred to as the Committee) consisting, at the time of entry into force of the Convention, of eighteen and, after ratification of or accession to the Convention by the thirty-fifth State Party, of twenty-three experts of high moral standing and competence in the field covered by the Convention. The experts shall be elected by States Parties from among their nationals and shall serve in their personal capacity,

consideration being given to equitable geographical distribution and to the representation of the different forms of civilization as well as the principal legal systems.

2. The members of the Committee shall be elected by secret ballot from a list of persons nominated by States Parties. Each Party may nominate one person from among its own nationals.

3. The initial election shall be held six months after the date of the entry into force of the present Convention. At least three months before the date of each election, the Secretary General of the United Nations shall address a letter to the States Parties inviting them to submit their nominations within two months. The Secretary General shall prepare a list in alphabetical order of all persons thus nominated, indicating the States Parties which have nominated them, and shall submit it to the States Parties.

4. Elections of the members of the Committee shall be held at a meeting of States Parties convened by the Secretary General at United Nations Headquarters. At that meeting, for which two thirds of the States Parties shall constitute a quorum, the persons elected to the Committee shall be those nominees who obtain the largest number of votes and an absolute majority of the votes of the representatives of States Parties present and voting.

5. The members of the Committee shall be elected for a term of four years. However, the terms of nine of the members elected at the first election shall expire at the end of two years; immediately after the first election the names of these nine members shall be chosen by lot by the Chairman of the Committee.

6. The election of the five additional members of the Committee shall be held in accordance with the provisions of paragraphs 2,3 and 4 of this article, following the thirty-

fifth ratification or accession. The terms of two of the additional members elected on this occasion shall expire at the end of two years, the names of these two members having been chosen by lot by the Chairman of the Committee.

7. For the filling of casual vacancies, the State Party whose expert has ceased to function as a member of the Committee shall appoint another expert from among its nationals, subject to the approval of the Committee.

8. The members of the Committee shall, with the approval of the General Assembly, receive emoluments from United Nations resources on such terms and conditions as the Assembly may decide, having regard to the importance of the Committee's responsibilities.

9. The Secretary-General of the United Nations shall provide the necessary staff and facilities for the effective performance of the functions of the Committee under the present Convention.

Article 18

1. States Parties undertake to submit to the Secretary General of the United Nations, for consideration by the Committee, a report on the legislative, judicial, administrative or other measures which they have adopted to give effect to the provisions of the present Convention and on the progress made in this respect:

   (a) Within one year after the entry into force for the State concerned;

   (b) Thereafter at least every four years and further whenever the Committee so requests.

2. Reports may indicate factors and difficulties affecting the degree of fulfilment of obligations under the present Convention.

Article 19

1. The Committee shall adopt its own rules of procedure.
2. The Committee shall elect its officers for a term of two years.

Article 20

1. The Committee shall normally meet for a period of not more than two weeks annually in order to consider the reports submitted in accordance with article 15 of the present Convention.
2. The meetings of the Committee shall normally be held at United Nations Headquarters or at any other convenient place as determined by the Committee.

Article 21

1. The Committee shall, through the Economic and Social Council, report annually to the General Assembly of the United Nations on its activities and may make suggestions and general recommendations based on the examination of reports and information received from the States Parties. Such suggestions and general recommendations shall be included in the report of the Committee together with comments, if any, from States Parties.
2. The Secretary General of the United Nations shall transmit the reports of the Committee to the Commission on the status of Women for its information.

Article 22 : The specialized agencies shall be entitled to be represented at the consideration of the implementation of such provisions of the present Convention as fall within the scope of their activities.

The committee may invite the specialized agencies to submit reports on the implementation of the Convention in areas falling within the scope of their activities.

Article 23 : Nothing in the present Convention shall

affect any provisions that are more conducive to the achievement of equality between men and women which may be contained:

(a) In the legislation of a State Party; or

(b) In any other international convention, treaty or agreement in force for that State.

Article 24 : States Parties undertake to adopt all necessary measures at the national level aimed at achieving the full realization of the rights recognized in the present Convention.

Article 25

1. The present Convention shall be open for signature by all States.
2. The Secretary-General of the United Nations is designated as the depositary of the present Convention.
3. The present Convention is subject to ratification. Instruments of ratification shall be deposited with the Secretary-General of the United Nations.
4. The present Convention shall be open to accession by all States. Accession shall be effected by the deposit of an instrument of accession with the Secretary General of the United Nations.

Article 26

1. A request for the revision of the present Convention may be made at any time by any State Party by means of a notification in writing addressed to the Secretary-General of the United Nations.
2. The General Assembly of the United Nations shall decide upon the steps, if any, to be taken in respect of such a request.

Article 27

1. The present Convention shall enter into force on the

thirtieth day after the deposit with the Secretary General of the United Nations of the twentieth instrument of ratification or accession.

2. For each State ratifying the present Convention or acceding to it after the deposit of the twentieth instrument of ratification or accession, the Convention shall enter into force on the thirtieth day after the date of the deposit of its own instrument of ratification or accession.

Article 28

1. The Secretary General of the United Nations shall receive and circulate to all States the text of reservations made by States at the time of ratification or accession.
2. A reservation incompatible with the object and purpose of the present Convention shall not be permitted.
3. Reservations may be withdrawn at any time by notification to this effect addressed to the Secretary-General of the United Nations, who shall then inform all States thereof. Such notification shall take effect on the date on which it is received.

Article 29

1. Any dispute between two or more States Parties concerning the interpretation or application of the present Convention which is not settled by negotiation shall, at the request of one of them, be submitted to arbitration. If within six months from the date of the request for arbitration, the Parties are unable to agree on the organization of the arbitration, any one of those parties may refer the dispute to the International Court of Justice by request in conformity with the statute of the Court.
2. Each State Party may at the time of signature or ratification of the present Convention or accession thereto declare that it does not consider itself bound by paragraph 1 of

this article. The other States Parties shall not be bound by that paragraph with respect to any State Party which has made such a reservation.

3. Any State Party which has made a reservation in accordance with paragraph 2 of this article may at any time withdraw that reservation by notification to the Secretary General of the United Nations.

Article 30 : The present Convention, the Arabic, Chinese. English, French, Russian and Spanish texts of which are equally authentic, shall be deposited with the Secretary-General of the United Nations.

In Witness Whereof the undersigned, duly authorized, have signed the present Convention.

Extirpating Discrimination

The General Assembly : Considering that the peoples of the United Nations have, in the Charter, reaffirmed their faith in fundamental human rights, in the dignity and worth of the human person and in the equal rights of men and women.

Considering that the Universal Declaration on Human Rights asserts the principle of non-discrimination and proclaims that all human beings are born free and equal in dignity and rights and that everyone is entitled to all the rights and freedoms set forth therein without distinction of any kind, including any distinction as to sex.

Taking into account the resolutions, declarations, conventions and recommendations of the United Nations and the specialized agencies designed to eliminate all forms of discrimination and to promote equal rights for men and women.

Concerned that, despite the Charter of the United Nations the Universal Declaration of Human Rights, the International Covenants on Human Rights and other instruments of the United Nations and the specialized agencies and despite the progress made in the matter of equality of rights, there continues to exist considerable discrimination against women.

Considering that discrimination against women is incompatible with human dignity and with the welfare of the family and of society, prevents their participation, on equal terms with men, in the political, social, economic and cultural life of their countries and is an obstacle to the full development of the potentialities of women in the service of their countries and of humanity.

Bearing in mind the great contribution made by women to social, political, economic and cultural life and the part they play in the family and particularly in the rearing of children.

Convinced that the full and complete development of a country, the welfare of the world and the cause of peace require the maximum participation of women as well as men in all fields.

Considering that it is necessary to ensure the universal recognition in law and in fact of the principle of equality of men and women, Solemnly proclaims this declaration:

Article 1 : Discrimination against women, denying or limiting as it does their equality of rights with men, is fundamentally unjust and constitutes an offence against human dignity.

Article 2 : All appropriate measures shall be taken to abolish existing laws, customs, regulations and practices which are discriminatory against women, and to establish adequate legal protection for equal rights of men and women, in particular:

(a) The principle of equality of rights shall be embodied in the constitution or otherwise guaranteed by law;

(b) The international instruments of the United Nations and the specialized agencies relating to the elimination of discrimination against women shall be ratified or acceded to and fully implemented as soon as practicable.

Article 3 : All appropriate measures shall be taken to educate public opinion and to direct national aspirations towards the eradication of prejudice and the abolition of customary and all other practices which are based on the idea of the inferiority of women.

Article 4 : All appropriate measures shall be taken to ensure to women on equal terms with men, without any discrimination:

(a) The right to vote in all elections and be eligible for election to all publicly elected oodles;

(b) The right to vote in all public referenda;

(c) The right to hold public office and to exercise all public functions.

Such rights shall be guaranteed by legislation.

Article 5 : Women shall have the same rights as men to acquire, change or retain their nationality. Marriage to an alien shall not automatically affect the nationality of the wife either by rendering her stateless or by forcing upon her the nationality of her husband.

Article 6

1. Without prejudice to the safeguarding of the unity and the harmony of the family, which remains the basic unit of any society, all appropriate measures, particularly legislative measures, shall be taken to ensure to women, married, or unmarried, equal rights with men in field of civil law, and in particular:

   (a) The right to acquire, administer, enjoy, dispose of and inherit property, including property acquired during marriage;

   (b) The right to equality in legal capacity and the exercise thereof;

   (c) The same rights as men and with regard to the law on the movement of persons.

2. All appropriate measures shall be taken to ensure the principle of equality of status of the husband and wife, and in particular:

    (a) Women shall have the same right as men to free choice of a spouse and to enter into marriage only with their free and full consent;

    (b) Women shall have equal rights with men during marriage and at its dissolution. In all cases the interest of the children shall be paramount;

    (c) Parents shall have equal rights and duties in matters relating to their children. In all cases the interest of the children shall be paramount.

3. Child marriage and the betrothal of young girls before puberty shall be prohibited, and effective action, including legislation, shall be taken to specify a minimum age for marriage and to make the registration of marriages in an official registry compulsory.

Article 7 : All provisions of penal codes which constitute discrimination against women shall be repealed.

Article 8 : All appropriate measures, including legislation, shall be taken to combat all forms of traffic in women and exploitation of prostitution of women.

Article 9 : All appropriate measures shall be taken to ensure to girls and women, married or unmarried, equal rights with men in education at all levels, and in particular:

(a) Equal conditions of access to, and study in educational institutions of all types, including universities and vocational, technical and professional schools;

(b) The same choice of curricula, the same examinations, teaching staff with qualifications of the same standard, and school premises and equipment of the same quality, whether the institutions are co-educational or not;

(c) Equal opportunities to benefit from scholarships and other study grants;

(d) Equal opportunities for access to programmes of continuing education, including adult literacy programmes;

(e) Access to educational information to help in ensuring the health and well-being of families.

Article 10

1. All appropriate measures shall be taken to ensure to women, married or unmarried, equal rights with men in the field of economic and social life, and in particular:

   (a) The right, without discrimination on grounds of marital status or any other grounds, to receive vocational training, to work, to free choice of profession and employment, and to professional and vocational advancement;

   (b) The right to equal remuneration with men and to equality of treatment in respect of work of equal value;

   (c) The right to leave with pay, retirement privileges and provision for security in respect of unemployment, sickness, old age or other incapacity to work;

   (d) The right to receive family allowances on equal terms with men.

2. In order to prevent discrimination against women on account of marriage or maternity and to ensure their effective right to work, measures shall be taken to prevent their dismissal in the event of marriage or maternity and to provide paid maternity leave, with the guarantee of returning to former employment, and to provide the necessary social services, including child-care facilities.

Nod for Marriage

Recommendation on consent to marriage, minimum age for marriage and registration of marriages.

The General Assembly, recognizing that the family group should be strengthened because it is the basic unit of every society, and that men and women of full age have the right to marry and to found a family, that they are entitled to equal rights as to marriage and that marriage shall be entered into only with the free and full consent of the intending spouses, in accordance with the provisions of article 16 of the Universal Declaration of Human Rights, Recalling its resolution 843(IX) of 17 December 1954.

Recalling further article 2 of the Supplementary Convention on the Abolition of Slavery, the Slave Trade, and Institutions and Practices Similar to Slavery of 1956, which makes certain provisions concerning the age of marriage, consent to marriage and registration of marriages.

Recalling also that Article 13, paragraph lb. of the Charter of the United Nations provides that the General Assembly shall make recommendations for the purpose of assisting in the realization of human rights and fundamental freedoms for all without distinction as to race, sex, language or religion.

Recalling likewise that, under Article 64 of the Charter, the Economic and Social Council may make arrangements with the Members of the United Nations to obtain reports on the steps taken to give effect to its own recommendations and to recommendations on matters falling within its competence made by the General Assembly.

Recommends, that, where not already provided by existing legislative or other measures, each Member State should take the necessary steps, in accordance with its constitutional processes and its traditional and religious practices, to adopt such legislative or other measures as may be appropriate to give effect to the following principles:

Principle I

(a) No marriage shall be legally entered into without the full and free consent of both the parties, such consent to be expressed by them in person, after due publicity and in the presence of the authority competent to solemnize the marriage and of witnesses, as prescribed by law,

(b) Marriage by proxy shall be permitted only when the competent authorities are satisfied that each party has, before a competent authority and in such manner as may be prescribed by law, fully and freely expressed consent before witnesses and not withdrawn such consent.

Principle II : Member States shall take legislative action to specify a minimum age for marriage, which in any case shall not be less than fifteen years of age; no marriage shall be legally entered into by any person under this age, except where a competent authority has granted a dispensation as to age, for serious reasons, in the interest of the intending spouses.

Principle III

1. All marriages shall be registered in an appropriate official register by the competent authority.
2. Recommends that each Member State should bring the Recommendations on Consent to Marriage, Minimum Age for Marriage and Registration of Marriages contained in the present resolution before the authorities competent to enact legislation or to take other action at the earliest practicable moment and, if possible, not later than eighteen months after the adoption of the Recommendation;
3. Recommends that Member States should inform the Secretary General, as soon as possible after the action referred to in paragraph 2 above, of the measures taken under the present Recommendation to bring it before the competent authority or authorities, with particulars

regarding the authority or authorities considered as competent;

4. Recommends further that Member States should report to the Secretary General at the end of three years, and thereafter at intervals of five years, on their law and practice with regard to the matters dealt within the present Recommendation, showing the extent to which effect has been given or is proposed to be given to the provisions of the Recommendation and such modifications as have been found or may be found necessary in adapting or applying it;
5. Requests the Secretary General to prepare for the Commission on the Status of Women a document containing the reports received from Governments concerning methods of implementing the three basic principles of the present Recommendation;
6. Invites the Commission on the Status of Women to examine the reports received from Member States pursuant to the present Recommendation and to report thereon to the Economic and Social Council with such recommendations as it may deem fitting.

Bibliography

Adrienne, R. : *Of Woman Born— Motherhood as Experience,* Norton and Roman Company, New York, 1976.

Ahamed, S. : *Women in Profession — a Comparative Study of Hindu and Muslim Women*, Royal Publishers, New Delhi, 1996.

Aileen, D. R. : *The Hindu Family in its Urban Society*, Univ. of Toronto Press, Toronto, 1961.

Altekar, A.S. : *The Position of Women in Hindu Civilization*, Motilal Banarsidas, Varanasi, 1962.

Andrea, M. Singh and Alfred, de Souza : *The Position of Women in Migrant Bastis in Delhi,* New Delhi, 1976.

Anis, Ahmad : *Woman and Social Justice*, Royal Publishers, New Delhi, 1997.

Anita, A. : *Indian Women*, Gyan Books Pvt. Ltd., New Delhi, 2000.

Asthana, P. : *Women's Movement in India*, Vikas Publishing House, Delhi, 1974.

Baig, T.A. : *India's Woman Position*, S. Chand & Company Pvt. Ltd., Delhi, 1976.

Bala, U. : *Indian Women Freedom Fighters*, Manohar Publications, New Delhi, 1986.

Balakrishnan, A. : *Problems of Rural Landless Women Labourers*, Gyan Books Pvt. Ltd., New Delhi, 2004.

Barot, Jyoti : *The Indian Family in the Change and Challenge of the Seventies,* Sterling Publishers, New Delhi, 1972.

Bebel, August : *Women in the Past, Present and Future*, Deep and Deep Publications, New Delhi, 1996.

Beteille, A. : *Position of Women in India Society*, Publication Division, Government of India, Delhi, 1975.

Bhasin, K. : *The Position of Women in India*, Leslie Sawny, Bambay, 1971.

Billington, Mary F. : *Women in India*, Amarka Book Agency, Delhi, 1973.

Blalock, H.M. and Blalock, A.B. : *Methodology in Social Research*, McGraw-Hill, New York, 1969.

Caplow, T. : *Sociology of Work*, Mc-Graw Hill, New York, 1954.

Carden, Maren L. : *The New Feminist Movement*, Sage Foundation, New York, 1974.

Chakrapant, C. K. S. Vijaya : *Changing Status and Role of Women in Indian Society*, M.D. Pub., New Delhi, 1994.

Chattapadhya, Kamladevi , *The Romantic Rebel,* Sterling Publishers Pvt. Ltd., New Delhi, 1999.

————: *The Awakening of Indian Women*, Everyman's Press, Madras, 1939.

Chaturvedi, G. : *Women Administration in India— a study of the socio-economic background*, RBSA Publication, Jaipur, 1985.

Chaube, Ramesh S. M. Kalpana : *Status of Women in Rural Societies*, Gyan Books Pvt. Ltd., New Delhi, 2002.

Dahiya, M. : *Extension Education and Rural Women*, Anmol Publications, New Delhi, 1998.

Dasgupta S. : *In Search of Alternatives Tribal Woman in Desert Scenario*, Gyan Books Pvt. Ltd., New Delhi, 1995.

Davis, Elizabeth G. : *The First Sex*, Penguin, Delhi, 1978.

De'Souza A. : *Women in Contemporary India and South Asia*, Manohar Pub., Delhi, 1980.

Deckard, B.S. : *The Women's Movement*, Harper and Row, New York, 1979.

Desai, Neera and Patel V. : *Indian Women*, Popular Prakashan, Bombay, 1975.

Devangana, Desai : *Erotic Sculpture of India— a Socio Cultural Study*, Tata McGraw Pub., New Delhi, 1975.

Devasia, L. Devasia, V.V. : *Empowering Women for Sustainable Development*, Ashish Pub. House, New Delhi, 1994.

Devi, Mahesweta : *Bonded Labour in India,* Radhakrishna Publishers, New Delhi, 1981.

Dutt, S. : *Women and Education*, Anmol Publications, New Delhi, 1997.

Engineer, A. A. : *Islam, Women and Gender Justice*, Gyan Books Pvt. Ltd., New Delhi, 2001.

Evans, Sara M. : *Born for Liberty,* Collier Macmillan Publishers, New York, 1989.

Everett, J.M. : *Women and Social Change in India*, Heritage Pub., New York, 1979.

Gandhi, M.K. : *The Role of Women*, Bhartiya Vidhya Bhavan, Bombay, 1964.

Geetha, R. Gowri : *Elderly Women,* Discovery Publishing House, New Delhi, 2003.

Giri, Mohani V. : *Kanya— Exploitation of Little Angels*, Gyan Books Pvt. Ltd., New Delhi, 1999.

————— : *Women*, Gyan Books Pvt. Ltd., New Delhi, 2004.

Gloria, Steinem : *Outrageous Acts and Everyday Rebellions,* Rinehart and Winston, New York, 1980.

Good, W.J. : *World Revolution and Family Patterns*, Collier MacMillan, London, 1963.

Gorwaney, N. : *Self Image and Social Change— a Study of Female Students*, Sterling Publishers, Delhi, 1977.

Gullahorn, J.E. : *Psychology and Women in Transition*, John Wiley, New York, 1979.

Gupta, A.K. : *Women and Society*, Criterion Pub., New Delhi, 1986.

Gupta, A.R. : *Women in Hindu Society,* Jyotsana Prakashan, Delhi, 1982.

Gupta, S. : *Role of Women in the 21st Century,* Anmol Publications, New Delhi, 2000.

Harish, Ranjana : *The Female Footprints*, Sterling Publishers Pvt. Ltd., New Delhi, 1996.

Horney, I.B. : *Women in Farly Buddhist Literature*, Buddhist Publication Society, Kandy, 1961.

Horney, K. : *Feminine Psychology*, W.W. Norton & Co., New York, 1967.

Inkeles, A. Smith, D. : *Becoming Modern*, Heinmann Educational Books Ltd., London, 1974.

Jain, Amina, Jasbir and Amin : *Margins of Erasure— Purdah in the Subcontinental*, Sterling Publishers Pvt. Ltd., New Delhi, 1996.

Jain, D : *Indian Women*, Publication Division, Government of India, Delhi, 1975.

Jain, S. : *Encyclopaedia of Indian Women,* Gyan Books Pvt. Ltd., New Delhi, 2003.

Janapathy, V. : *Indian Women through the Ages,* Gyan Books Pvt. Ltd., New Delhi, 2002.

Jayashree : *India and Indian Women*, Granthayan, Aligarh, 1980.

John, N. J. : *Suppressed Childhood*, Dominant Books, New Delhi, 2003.

Joshi, K. : *Sex Roles in Transition,* Gyan Books Pvt. Ltd., New Delhi, 2003.

Joyce, T. Athol Thomas N. W. : *Women of Universe*, Gyan Books Pvt. Ltd., New Delhi, 1997.

Kalarani : *Role Coriflict in Working Women*, Chitra Pub., New Delhi, 1976.

Kalawati : *Educational Status of Rural Girls,* Discovery Publishing House, New Delhi, 1994.

Kapur, P. : *Marriage and the Working Woman in India*, Vikas Pub., Delhi, 1975.

Karmakar, Sumati : *The Better Half — Mothers, Sisters, Wives and Homemakers,* Dominant Books, New Delhi, 2001.

Kaul, V. : *Women and the Wind of Change,* Gyan Books Pvt. Ltd., New Delhi, 2000.

Kaur, M. : *Rural Women and Technological Advancement*, Discovery Publishing House, New Delhi, 1988.

———— : *Women in India's Freedom Struggle*, Sterling Publishers Pvt. Ltd., New Delhi, 1990.

Kelker, D. B. M. : *A Subordination of Women*, Discovery Publishing House, New Delhi, 1995.

Khan, B. A. : *Economic Rights of Women under Islamic Law & Hindu Law*, Royal Publishers, New Delhi, 1995.

Khanna, G : *Indian Women Today*, Discovery Publishing House, New Delhi, 1978.

Kidwai, S.M.H. : *Women under Different Social and Religious Law*, Seema Pub., New Delhi, 1976.

Kiran, Devendra : *Status and Position of Women in India*, Vikas Publishing House Pvt. Ltd., 1985.

Kirpal, V. : *The Girl Child in 20th Century Indian Literature*, Sterling Publishers Pvt. Ltd., New Delhi, 1992.

Kishwar, M. : *Off the Beaten Track Rethinking Gender Justice for Indian Women*, Oxford, New York, 1999.

Kotani, H. : *Caste System, Untouchability and the Depressed*, Manohar Publishing House, New Delhi, 1999.

Kulshreshtha, I.N. : *The War Against Gender Bias*, Sterling Publishers Pvt. Ltd., New Delhi, 1993.

Kumar, A. : *Women and Development*, Anmol Publications, New Delhi, 2004.

Kuppuswamy, B. : *Social Change in India*, Vikas Publishing House, Delhi, 1972.

Lakshmikumari, M. : *The Role of Women in Society*, Sterling Publishers Pvt. Ltd., New Delhi, 1997.

Law, Bimla C. : *Women in Buddhist Society*, N.E. Bastian, Ceylone, 1927.

Laxmi, D. : *Encyclopaedia of Women Development and Family Welfare*, Anmol Publications, New Delhi, 1998.

Madhurima : *Violence Against Women*— Dynamics of Conjugal Relations, Gyan Books Pvt. Ltd., New Delhi, 1996.

Malhotra, M. : *Dimensions of Women Exploitation*, Gyan Books Pvt. Ltd., New Delhi, 2004.

———— : *Empowerment of Women*, Gyan Books Pvt. Ltd., New Delhi, 2004.

Mandal, A. : *Women in Panchayati Raj Institutions,* Kanishka Publishers, New Delhi, 2002.

Mandal, J. : *Women and Reservation in India*, Gyan Books Pvt. Ltd., New Delhi, 2003.

Manna, S. : *The Fair Sex in Tribal Cultures— Problems and Development*, Gyan Books Pvt. Ltd., New Delhi, 1989.

Marshall, Katherine : *Employed Family and Division of Housework*, Autumn, 1993.

Mathur, R.N. : *Quality of Working Life of Women Construction Workers,* Commonwealth Publishers, New Delhi, 1997.

Mcleod, A. L . : *Commonwealth and American Women's Discourse*, Sterling Publishers Pvt. Ltd., New Delhi, 1996.

Meena, Anand : *Dalit Women — Fear and Discrimination*, Gyan Books Pvt. Ltd., New Delhi, 2004.

Mehta, H. : *Indian Woman*, Batula & Co., New Delhi, 1981.

Mehta, R. : *Socio Legal Status of Women in India*, Metropolitan Book Co., Delhi, 1982.

———— : *The Western Educated Hindu Woman*, Asia Pub. House, New York, 1970.

Mehta, S. : *Revolution and Status of Women in India*, Metropolitan Book Co., Delhi, 1982.

Menon, L. : *Women Empowerment and Challenge of Change*, Kanishka Publishers, New Delhi, 1998.

Menon, M. Indu : *Status of Muslim Women in India*, Uppal Pub. House, Delhi, 1981.

Mies, M. : *Indian Women and Patriarchy— Conflicts and Dilemmas of Students and Working Women*, Concept Publishers, New Delhi, 1980.

Mishra, J. : *Women and Human Rights*, Gyan Books Pvt. Ltd., New Delhi, 2000.

Mishra, S. : *Status of Indian Women,* Gyan Books Pvt. Ltd., New Delhi, 2002.

Misra, R. : *Women in Mughal India*, Munshiram Manoharlal, Delhi, 1991.

Mitra, J. : *Women and Society —Equality and Empowerment,* Kanishka Publishers, New Delhi, 1997.

Mittal, M. : *Women in India— Today and Tomorrow*, Anmol Pub., New Delhi, 1995.

Mohanty, J. : *Glimpses of Indian Women in Freedom Struggle*, Discovery Publishing House, New Delhi, 1996.

Moneil, Elton B. and Rubin Z. : *The Psychology of Crime*, Canfield Press, San Francisco, 1979.

Morgan, Robin : *Sisterhood is Powerful— an Anthology of Writings from the Women's Liberation Movement,* Random House, New York, 1970.

Mukherjee, D. : *Status on Crime Against Women in Different Countries*, Gyan Books Pvt. Ltd., New Delhi, 2004.

Nancy, F. : *The Grounding of Modern Feminism*, Yale University Press, New Haven and London, 1987.

Nanda, B.R. : *Indian Women*, Vikas Pub. House, Delhi, 1976.

Naseef, Fatima Umar : *Women in Islam — Discourse in Rights and Obligations*, Sterling Publishers Pvt. Ltd., New Delhi, 1999.

Neeraja, K. P. : *Rural Women*, Discovery Publishing House, New Delhi, 2003.

Pal, B.K. : *Problems and Concerns of Indian Women*, ABC Pub. House, New Delhi, 1989.

Pandit, S. K. : *Women in Society*, Rajat Pub., Delhi, 1998.

Papanek, Hanna and Gail M. : *Separate Worlds — Studies of Purdah in South Asia,* Chanakya Publications, New Delhi, 1982.

Pinkham, Mildreth Worth : *Female in the Sacred Scripts of Hinduism,* AMS Press, New York, 1941.

Pujari, Premlata and Kaushik, Vijay K. : *Women Power in India,* Kanishka Pub., Delhi, 1994.

Puri, Jyoti : *Woman, Body, Desire in Past-Colonial India — Narratives of Gender and Sexuality*, Manohar Publishing House, New Delhi, 1999.

Rajgopal, T.S. : *Indian Ideal of Womanhood*, Ramakrishna Mission, Calcutta, 1969.

Ramabal, Saraswati Pundita : *The High Caste Hindu Woman*, Jas. B. Podgers Printing Co., Philadelphia, 1888.

Ranganathan, S. : *Women and Social Order — a Profile of Major Indicators and Determinants*, Kanishka Publishers, New Delhi, 1998.

Rani, K. : *Role Conflict in Working Wives*, Chetana Publications, New Delhi, 1976.

Rao, D. Bhaskara : *International Encyclopaedia of Women*, Discovery Publishing House, New Delhi, 1998.

Reddy & Ramesh : *Girl Child Labour — a World of Endless Exploitation*, Dominant Books, New Delhi, 2002.

Rege, Y.M. : *Whither Women*, The Popular Book Depot, Bombay, 1938.

Rohibaugh, J. Bunker : *Women— Psychology's Puzzle*, Basic Books, New York, 1979.

Rosemeyer, S. S. : *Women's Rights— Search for Identity*, Dominant Books, New Delhi, 2000.

Roy, Kumkum : *Women in Early Indian Societies*, Manohar Publishing House, New Delhi, 1999.

Sahay, S. : *Women's Education in Ancient and Muslim Period*, Discovery Publishing House, New Delhi, 1996.

Samant, V. : *Health Awareness for Women*, Gyan Books Pvt. Ltd., New Delhi, 2000.

Sarada, D. : *Family Life Education for Adolescent Girls*, Discovery Publishing House, New Delhi, 1999.

Saxena, K. : *Women and Politics*, Gyan Books Pvt. Ltd., New Delhi, 2000.

Sen, A. : *Problems and Potentials of Women Professionals*, Gyan Books Pvt. Ltd., New Delhi, 1999.

Sengupta, P. : *The Story of Women in India*, Indian Book Co., New Delhi, 1974.

Sheela, J. : *Women Marriage in India,* Dominant Books, New Delhi, 2003.

Shirwadkar, S. : *Women and Socio-Cultural Changes*, Gyan Books Pvt. Ltd., New Delhi, 1998.

Shridevi : *A Century of Indian Womanhood*, Rao and Raghavan, Mysore, 1965.

Singh, S. S. & Jyoti S. : *The Fiftieth Milestone— a Feminine Critique*, Sterling Publishers Pvt. Ltd., New Delhi, 1998.

Singh, S., Gupta S. : *Women Leadership in Organisations—Socio-Cultural Determinants,* Gyan Books Pvt. Ltd. New Delhi, 2002.

Singh, I. P. : *Women, Law and Social Change in India*, Radiant Pub., New Delhi, 1989.

Sinha, Niroj : *Women in Indian Politics—Empowerment of Women through Political Participation*, Gyan Books Pvt. Ltd., New Delhi, 2000.

Sonali, K., Wadhwa J. : *Gender—a Cross-Cultural Perspective*, Gyan Books Pvt. Ltd., New Delhi, 2000.

Srinivasan, M.N. : *The Changing Position of Indian Women*, Oxford Univ. Press, Delhi, 1970.

Subbamma, M. : *Women, Tradition and Culture*, Sterling Pub., Delhi, 1985.

Sunita, and Others : *Rural Women work —Differential Treatment by Land Lord-elites*, 1987.

Swarnalatha, E. V. : *Empowerment of Women—through Self Help Groups,* Discovery Publishing House, New Delhi, 1997.

Swarup, Justice Hari : *Women in Crisis— New Approaches to Happiness,* Gyan Books Pvt. Ltd., New Delhi, 2001.

Thanvi, Ashraf Ali : *Pecular Personal Problems of Men & Women,* Royal Publishers, New Delhi. 1993.

Thomas, P. : *Indian Women through the Ages*, Asia Pub. House, New York, 1964.

Tikoo, P. N. : *Indian Women*, B.R. Publishing Corporation, Delhi, 1985.

Tripathy, S. N. : *Bonded Labour in India,* Discovery Publishing House, New Delhi, 1989.

Tripathy, S. N. : *Unorganised Women Labour in India,* Discovery Publishing House, New Delhi, 1996.

Tripathy, S. N. : *Women in Informal Sector,* Discovery Publishing House, New Delhi, 2003.

Trivedi, H. R. : *Scheduled Caste Women Studies in Exploitation, with Reference to Superstition, Ignorance and Poverty*, Concept Pub. Co., Delhi, 1976.

U. B. Bhoite, Jogdand, P. G., and : *Dalit Women — Issues and Perspectives,* Gyan Books Pvt. Ltd., New Delhi, 1995.

Usha, R.N.J. : *Women in Developing Society*, Ashish Pub. House, Delhi, 1983.

Utpala, N. : *Women's Development and Social Conflicts—Historical Perspectives on Indian Women,* Kanishka Publishers, New Delhi, 1999.

Vitels, M.S. : *Motivation and Morale of Women*, Morton, New York, 1998.

Vreede, de Stuers. : *Girl Students in India — a Study in Attitude towards Family Life, Marriage and Career*, Assen, Van Gorcum and Co., New York, 1993.

Whyte, F.W. : *Money, Motivation & Crime in Women*, Harper and Row, New York, 1992.

Wolfgang, Lederer : *The Fear of Female*, Arun and Strattan, New York, 1968.

Yaqin, Anwarul and Anwar B. : *Protection of Woman under Law*, Deep and Deep Publications, New Delhi, 1982.

Young, Serinity : *Anthology of Sacred Texts by and about Women,* Pandora, Harper Collins, New York, 1993.

Zeitlin, Irving, M. : *Rethinking Sociology*, Appleton-Century Crafts, New York, 1990.

Zillah, R. Eisenstein : *The Radical Future of Liberal Feminism,* Longman, New York, 1981.

Index

A

B

C

D

E

F

G

H

N

O

P

Q

R

S

T

U

V

W

Y

❑❑❑